The Multimediated Rhetoric of the Internet

This project is a critical, rhetorical study of the digital text we call the Inter-net, in particular the style and figurative surface of its many pages as well as the conceptual, design patterns structuring the content of those same pages. Handa argues that as our lives become increasingly digital, we must consider rhetoric applicable to more than just printed text or to images. Digital analysis demands our acknowledgement of digital fusion, a true merging of analytic skills in many media and dimensions. CDs, DVDs, and an Internet increasingly capable of streaming audio and video prove that literacy today means more than it used to, namely the ability to understand information, however presented. Handa considers pedagogy, professional writing, hypertext theory, rhetorical studies, and composition studies, moving analysis beyond merely "using" the web towards "thinking" rhe-torically about its construction and its impact on culture. This book shows how analyzing the web rhetorically helps us to understand the inescapable fact that culture is reflected through all media fused within the parameters of digital technology.

Carolyn Handa is Professor of English and a member of the Composi-tion, Rhetoric & English Studies (CRES) Program at the University of Alabama, USA.

Routledge Studies in Rhetoric and Communication

The Multimediated Rhetoric of the Internet
Digital Fusion

Carolyn Handa

Routledge
Taylor & Francis Group

LONDON AND NEW YORK

First published 2014 by Routledge

2 Park Square, Milton Park, Abingdon, Oxon OX14 4RN
711 Third Avenue, New York, NY 10017, USA

Routledge is an imprint of the Taylor & Francis Group, an informa business

First issued in paperback 2017

Library of Congress Cataloging-in-Publication Data
Handa, Carolyn.
   The multimediated rhetoric of the Internet : digital fusion / Carolyn
Handa.
      pages cm. — (Routledge studies in rhetoric and communication ; 10)
   Includes bibliographical references and index.
   1.   Online authorship.   2.   Interactive multimedia.   3.   Hypertext
systems.   4.   Web sites—Design.   5.   Rhetoric—Social aspects.
   6.   Internet—Social aspects.   7.   Communication—Technological
innovations.   8.   Communication and culture.   I.   Title.
   PN171.O55H36 2014
   302.23'1—dc23
   2013026624

ISBN13: 978-0-415-89325-1 (hbk)
ISBN13: 978-1-138-30602-8 (pbk)

Typeset in Sabon
by IBT Global.

Finally for my sibs:
Diane, Emily, Robert, Stephen, and Susan

And always in memory of my parents:
Patricia Sakon Handa
and
George J. Handa

Contents

Figures

Acknowledgments

This book would never have been written had I not enrolled in a class back in the dark ages of my graduate student career at UCLA: a seminar in Renaissance non-fiction prose. Richard Lanham taught the class about rhetoric, rhetorical analysis, and most of all, writing. While that class remains the most influential one I ever took, Richard Lanham's work continues to this day to influence my thinking by leading me, sometimes in roundabout ways, to sources that prove invaluable for my own research in multimediated rhetoric. My thanks always to Richard Lanham, a true teacher and professor of the art of rhetoric.

Parts of Chapter 6 appeared in an earlier, much different version. Thanks to Emily Golson and Toni Glover for permission to reprint parts of the essay included in their volume *Negotiating a Meta-pedagogy: Learning from Other Disciplines*, 2009, © Emily Golson and Toni Glover.

Kira Cramer created the partial reproduction of the 1999 MLA Convention Web site's opening page, Figure 2.1, and also saved readers from having to look at my original rough line sketches for Figures 3.4, 3.5, 3.6, 4.1, and 5.1. Kira, thank you for your help transforming my amateurish attempts. I am proud that you are both a scientist and an artist, but most of all, a good friend. Chris Komai at the Japanese American National Museum answered questions I had about a Chiura and Gyo Obata exhibit. Kelly Bathe and Corinne Drobot at HOK helped put me in contact with the photographers whose work is included here. HOK's Corinne Drobot and Megan McClure kept me abreast of work on the company's *Genius of Biome* report and notified me when it was published online. Nick Carbone, lookout extraordinaire, first spotted the Slate piece I quote from in Chapter 1. Nick sent the link to the TechRhet list so that someone like me, who never manages to be quite as good a lookout, could find it. Peg Syverson first introduced me to the work of Edwin Hutchins along with the concepts of distributed and situated cognition during a long conversation in a Computers and Writing Conference hotel lobby many years ago.

I am grateful to the following people who granted permission to reproduce the following figures in this book:

Chris Gascoigne (Figure 1.1, Carnival UK headquarters)

Barry Grossman (Figure 1.2, Office Depot headquarters)

Sam Fentress (Figure 1.3, Indianapolis International Airport)

Moris Moreno (Figure 1.4, Salvador Dali Museum)

Stuart Moulthrop (Figure 3.1, Storyspace map of "forking paths" hypertext)

The Chrysler Group LLC (Figure 4.2, This is Chrysler)

Tristan Denyer and Marci Daniels for the Black Studies Project banner (seen in Figure 5.1) that they originally designed for Howard Rambsy II's Black Studies Project and Web site at Southern Illinois University, Edwardsville

Howard Rambsy II (Figure 5.1, Black Studies Web site banner, SIUE)

A big thank you to Ryan Kenney and his group, as well as to Susan Park, for shaping this book into its final form. Finally, thanks to Emily Ross and Nancy Chen at Routledge. Emily must be the most patient editor in the world.

Introduction
Rhetoric, Fusion, Borders, and Liminality

From the moment of the appearance of the book, the linking of text and image is frequent, though it seems to have been little studied from the structural point of view.

~ Roland Barthes

This book's title may have arisen because I watch far too much of the Food Network. Or it could be that I wish I could cook my way out of a paper bag or improvise with the best jazz musicians on the planet. Truthfully, the concept of "fusion" in all its permutations occurred to me as the most appropriate metaphor on which to base my argument and analysis in this work: that writing for, and analyzing, the World Wide Web demands a set of rhetorical skills that apply not only to the Web's texts, not just to its images, not solely to mute, black and white, onscreen displays, and not exclusively to two-dimensional surfaces. As our lives in this twenty-first century become increasingly digital, we must consider rhetoric applicable to more than just printed text, as we in composition/rhetorical studies have long been accustomed to, or to images, as our colleagues in art history and communication studies have long done. Digital analysis demands our acknowledgment of, and adeptness in, digital analytic fusion, a true merging of analytic skills in many media and dimensions (see for example Handa, special issues of *Computers and Composition*; Handa, *Visual Rhetoric in a Digital World*; Hilligoss and Williams; Hocks and Kendrick; Kimme Hea; Kress; Williams). CDs, DVDs, and a World Wide Web increasingly capable of streaming audio and video, all in various digitized forms, prove that literacy today means more than it used to. "[T]he word 'literacy,' meaning the ability to read and write, has gradually extended its grasp in the digital age until it has come to mean the ability to understand information, however presented" (Lanham, "Digital Literacy," 198). Embedded in the word "understand", however, are discrete types of analytic ability.

This project is a critical, rhetorical study of the digital text we call the World Wide Web, most recently Web 2.0, in particular the style and figurative surface of its many pages as well as the conceptual, design patterns structuring the content of those same pages. I analyze the Web rhetorically in order to reflect on its structures and devices so that I might address the call made by some recent scholars of rhetoric and of visual language that we study, in a more sustained rhetorical manner, the combined instances of words threaded with images and of designed objects, both of which we find on the Web. I am attempting to move our studies beyond merely "using" the Web towards "thinking" rhetorically about its construction and its impact on culture, as Cynthia Selfe urges:

> We have paid technology issues precious little focused attention over the years. Allowing ourselves this luxury of ignoring technology, however, is not only misguided at the end of the twentieth century, it is dangerously shortsighted. . . . [We are only] *using* computers—or having students do so—but not . . . *thinking* about what we are doing and understanding at least some of the important implications of our actions. . . . Composition studies faculty have a much larger and more complicated obligation to fulfill—that of trying to understand and make sense of, *to pay attention* to, how technology is now inextricably linked to literacy and literacy education in this country. (CCCC Keynote Address, Chicago, April 2, 1998)[1]

Almost two decades ago, researchers like Sonja K. Foss bemoaned the lack of rhetorical attention paid to visual imagery ("Visual Imagery," 85). Designers like Richard Buchanan argued, furthermore, that the design field needed a theory of rhetoric appropriate for and applicable to the collection of activities involved in design decisions with regard to objects as large as cities or towns to those as small as a tool or an advertisement (91, 109). Other educators like Jay Lemke ("Multiplying Meaning") addressed the idea of analyzing both text and image from the angle of semiotics, and the New London Group proposed a pedagogy of multiliteracies. We moved from calls to study images to calls for multiple media analysis. I am continuing, advancing, and stressing those arguments here: rhetoric needs to figure prominently in all such analysis.

Within a decade and a half the Web has come to surround us, the degree of its ubiquity sometimes threatening to make invisible the rhetoric and cultural influences reflected therein. Ubiquitous, yes. But *ubi sunt*? Because the Web envelops so much of our lives, stopping to look critically at it or its rhetoric is a rare act. However,

> nothing is free of rhetoric, . . . visual manifestations emerge from particular historical circumstances, . . . [and] ideological vacuums do not exist. . . . But, among information designers, there has been a tendency to escape from the assaults of the wider world, to deny any idea of rhetorical persuasion, and to take refuge in immaculate black machine casings. Indeed, the whole revolution of information technology seems to encourage the view that ideology becomes increasingly reduced—miniaturized—in step with the development of ever smaller and more

powerful computing devices. Therefore, we need to keep awake, applying our critical intelligences outside, as well as inside, the black box:
questioning and resisting. (Kinross, 143)

Forgetting about the Web's rhetoric and remaining untutored in the ways we
can identify it or forgetting about technological situatedness, forgetting that
culture and ideology are ever-present, could be dangerous. While arguing for
an approach to digital research that accounts for the questions articulation
theory raises, Amy Kimme Hea states: "Research projects that either fail to
consider the influence of technical and cultural practices, or attempt . . . to
create seamless narratives about our research run the risk of re-inscribing the
very inequities we seek to disrupt" ("Riding the Wave," 270).

My intended audience for this volume on the digital rhetoric of the
World Wide Web is primarily scholars involved in studying the World Wide
Web as a cultural artifact and using the World Wide Web to teach, more
specifically, writing specialists in composition and rhetoric, technical writing, professional writing. However, I hope that the volume's readers will
also consist of students in graduate programs in Rhetoric and Composition
whose curricula include courses in using the Web to teach, Web design, and
technical as well as professional writing. The groups below are those that I
hope will gain from the point of view I write from in this text:

- New media scholars
- Rhetoric scholars trying to understand the ways in which rhetoric
  applies to images and graphics
- Visual culture specialists
- Rhetoric/composition and communication specialists studying and
  teaching new media analysis
- Technical and professional writing teachers interested in the rhetori-
  cal foundations of visual elements combined with text
- Graduate courses in rhetoric, communication, and new media
- Graduate courses in computers and composition and in visual
  rhetoric
- Graduate and undergraduate courses in writing for the World Wide
  Web
- Graduate and undergraduate classes in visual communication
- Graduate and undergraduate courses in technical and professional
  writing
- Individuals involved in Web page construction and design

These days, writing teachers in college classrooms often ask students to
use digital media to construct texts incorporating images and sound for
posting on class Web sites, or for inclusion in electronic portfolios stored
on the Web (Yancey). Furthermore, as the World Wide Web, graphics software, presentation software, and multimedia authoring packages have

become easier to use and increasingly widespread, those of us involved in the rhetoric and composition field have begun incorporating images and design elements into our own instructional presentations in addition to using graphics and design elements to enhance our professional presentations. As these digitized forms proliferate, therefore, writing instructors come face to face with the task of thinking more critically about the many ways in which these digital innovations impact both our writing classes as well as our own profession in terms of rhetoric and literacy.

While not many of us these days will argue against the need to be visually literate, this study will not examine visual literacy *per se*, a topic covered in much detail elsewhere over the past decade.[2] This study is also not scrutinizing visual rhetoric, a type of study often housed in communications departments that focuses primarily on images. I am focusing instead on digital rhetoric, or in other words, the ways rhetoric impacts various digital media that are now fused together on the Web, and arguing about our need to apply rhetorical elements more deeply and analytically to all the Web's facets. My ultimate goal, finally, is to help us understand how analyzing the Web rhetorically helps us to grasp the inescapable fact that culture always undergirds, and is reflected through, all media fused within the parameters of digital technology.

Although the composition profession as a whole has yet to focus much sustained critical attention on what happens to rhetoric and rhetorical analysis in our classrooms when we incorporate visual and aural elements into the texts of writing assignments, such research is becoming increasingly important. I began this project with several overarching questions: does the rhetoric that emerges on the World Wide Web differ from the rhetoric we find in print, in the codex book, and from the visually focused rhetoric that studies images or three-dimensional objects such as sculptures or monuments? Embedded within this question are a series of sub-questions that provide the impetus for each chapter. The first of these sub-questions is: how do we analyze this multimediated rhetoric? The second is: are we conducting satisfactory rhetorical analyses of all media fused on digital sites, or are we concentrating primarily on one type of media, namely the visual? My final overarching question is: how could we push such analysis and multimediated composition further?

Below, I extend my research into other areas that I explain briefly. Readers can then understand why I consider questions of digital rhetoric and literacy in their many applications to subjects that writing teachers think about everyday: pedagogy, professional writing, hypertext theory, rhetorical studies, and the future of composition studies. I devote different chapters of my book to subjects that will encourage rhetoricians, compositionists, and communications scholars to engage in some much-needed dialogue on the subject and to further our existing scholarship. Because I am studying the rhetoric of many different World Wide Web pages, furthermore, I attempt to ground the discussion practically, that is, with references to and analyses of actual pages that illustrate my theories and claims. I also show writing teachers how to use Web pages for illustrating many rhetorical and writing techniques to their students.

The study of digital rhetoric today needs to be conducted by humanists, that is, by rhetoricians and compositionists, just as much as by artists, computer technicians, multimedia designers, and Web technologists. The word "fusion" in my title applies also to my fusion of theories from varied disciplines as I make my case for serious rhetorical analysis of the Web. My final arguments are: the multimediated "texts" of the World Wide Web, which now include images, graphic elements, and sound, build on traditional notions of text and rhetoric but challenge us to apply them and our analytic skills to the digital page. Such a challenge is significant for our writing classrooms and higher education not merely because so much information is now housed on the Web, but because rhetorical study of this material contributes to our understanding of ethos, logos, pathos, culture, and the importance of cultural context to any study. Expanded rhetorical notions of text thus impact literacy and literacy education. Such a challenge matters to the practice of human signification for today's various cultures throughout the world because as humanists we contribute a special kind of insight that designers, computer scientists, programmers, or digital architects, to name a few, do not often search for.

One final caveat: young people today surround themselves with multimedia and cyber-texts outside of the classroom; scholars, teachers, and their parents need to understand these forms as they emerge in both the classroom, society, and culture. Without research and studies analyzing the ways in which we can begin to understand this digital age rhetorically, however, both young and, well, "older" folks will feel disenfranchised in classrooms that do not acknowledge the influence of new media in twenty-first century learning. The university will become irrelevant to the ways future generations learn and live in the world.

* * * * *

CHAPTER 1

Chapter 1 discusses how, exactly, we can consider the digital to be rhetorical, cognitive, and cultural. Over the past two decades, hypertexts have often elicited commentary and scholarship highlighting their untraditional structure and the challenges of reading them in non-linear ways. With the advent of Web 2.0, hypertexts became more visually oriented, embedded with graphics, and video—live or otherwise. Such non-linear, digital constructions would seem, then, to challenge—even more seriously—our notions of reading and conceiving of text because images and graphics hardly seem to share the same rhetoric as words.

If we rethink our notions of text, however, we need not necessarily discard traditional notions of print literacy. Rather, we should attempt to identify those traditional textual notions in other forms, to re-envision them—in this case, visually and even spatially. Jay Bolter, calling the Web a vast global hypertext with millions of readers, has noted that electronic communication, hypertext in particular with its defining form, the Web site, threatens the modern definition of rhetoric. Our definition of text, he argues, must expand today to allow images and alternative forms of persuasion to figure more prominently in that definition of rhetoric ("Hypertext and the Question"). Henrietta Nickels Shirk understood this concept of broadening our understanding of "rhetoric" two decades ago when she wrote that "[f]rom the composing perspective, hypertext authors must be alert to two new ways of thinking about the presentation of information. . . . [T]hese new ways . . . actually relate to broad areas of study and trends that have long been of concern to students of composition studies who have been interested in metaphorical theory and cognitive science as these fields relate to the creation of text" (181, 182).

An expanded definition of rhetoric will help us draw on our knowledge and practices as textual scholars. It will clarify and identify how that knowledge and those practices have been refashioned. Because our analytic, cognitive acts—thinking, acting, writing—are historically contingent (see, for example, Hutchins or Sutton, especially 222–230), we would be hard-pressed, in fact, to escape centuries of culturally honed cognitive skills. Jay Bolter and Richard Grusin argue that the new media can only achieve significance culturally by "paying homage" to earlier media—the argument throughout their volume *Remediation*. Along these lines, any new or expanded definition of rhetoric must draw on pre-existing, historically contingent cognitive skills and pay homage to pre-existing forms of rhetoric and literary skills. Luckily, because of the increasingly visual nature of hypertext as embodied in the World Wide Web, we can more easily "see" these theoretical parallels.

To clarify: I use the term "cognition" here to refer to a general process of understanding rather than a specific scientific explanation of brain functions used during the act of writing. Studies of writing in the late 1970s and early 1980s, according to Deborah McCutchen, Paul Teske, and Catherine Bankston, especially the studies of Richard Young, J.R. Hayes, and Linda Flowers, approach writing by following "the example of AI [artificial intelligence] models, emphasizing constraint identification, problem decomposition, and hierarchical planning processes" (451). McCutcheon, Teske, and Bankston trace the paths that research on writing and cognition followed in the field of composition and rhetorical studies. When I use the term, however, I am not drawing on this approach to writing and cognition. Instead, I am referring to cognition as a mode of apprehension that is historically and culturally contingent; the ways that we think depend on the culture in which we were raised. One of the best examples of a culture's influence on cognition can be found in Edwin Hutchins' *Cognition in the Wild*, specifically the chapter titled "Navigation as Computation". Perception and analysis depend on culture. Hutchins explains and demonstrates exactly how the Western tradition of piloting places constraints on the algorithms and computation Western navigators use in order to pilot ships. His chapter and the entire book "contrast the culturally specific representations and algorithms used by our technological Western culture with those used by a nonliterate Micronesian culture to solve the navigation problem" (51).

Chapter 1, therefore, argues that although Web pages look different from codex books, the rhetoric and rhetorical strategies that Web pages embody, their visual figures and tropes, arise from ones with which we are already familiar. We can find visual examples of metaphor and other figures of speech such as anaphora and accumulatio. Furthermore, if associative thinking is the hallmark of hypertextual argumentation, we are already accustomed to the associative argumentation of poems. Mapping a sonnet with its metaphoric links and associative connections between quatrains and couplet produces a document resembling a series of linked Web pages. Reconceiving of rhetorical and poetic figures in visual terms can help us to teach digital texts which include images, to understand and map the thinking processes reflected through the choices involved in more complex Web site construction, and to realize that images and words are complementary, together forming a more complete rhetoric than a singular concentration on words could ever provide.

Once we begin analyzing, in more informed ways, the degree to which Web pages and sites have absorbed a culture and rhetoric that they reflect back to us in refigured, refashioned forms, we can become digitally literate, skilled, as Richard Lanham has put it, at "deciphering complex images and sounds as well as the syntactical subtleties of words . . . [so that we feel] at home in a shifting mix of words, images and sounds" ("Digital Literacy," 198, 200).

CHAPTER 2

Chapter 2 tackles the subject of the organizational principles, schemes, and figures we can discover in Web sites. Whether writing is creative or expository, rhetorical schemes, figures, and organizational principles emerge whenever people attempt to convey information, to reason, to describe emotions, to make sense of our world. Now in the twenty-first century, creative and expository writing no longer take place only on paper. Today's written "page" is both paper and digital, and with digitality comes the increased ability to include images and graphic elements as integral parts of a text. To an extent that they never were for paper texts, images and graphics have become necessary, expected parts of World Wide Web pages.

Figures of thought and speech previously considered primarily characteristics of oral or written texts must no longer be attributed only to words. They can be identified in visual images and also in digital texts that fuse images and graphic elements to their surrounding text on the Web. If, for example, metaphor and metonymy occur visually on the Web, I believe that they serve as more than mere illustrations of the words they accompany: they are crucial components of the rhetoric of their Web pages and the arguments that those Web texts make. Barbara Stafford's *Visual Analogy: Consciousness as the Art of Connecting*, while specifically exploring an area this chapter will not touch—"imaging and imagists in the middle of the philosophical, neurobiological, and cognitive science debates surrounding the nature of consciousness" (xvi)—opens a line of inquiry for rhetoricians because we can start to analyze how the rhetorical figure of analogy is adapted in order to truthfully or falsely represent circumstances, or whether digital writers ignore analogy in places where we might expect it because the authors are unaware of the rhetorical nature of the images enmeshed within their texts. In other words, if they do not realize that an image can have analogous text, then they cannot create an analogy.

This chapter considers rhetorical arrangement as it is reflected through larger design patterns on both individual pages and within separate sentences and images. Because of the Web's hypertextual nature, I explore the degree to which parataxis is used successfully within a Web site's overall design, that is, whether the individual screens are helped or hindered either by an awareness of digital paratactic structure, or whether the pages try to rely on the more hypotactic structure of the printed page, chapter, and book. I do not discuss the larger figurative structure of classification here because I devote a separate chapter to it. I analyze particular clusters of pages on the World Wide Web in order to determine:

- the extent to which visual metaphor, visual metonymy, visual parataxis, visual hypotaxis, visual anaphora, and visual analogies are occurring, and to discover whether they are working with or against their surrounding verbal contexts,
- how Web writers use rhetorical figures and tropes, for instance, whether they appear as clichés and stereotypes, and if so, in which particular situations,
- what digital metaphor and metonymy reveal about the particular cultures from which they arise,
- whether they occur on pages where we would expect *verbal* metaphors, for instance, pages containing poetry or devoted to poets and poetry organizations,
- and finally, what these digital figures of speech and tropes reveal about the power of the World Wide Web in conveying information or misinformation, and about the types of cultures (in the most general sense of groups or classes) that give rise to specific instances of metaphor and metonymy.

CHAPTER 3

Chapter 3 analyzes classification as we see it displayed on the World Wide Web and argues that classification relates directly to the ways we think about our world. In their chapter entitled "Classification and Control", Robert Hodge and Gunther Kress argue that "[c]lassification is at the basis of language and thought. Without acts of classification no one could relate concepts or words to new concepts or messages, because words and concepts only exist through classification" (62). One of the most ubiquitous techniques we see on Web pages everywhere we look is classification. Actually, a Web site itself—apart from the information it contains—is a *designed* classification system, a system that is fundamentally rhetorical. Whether it is rhetorically designed remains to be seen. By my calculations, a Web site fuses:

- a design
- an outline
- a classification system
- rhetorical elements
- its creator's social and cultural contexts

Search engines, online retail, university sites all rely on classifying their information, products, or services so that they will be easily accessible to their viewers. The way Web sites break down their subject's identity, the way they classify their offerings, offers a window into the culture creating that classification. Analyzing classification systems, moreover, offers insight into the ways the sponsoring institutions want to control their identities and the ways we perceive them.

The seemingly simple act of putting items in groups, however, can and has caused heated discussions in some disciplines. The biological sciences, in particular, come to mind. Even the humanities have had problems when it comes to classification, where the categories involved in canon formation have led to serious problems of exclusion and anthology wars: scholars squabble over the groupings and representative authors selected for major literary anthologies. Classification or categorization clearly has far-reaching consequences.

Many of us have had the experience of being frustrated while trying to find information on some Web sites because the categories we expect to find before reaching the site are quite different from the ones we actually see once we arrive. We experience a sort of cognitive disjunction, possibly because the classification scheme we have been acculturated to expect has completely different categories from the ones created by the site designers. Richard Lanham makes the case that rhetorical figures are evolutionary strategies that developed to help the brain with memory, computation, and iterative searching (*A Handlist of Rhetorical Terms*). So too with classification systems, which fall under one of the five parts of rhetoric, along with invention, arrangement, style, and delivery (Lanham, 165). In their introduction to *Cognition and Categorization*, editors Eleanor Rosch and Barbara Lloyd gather essays arguing that "the segmentation of the world [is not] essentially arbitrary" (2). And in her chapter "Principles of Categorization", Rosch outlines two general assertions:

> [1] the task of category systems is to provide maximum information with the least cognitive effort; . . . [2] the perceived world comes as structured information rather than arbitrary or unpredictable attributes. Thus maximum information with the least cognitive effort is achieved if categories map the perceived world structure as closely as possible. (28)

Other scholars whose research serves as the foundation for my inquiry in this chapter are James Elkins ("Problems of Classification" in *The Domain of Images*), George Lakoff ("The Importance of Classification" in *Women, Fire, and Dangerous Things: What Categories Reveal about the Mind*), and Geoffrey C. Bowker along with Susan Leigh Star (*Sorting Things Out: Classification and Its Consequences*). Bowker and Star contend that "as a culture we have not yet developed conventions of classification for the Web that bear much moral or habitual conviction in daily practice" (8). What, then, are the implications for Web study, because building classification systems has many more far-reaching consequences than just putting objects into groups or representing these groups in charts and images. Bowker and Star contend that classification impacts epistemology, politics, and ethics (10). If we cannot escape the ever-growing, innumerable categories and classification systems proliferating digitally on the Web, will there be consequences that we need to envision today?

This chapter explores the graphical constructions through which classification schemes are exhibited on the World Wide Web, along with the text filling those constructions. I analyze several suites of pages in order to uncover the hidden taxonomies with their underlying laws and principles, if indeed there are any. I wanted to determine whether the categories represented have further impact, so I asked the following questions:

- Is there any difference when classification is presented digitally rather than in print?
- Does a classification system and the way it is represented graphically on the Web show any bias in its information display?
- Will the classification scheme have any impact on the way users may perceive themselves?
- Are classification schemes on the Web used more often for persuasive purposes than classification on a printed page?
- Is the classification system built on historic principles which may now be outdated?

- Does the classification scheme have immediate, direct effects on the lives of its users?
- What can a classification system tell us about the perceived world of its designers and the cultural attitudes of that world?

CHAPTER 4

Chapter 4 analyzes rhetoric, context, and culture as they appear in retail sites on the Internet. Digital texts inundate our students as they conduct research, purchase items, download music, play games, and generally live their lives online. Countless numbers of Web sites whose designs are often motivated by commercial interests that may prove reductive or simplistic when we examine these sites rhetorically assault these students' eyes and minds, thus consciously and subconsciously reinforcing sometimes questionable rhetorical displays.

I argue that the old problem of textual study needs refreshing in this age of the ubiquitous, digital, visually loaded Web text. Our students need the same critical skills that they apply to advertising ploys and appeals found in other media. They need the same attention paid to critiques of the organizations funding these Web sites as they might to markedly propagandistic texts. They need the same analysis of the cultures giving rise to organizations holding particular company philosophies as they might to a study of the documents authored by a society that would side with music conglomerates to outlaw a collaborative online venture like Napster.[3] And finally they need skills that will help them to assess what sites are more open than others about using rhetorical strategies that display their motives clearly. As instructors of rhetoric and composition we can train our students to apply traditional rhetorical tools to analyzing the visual/verbal hybridity of the Web site, and in this way to develop an analytic competence and cultural awareness that will serve them as public citizens and employees once they move into lives and careers beyond our classrooms.

This chapter examines the rhetoric of professional organizations and businesses as conveyed through the words and images displayed on their company Web sites in order to analyze the effects of different rhetorical strategies and the company qualities and philosophies reflected by those effects. By studying sites that display clear company philosophies and by analyzing the way the sites use visuals, including visual rhetorical devices—that is, figures of speech such as metaphor, metonymy, and synecdoche portrayed visually—and the visual syntax of complete Web sites, I argue that some organizations have a more complex presence than the appearance they present on their splash pages. A few of these sites can also reflect either a misunderstanding of audience or a subconscious blindness to the global audience present on the World Wide Web. Throughout this entire chapter I offer specific strategies for examining the digital rhetoric of Web sites.

CHAPTER 5

While other chapters in this volume touch on relatively contained individual rhetorical elements like syntax, tropes, and figures, Chapter 5 focuses on the more expansive topic of delivery, one of the five rhetorical canons, explaining how this once somewhat overlooked single canon has lately come to play a pivotal role in digital texts displayed today on the Web. Within the past decade scholars in composition and rhetoric have begun paying increasingly more attention to delivery, realizing that technology allows a more performative aspect to text displayed online than text in a codex book. "Delivery" has traditionally referred to those non-verbal cues such as facial expressions, body movement, or voice modulation that help speakers present information convincingly. Largely fallen by the wayside for composers of written text, delivery is also missing from composition textbooks discussing effective writing strategies such as invention, arrangement, or style.

Tom Beghin, a scholar who has studied the rhetoric of musical performances, mentions that rhetoric provides us with a means of explaining communication that may also be non-verbal, for him of course, musical performances (2); he also mentions that rhetoric is useful for artists who perform and composers who create, for audiences who witness the performances, and for critics or scholars analyzing or studying effective deliveries and performances. His breakdown, then, can just as easily apply to digital performances embodied in Web pages. In this age of Web 2.0, those writing digital text for the Web must consider including a variety of "delivery" cues to make convincing and clear points and thus a successful performance. Those viewing such sites, both audiences and users, must be mindful of the range of digital rhetorical elements available to the creator in order to understand the delivery fully and respond appropriately. Finally, for those critiquing or analyzing such constructions, rhetoric offers ways to understand the entire construction and thus the site's delivery or performance as a whole. Digital delivery today fuses images, video clips, and sound with texts, so it merits our critical attention and study as such. This chapter focuses more on the "deliverer" rather than the method of "delivery", differing partly from the work of James Porter, for instance, whose important work "Recovering Delivery for Digital Rhetoric" analyzes digital delivery in terms of technological production and topics such as distribution and accessibility. However, this chapter resembles part of Porter's work in that I do not focus on remediation or distribution with regard to this canon. In oversimplified terms, I suppose I could say that I am more concerned with the delivery driver and 1) whether that driver has a firm understanding of how to reach her destination successfully, and 2) what amalgamation of tools—

- a GPS with spoken directions?
- maps with routes highlighted in bright colors? Turn by turn written directions?

- veteran driver lore and advice about problematic roads, tricky highway interchanges, or confusing street signs?
- a good personal sense of direction?

—she brings to bear on the problem of reaching her goal efficiently and successfully, than I am with the model of delivery truck and whether that truck is capable of handling all types of traffic congestion or rough roads leading to the most rural of areas on its route.

After an overview of current research on rhetorical delivery and the wide variety of topics being covered recently, this chapter focuses on analyzing rhetorical delivery as we find it embodied in the suites of pages that comprise a Web site. It asks what makes Web sites' performances, their delivery, more memorable. I analyze delivery as it is digitally performed, after examining purposes of some types of performances that at first glance seem unrelated to rhetorical delivery and performance, namely athletic and musical performances. This chapter discusses the idea that we can distinguish rhetorical performances from simple communication by understanding that rhetoric has social effects.

The chapter argues that we can understand rhetorical delivery by studying what we mean by rhetorical performance and then digital equivalents of performance. The chapter ends by presenting four different cases where we can see the social effects of their rhetorical performances as these different sites address exigent situations particular to their specific communities.

CHAPTER 6

The twenty-first century's visual and aural Web presses us to increase contact with other disciplines and with sub-specialties of our own discipline (see for instance the work of Cynthia Selfe, "The Movement of Air, the Breath of Meaning: Aurality and Multimodal Composing" [2009]; and a recent collection [2009] edited by Emily Golson and Toni Glover: *Negotiating a Meta-Pedagogy: Learning from Other Disciplines*) whose theories and analytic approaches can help us examine the Web more critically and more intelligently; semiotics, the fine arts, architecture, design, visual literacy, technical writing, and perhaps even geography are some of these disciplines. While composition studies has early on adopted a cross-disciplinary predisposition (see Janice Lauer), such a cross-disciplinary bent is even more important for digital rhetoricians.

Chapter 6 discusses the "Border Work" that we need to do because of today's hybrid texts and the digital situation I have been calling rhetorical fusion: the border between two-dimensional and three-dimensional texts; the border between geographical locations and their online Web sites; the border between disciplines. Because the World Wide Web is a commonplace technology everywhere today for education, commerce, and cultural institutions, its speed and easy access have made sitting in a classroom or lab unnecessary for participating fully in Web-related educational activities. Students can check their class syllabi and assignments on the Web, post their own Web pages, search for research materials, and conduct email correspondence—from their classrooms, dorm rooms, or homes. The ubiquitous technology of the Web is now heavily impacting our labor in general and our academic workforce in particular. These external pressures have forced us to grapple with digital literacy and ultimately to use rhetoric digitally. To shape ourselves as compositionists and rhetoricians of the future and maintain accountability to our Web-savvy students, we must challenge ourselves as teachers and scholars to apply our rhetorical skills in previously unforeseen ways because of this media explosion. This chapter suggests areas that educators can study in order to establish rhetoric as equally important to digital studies as design and computer programming are already. It also extends rhetoric's applicability to spatial analysis.

Once we understand the spatial characteristics of fused texts, we can begin to consider collections of pages themselves as being akin to three-dimensional places through which we navigate. We can also investigate disciplines related to studying space for helpful theories and analytic techniques, for instance Jean Trumbo's differentiation between several different types of space that designers—and I would add now, rhetoricians—must consider. This chapter also argues that the collection of Web sites representing some geographic locations like museums and memorials need to be read rhetorically together to get a complete rhetorical picture of the physical site's ethos, logos, and pathos. Finally, this chapter touches briefly on the concept of liminality in a broad sense as being a threshold for change, that elusive spot between borders where we might escape the confines of either side.

* * * * *

In between the time I began writing this project and its publication, the Web addresses or URLs of some Web pages may have changed. The placement of individual pages within an entire suite may also be different. Such changes would have happened whether this book was first published in print or online and are impossible to prevent given the amorphic, ever-changing structure of the Web. Most pages are still available through the addresses cited here, whether or not their links from original locations still exist. Much more important than links, however, is the inclusion of a page within a whole suite or larger Web site rather than the exact way it is linked. I realize that I, myself, having been so long accustomed to reading codex books and traditional journal articles, rely on the hierarchical significance of subordination while analyzing documents, whether print or digital. Or, to put this habit in rhetorical terms, I rely on hypotaxis more than parataxis to signify the primacy of certain ideas. The associative quality of paratactic connections, however, does not prevent or nullify an argument. Parataxis just changes an argument slightly so that claims become equal. The evidence I point to on Web pages, then, still applies, because it contributes to the message of the whole fused site. As I indicated above in my synopsis of Chapter 1, I explain more there about hypertextual organization, associative argumentation, and the historical contingency often affecting the act of analysis.

1 How the Digital is Rhetorical, Cognitive, and Cultural

In the next ten years, we will probably have to confront serious challenges to our reception and conception of text.

~ Stuart Moulthrop

If our definition of text expands to include electronic communication, then we will have to give graphics a prominent place in that definition.

~ Jay Bolter

Well over a decade ago, I noted that when my youngest relatives reached college, their generation would have never known a world without the Internet, would never have lived in a household lacking access to the Web, and would never have experienced text as completely independent of images. Many of us saw the digital world forming; I was hardly alone or psychic in anticipating our current situation. Young adults, teens, and children today, collectively designated the Net Generation a.k.a. Millennialists, think differently from previous generations and rely automatically on digital technology instead of paper.[1] Preparing for a recent trip a few years back, I remarked to a niece that I would be gathering maps and guide books from the Automobile Association. I've always done so and done so automatically. My then 17-year-old traveling companion looked perplexed. She simply said: "I'm just going to borrow Dad's GPS." Hmmmm. My turn: befuddlement. No paper? No maps? Well actually, why would I or anyone, for that matter, want paper maps that never seem to fold correctly, that take another person to read them while the driver tries to follow verbal directions? Despite my being adept with technology, that is, using email, texting, managing to figure out and use photographic software, shopping online, incorporating technology into my teaching, carrying a laptop and cell phone whenever I travel, and considering myself digitally sophisticated compared to most baby-boomers my age, I still distinguish between text and the technological or the digital, and I automatically choose text. Despite the ubiquitous presence of a popularized Web that has instigated a visual and aural proliferation of digital texts embedded with graphics, sound, and often video, my mind still persists in maintaining this unfortunate division.

Reading a codex book (i.e. one with paper pages that turn and are numbered sequentially) supports a linear logic and an ordered movement from one page to the next. The codex book may possibly contain illustrations, but these illustrations are usually ancillary to the book's main points and do not hinder the linear movement. While we can skip around in a codex book, perhaps checking the "Works Cited" page before starting the book or reading a middle chapter first, or skimming a few later pages, we understand the author's organizational principle: to state a concept or point that is developed, elaborated on, and supported as the book progresses through its sequentially numbered pages and chapters. The fundamental ordering principle is linear and progressive.

Among some groups of scholars, designers, and artists, however, the Web has caused a growing sense that we need to reconsider the shape of text now and in the future, and develop the skills we will need in order to understand the *apparently* new, complex rhetoric shaping such texts. They reason that digital texts (i.e. text appearing in digitized form on a computer screen in the form of CD-ROMs or Web pages) may be, but usually are not, numbered sequentially and support a non-linear textual movement from any one link or unit to any other. In this type of text, illustrations, graphics, and colors are givens. Any simple black and white text seems odd. And while we can move linearly through a digital text, going from one screen to the next and ignoring intervening links or highlighted hot spots, we understand the author's premise here is to encourage readers to choose links in a random, personally chosen order rather than an authorially dictated pattern.

We can take as an example one of the online articles I quote from a few pages below. When I download Doug Brent's hypertext article "Rhetorics of the Web: Implications for Teachers of Literacy" for offline reading, I get a folder full of .htm files. The files are ordered alphabetically, but reading them alphabetically may be the least coherent way to figure out the article's point—although it is definitely one way of proceeding. A better bet is to find the one page with the article's abstract, then its first or primary page, and to proceed in any order from there. The fundamental ordering principle for this hypertext is associative—or in rhetorical terms—asyndetic. For such multimediated digital texts, traditional notions of reading and conceiving would seem to be seriously challenged, as Stuart Moulthrop suggested in 1991 (255).

Even if we accept this challenge then redefine what we mean by "text" in order to accommodate digital text, we will need to revise our concept of rhetoric, too. Jay Bolter, calling the Web a vast global hypertext with millions of readers, has noted that electronic communication, hypertext in particular with its defining form, the Web site, threatens the modern definition of verbal rhetoric, primarily because this definition has no place for visual elements. Our definition of text, he says, must expand today to allow images and alternative forms of persuasion to figure more prominently in that definition ("Hypertext and the Question of Visual Literacy," 7). More recently (2007) Barbara Warnick argues that "the use of rhetoric in new media environments has been understudied by scholars and critics of rhetoric. The need for more research and theory in this area is great" (*Rhetoric Online*, 13). Warnick quotes Gunther Kress, who argues that today's modes of oral and written communication have been destabilized by today's multimediated texts, so much so that we urgently need tools and theories to aid in analyzing these hybrid forms (ibid.).

DIGITAL RHETORIC

The rhetorical tradition that began in Greece applied more to oral presentations than to textual artifacts. Greek citizens needed to arrange their words in a manner understandable to any listeners who might hear such words whenever the citizens spoke publicly.[2] Currently, rhetoric, while still associated with the spoken word, has come to be considered predominantly as a language art and a discipline classified as part of the humanities and the communications fields. While we study its effects on both the spoken and written word as an art of presentation and arrangement, we most often use printed transcripts of those words for such scrutiny, or we examine documents written without any intent to be presented orally. Traditional views of rhetoric have made little provision for visual persuasion.

Henrietta Nickels Shirk understood Bolter's concept of broadening our understanding of "rhetoric" nearly two decades ago when she wrote that "[f]rom the composing perspective, hypertext authors must be alert to two new ways of thinking about the presentation of information. . . . [T]hese new ways . . . actually relate to broad areas of study and trends that have long been of concern to students of composition studies who have been interested in *metaphorical theory* and *cognitive science* [my emphases] as these fields relate to the creation of texts" (181, 182).

Digital rhetoric is simply (or maybe not so simply) traditional rhetoric applied visually as well as textually. It is not another form of rhetoric. We do not switch from digital to traditional rhetoric. All of the components we are accustomed to discussing in traditional rhetoric, especially having to do with style and arrangement for the purposes of conducting logical, discursive, persuasive arguments, are elements that can occur visually. Digital rhetoric—the rhetoric that covers multimediated documents—builds on, uses the same cues as, already existing forms of traditional rhetoric.

"Digital rhetoric", as I use the term in this book, is not purely visual rhetoric and differs from verbal rhetoric, too: digital rhetoric includes visual elements—be they complete images, graphic elements, or colors—as equal to and fused with words, phrases, and sentences, in this online art of arrangement for the presentation of a "self" in civic or public discourse. Digital rhetoric differs from purely verbal rhetoric because it considers the simultaneous hybridity of digital text, that is, both the visual and verbal elements working together—fused, in other words—to convey a certain purpose. Digital rhetoric, unlike verbal rhetoric, does not ignore one of these two elements or privilege one over the other.

For those of us immersed in the study of digital rhetoric, claiming that written or spoken words and images share the same rhetoric, or using a term like "visual rhetoric", is commonplace. For rhetoricians accustomed to studying classical argumentation and persuasion in terms of the written or spoken word, however, including images in such study or talking about "digital rhetoric" could seem questionable. For these verbally based scholars, images and sounds hardly seem to share the same rhetorical parentage as words. And if we are, furthermore, claiming that images in the hypertextual environment of the Web possess rhetorical characteristics, we run up against those who, while supporting the revolutionary possibilities of the Web for reading and writing, still feel extreme ambivalence when considering hypertext's abilities to deliver one of the main staples of traditional rhetoric: the discursive argument. Doug Brent reflects, "[T]here are very good arguments to be made that hypertext, which privileges infinite hypotaxis [clauses in subordinate or dependent relationships] rather than parataxis [clauses in coordinate or independent relationships], can paralyse the ability of rhetoric to explore important questions of civil society through the creation and interpretation of rigorous arguments."[3]

Not solely logos or argumentation, however, rhetoric is also the art of persuading and representing the self in order to make that persuasion more effectively. In other words, ethos and pathos. Digital rhetoric makes easier our ability to apply the rhetorical triangle's three components—ethos, pathos, and logos—because we are actually able to see elements such as ethos and pathos at work, thus enhancing our critical, analytic ability to decide how effectively all three are working together in order to make an online text's case. Scholars like David Kaufer and Brian Butler have moved beyond the verbal alone to explore the connection between rhetoric and design elements in their two different volumes. *Rhetoric and the Arts of Design* identifies rhetoric as a relative of the design arts such as architecture, engineering, and graphics. *Designing Interactive Worlds with Words* describes a representational theory of composition that "envisions texts not as words and clauses forming sentences and higher-level linguistic units but rather as words, forming into design elements stimulating imagery-rich narrative worlds and invitations for readers to interact with them." This theory, they explain, "will become increasingly important in defining writing as the multimedia revolution follows its course" (xix).

To reiterate: before the Web and online documents became commonplace, most academic texts were only, and thus automatically, considered primarily as verbal constructs. Some rare exceptions, however, have always been technical, scientific, and fine arts texts. The nature of these disciplines dictates that their texts could not and still cannot exclude images as they convey their meanings. Jay Lemke says about the discipline of science: "Science is not done, is not communicated, through verbal language alone. It *cannot* be. The 'concepts' of science are not solely verbal concepts, though they have verbal components. They are semiotic *hybrids*, simultaneously and essentially verbal, mathematical, visual-graphical, and actional-operational" ("Multiplying," 87). Kathryn Northcut's recent work in technical writing studies the ways images work in popular scientific texts to draw a lay audience into a scientific argument. If, as Northcut argues, scientific illustrations help a lay audience better understand scientific arguments, then the images are working along with the texts to persuade and convince because without these illustrations, the texts would be far less likely to make their cases.

So much for the lay audience and popular scientific texts. What about scientists and the texts they write specifically for their fellow researchers? As Lemke argues above, scientific texts cannot rely on words alone because scientific texts are semiotic hybrids. Scientific research depends on illustrations—charts, schematic representations, tables, graphs, and photographic images of the subject—to make a point and prove that the research is both valid and replicable. We can use, as an example, a piece by Michael J. Weiser, Chad D. Foradori, and Robert J. Handa discussing estrogen receptor systems in the brain. The article distinguishes between two systems, Estrogen Receptor *alpha* and Estrogen Receptor *beta*, in order to make the case that the less researched *beta* system, unlike the *alpha* system, helps modulate some non-reproductive neurobiological systems. The figures and tables in this piece offer visual proof for the authors' claims, and since this piece partly discusses differences between two systems, it presents visual evidence in comparative schematic representations and tables as well as specific visual explanations in numeric form via tables to back up textual statements about differences. The images here are not "mere" illustrations but are necessary visual evidence crucial to the essay's argument.

Few other non-technical, non-scientific texts, however, especially in the language arts, have relied to any considerable degree on images, charts, or other graphics to make their arguments. In fact, the commonplace privileging of text over image prompted a number of scholars to argue for the legitimacy of the image as a cognitive tool.[4] And even if open to the possibility of visual argumentation, scholars generally seem to consider either text or image as a viable mode of argumentation, but not both together, much less both combined in the hypertextual format that has erupted in the shape of the World Wide Web. J. Anthony Blair, for instance, allows that philosophically "[t]here seems to be no reason in principle for thinking there cannot be visual arguments" (26). Blair ultimately concludes, however, that "the great advantages of visual argument, namely its power and its suggestiveness, are gained at the loss of clarity and precision, which may not always be a price worth paying" (39). While I might consider Blair's argument applicable to hypertext and strictly visual arguments, I think we can make a case for fused texts—those containing both text and images—as containing symbiotic elements that are all necessary for establishing and supporting a strong, persuasive, rhetorically sophisticated claim.

If we are to study the rhetoric of the World Wide Web seriously, we must expand our notion of text to include images and to concede that images and graphic elements are fundamentally rhetorical. For those texts such as Web pages, we must realize the degree to which the more effective texts rely on a rhetorical fusion of verbal and visual elements. Such an expanded definition of rhetoric will not only draw on our knowledge and practices as textual scholars. It will also clarify and identify how that knowledge and those practices have been refashioned. Reconceiving our notions of text cannot mean in any way that we discard traditional notions of print literacy. It means, rather, that we attempt to recognize in other forms those traditional textual modes of organizing information and reapply them—in this case, visually. We must come to understand that images speak rhetorically.

COGNITION, CULTURE, AND THE DIGITAL

> *We need to disestablish the view of cognition as dominantly and aggressively linguistic.*
>
> ~ Barbara Stafford

> *[T]he ways we have of doing things, the ways that seem to us to be natural and inevitable or simply the consequences of the interaction of human nature with the demands of a given task, are in fact historically contingent.*
>
> ~ Edwin Hutchins

In fact, because our cognitive acts—thinking, acting, writing—are historically contingent, escaping centuries of culturally honed cognitive skills seems unlikely: "[H]uman cognition is always situated in a complex sociocultural world and cannot be unaffected by it" (Hutchins, xiii). Rhetoric's modes and figures, whether we consciously identify them as such or not, permeate our culture, influencing the ways we come to shape, understand, and convey information. We may possess different levels of skills when calling on rhetoric as a composing tool, but rhetorical elements surround us because we are bombarded by a plethora of media and people attempting to persuade us and to convey information. Even basic writers, often erroneously presumed to lack any knowledge of rhetorical skills, are not clueless—just by virtue of being alert, functioning, intelligent members of a culture and society. They listen to their iPods and music CDs, they watch television and YouTube, they read newspapers either online or offline, they attend churches where they hear rhetorically crafted sermons. They have heard, then—and have subconsciously been affected by—anaphora, or extended repetition; they understand how to classify; they have seen and heard chiasmus whether they recognize its pattern as a rhetorical figure or not. They are part of a rhetorical culture, part of the number of its members who have attempted to communicate throughout history. "A good part of what any person knows is learned from other people. The teaching by others can be formal or informal, intended or unintended, and the learning can occur through observation or by being taught rules. However accomplished, the result is a body of learnings called culture, transmitted from one generation to the next" (D'Andrade, 179). The same transmission applies to a rhetorical culture.

My argument below is twofold. First, cognition and culture, as situated, social activities, influence the rhetoric we bring to new media's documents, both these documents' construction and the way we read them, including the visual components of Web pages: images, and graphics fused with text to achieve an overall design. Actually, because of their visual elements, we should consider Web pages in part as socially constructed sign systems whose signs, i.e. the images and graphics embedded within pages, are just as rhetorical as their texts alone. Second, with an expanded notion of rhetoric we can apply our pre-existing knowledge of verbal rhetoric to analyzing Web pages in their totality and to reading them critically. We can begin to ask how the visual components of Web pages contribute rhetorically to these pages' texts, to what the pages reveal and reflect about the individuals and cultures that create them, as well as to what degree the online pages function as successful examples of digital rhetoric.

* * * * *

Rhetorical structures constitute patterns of thinking that are historically and culturally ingrained—"original evolutionary equipment", as Richard Lanham would argue:

> We might . . . project rhetorical figures onto a yet larger scale. They may represent a basic evolutionary strategy for our species. The biologist Edward O. Wilson writes: "The brain depends upon elegance to compensate for its own small size and short lifetime. As the cerebral cortex grew from apish dimensions through hundreds of thousands of years of evolution, it was forced to rely on tricks to enlarge memory and speed computation. The mind therefore specializes on analogy and metaphor, on a sweeping together of chaotic sensory experience into workable categories labeled by words and stacked into hierarchies for quick recovery" (*Biophilia*, p. 60). Such a raison d'etre for figured language would make it finally into a kind of data-compression, an immensely rapid substitute for iterative searching. As such, it would be a part of our original evolutionary equipment, not an add-on; essential rather than ornamental. (*Handlist*, 80)

We have no reason to think that such cognitive structures would devolve or be inapplicable to images. We in the humanities and language arts simply have yet to make such connections as a matter of course even though our colleagues in communication studies have been doing so regularly, some for quite a while.[5]

Certain elements of textual rhetoric, then, apply obviously to ways in which we can understand visual rhetoric. Because we have already been acculturated to hearing and reading these verbal patterns, they should be relatively easy to "recognize" when they occur visually and thus seem less bewildering since our acculturation makes it nearly impossible for us to think in different, that is, alien or foreign ways. To illustrate the control that cultural traditions hold in seemingly unacculturated tasks like moving from one point to another, Edwin Hutchins uses the example of the differences in navigational computation for Western and Micronesian navigators (Hutchins, 49–116).

> The difficulties that were overcome in the creation of all these techniques [i.e. those used in navigation], and the power they provide relative to their predecessors, are not at all apparent to the modern practitioner. Only when we look at the history can we see just how many problems had to be solved and how many could have been solved differently in the course of the development of the modern practices. A way of thinking comes with these techniques and tools. The advances that were made in navigation were always parts of a surrounding culture. They appeared in other fields as well, so they came to permeate our culture. (Hutchins, 115)

A pattern of thinking will not cease if we move from words to images or to an amalgamation of both on the World Wide Web. We can see one example in the proliferation of indexes on the Web. People are attempting to sort and classify all manner of information in order to provide us all with a sense of control over this information and an ability to recover it quickly. People automatically classify, and they have also become accustomed to applying classifications to whatever they display on Web pages.

Almost any retail site on the Web will provide an example of just the type of classification or index I mean. While we are looking at such pages from Target, Best Buy, or Wal-Mart online, we might just as well be looking at an index from a city directory or a lifestyle magazine. The mental habit of classifying information for ready access does not look much different online on the Web than offline in a codex book. Finding the information is simply faster. Even if we do add more images, as for instance in a site like Amazon.com, we can still see that the form of an index does not change much. Images here are merely illustrations of current books, music CDs, or movie DVDs.

Rather than saying that we are pre-programmed to design and speak on the Web in culturally determined ways, I am saying instead that such an acculturation makes online organizational patterns and visual rhetoric more familiar than not. Jay Bolter and Richard Grusin argue that the new media can only achieve significance culturally by "paying homage" to earlier media. If they are correct, any new or expanded definition of rhetoric must draw on pre-existing, historically contingent cognitive skills and pay homage to pre-existing forms of rhetoric and literacy skills. The increasingly visual nature of hypertext as embodied in the World Wide Web must display its rhetoric visually as well as verbally.

Although the forms and stories—the syntax, vocabularies, and literacies—of Web pages look to be new and different, the rhetoric and rhetorical strategies the pages embody, their visual figures and tropes, arise from ones with which we are already familiar. For Susan Hilligoss, familiar techniques from classical rhetoric—invention, arrangement, style, delivery, and ethos—can all be communicated visually (2). Metaphor and other figures of speech such as anaphora and accumulatio (technically a heaping up of description for emphasis, summary, or inference) have their visual equivalents. Furthermore, if associative thinking is the hallmark of hypertextual argumentation, we are already accustomed to the associative organization and "argumentation" of poems.[6] Mapping a sonnet with its metaphoric links and associative connections between quatrains and couplet produces a document resembling a series of linked Web pages. Reconceiving rhetorical and poetic figures in visual terms will help us to analyze digital texts which include images, to understand and map the thinking processes reflected through the choices involved in more complex Web site construction, and to realize that images and words are complementary, together forming a more complete rhetoric than a singular concentration on words could ever provide.

Once we begin analyzing, in more informed ways, the degree to which these Web pages have absorbed a culture and rhetoric that they reflect back to us in refigured, refashioned forms, we can then also become digitally literate, skilled, as Richard Lanham has put it, at "deciphering complex images and sounds as well as the syntactical subtleties of words, . . . [so that we feel] at home in a shifting mix of words, images and sounds" ("Digital Literacy," 198, 200).

DIGITAL ORGANIZATION AND ANALYTIC FUSION

I have been stressing that visual and verbal elements become fused within a digital terrain. Online rhetorical analysis, then, should focus in part on how well both visual and verbal rhetorics work with each other to serve the document's final purpose. I want to move now to discussing digital rhetoric as it applies on different scales to both the online document's overall organization and its smaller pieces, that is, to different sizes of projects, whether we are viewing

1) the outlines of a Web site's design:
   the organizational patterns we identify as being constructed to contain individual screens of text, the forms used to sustain and develop the text's main point, the elements used to indicate that pieces of an online text belong to the same overall document, and any other elements that help an online text cohere—what we would describe as "global elements" when training our composition students to review their peers' written papers,
2) an individual Web page where visual and verbal elements contribute to a single page/screen's point, or finally
3) a micro scale within individual pages:
   that is, those elements that work in a paper text on a sentence level: syntax, clausal connection patterns, rhetorical figures, and transitions between sentences—what we would describe as "local".

Scholars in one branch of rhetorical study—rhetorical structure theory—have worked for years on characterizing rhetorical design structures of a variety of differently sized texts. While I claim no expertise in this field, I do want to point out that Web texts, too, have design patterns—whether we look globally or locally—and I especially want to emphasize the importance of considering a digital text's organization to be just as rhetorical as its individual elements.[7] Therefore, because digital rhetoric, with its fused visual and verbal parts, is—as I have been maintaining throughout this chapter—still *rhetoric* at its base, I want to concentrate now on rhetorical elements as such. When we begin to study how digital rhetoric on Web pages combines visual elements with text to contribute to a Web page's message or point, we should also realize that we can apply rhetoric—especially figurative tropes and schemes—on all digital levels, from essay organization to the individual sentence. So two questions we can begin asking are 1) whether graphics and images work together with their verbal contexts to support the larger text's point, or 2) whether these visual elements clash rhetorically with their contexts either to convey a different message or obliterate the original message altogether. More on this subject of clashing elements later.

But first a distinction. Visual elements on a digital Web page do not function in quite the same way as graphic elements on a printed page because the digital or online graphics possess a greater possibility for work, that is, a greater likelihood that they will do more than simple illustrations or graphic decorations would. I concede that graphics within a non-technical article or book have a higher chance of being more decorative than essential for the author's argument simply because of the rhetorical history of printed arguments: traditional texts rely on traditional hierarchical argumentative structures. Graphics have little place here. Online documents, however, more specifically Web pages, cannot rely on strict hierarchical argument to make their case or persuade viewers of an author's point. Therefore online graphics need to work harder as rhetorical elements because they are more involved than decoration in the art of persuasion. Richard Lanham actually discusses the pressure on online graphics although he does so in economic terms, that is, in terms of competition for scarce resources. When so much online material competes for our attention, what we see when we drift through different sites had better capture our attention lest we just keep drifting. In *The Economics of Attention: Style and Substance in The Age of Information*, Lanham also contends that

> the digital computer has created a new expressive space. The screen works differently from the page. Words don't stay put. They dance around. Images play a major role and they move too. Color is everywhere. And sound, too, spoken and synthesized. Above all, a different expressive economy prevails. The printed page depends on an economics of deprival. No color, no movement, images in careful moderation. All these sacrificed to create an expressive field that encourages concentration on conceptual thought. It is a monopolistic attention economy, directed from the top. The digital screen depends on an economics of plenty. It allows competition between word, image, and sound for our attention. It is a market attention economy, driven from the bottom. (19–20)

I agree with Lanham that many of our new expressive spaces contain competing words, images, and sounds. What I am illustrating during the course of this book, however, is that such a competitive expressive economy exists in an expressive space that forgets about some or all of rhetoric's features, from the larger such as ethos or pathos to the smaller such as synecdoche. If images or graphics are inconsistent with their verbal contexts, the only recourse for both is competition.

For those of us with language arts backgrounds—rhetoric, expository writing, and literature—the Web's visual/textual hybridity proves to be one big stumbling block regarding digital rhetoric on the Web. Rhetoric as a verbal discipline should not disappear when we analyze Web pages. I, for one example, keep having to catch myself, to retreat from investing text on the Web with primacy at the expense of images on the Web, even from overlooking the rhetorical function of graphics, small or large, which I often find so easy to ignore or dismiss subconsciously as decoration. I need to remember constantly that a Web page's images, as much as its text, can be analyzed rhetorically. They can be connotative, for instance, in addition to being denotative. They should follow the rules for rhetorical patterns, parallelism for instance, if there are two or more images in a row. If the images are also metaphoric, for instance, the metaphors should not be mixed. Slip-ups lead to competition between words and images in online spaces.

One of the prevailing dicta of Web page construction is to avoid overwhelming the viewer with text. The elaborate and detailed logical progressions of the printed page are not only more difficult to follow on a Web page. Complicated logic along with blocks of solid text will also make viewers move on to another site, thereby undermining all of the hard work involved in walking the tightrope of a finely crafted argument. Such difficulty does not mean we "dumb down" or eliminate strictly traditional arguments as hypertext critics are sometimes wont to do. It means, rather, that we put complexity into another form, one more compatible with viewing.

Invention, logical arguments, and persuasion need not necessarily be purely verbal; if we can begin studying Web pages as media hybrids, we can begin understanding how figures of thought, tropes, and schemes play out in terms other than verbal.[8] Doing so, we can begin to address a problem that Jay Bolter and others have raised:[9]

> Hypertext undermines the rhetorical foundation for the teaching of writing—that is, the need for a unified point of view and a coherent thesis. To include hypertextual writing and reading in the curriculum, we would need a rhetoric appropriate to the associative character of hypertext, as Landow (1992) argued. To comprehend the structure of a given hypertext, the reader must grasp how its links function. (Bolter, "Hypertext and the Question of Visual Literacy," 10)

To the last line above I would add: and grasp how its images are both literal and metaphoric. A rhetoric encompassing the visual would allow for asyndetic (or associative) forms of argument where the "missing" conjunctions, in this case, could be supplied by images or graphic elements. Visual elements would also enable links to be comparative or parallel or hierarchical or subordinate or coordinate, all structural critical thinking skills that currently form part of our rhetorical culture.[10]

As an example we might use any of the university Web sites whose opening pages contain pillars, books, or other typically academic-looking graphics. Often the pages have photos of faculty and students or administrators. Also embedded in menus either horizontal or vertical are categories opening up to aspects of the university students and visitors might want to explore. Whatever happens to show up there, however, is both denotative and connotative with a bit of synecdoche thrown in for good measure. These days many universities have their mission statements posted online, so one useful exercise is to consider that statement in conjunction with the photos and other graphics to see whether they show a consistent point of view. One would think the photos should connote some of the qualities described in the mission statement by suggesting metaphorically those characteristics and attitudes espoused by the university. If an institution of higher education prides itself on its teaching focus and on its teacher/student ratio, what better way to suggest these elements than by showing a single instructor, a professor and not a teaching assistant, advising a single student? The photo can then connote individual attention and an individualized education, as opposed to the lack of individual attention students confront at large research-oriented public universities where beginning undergraduates have little to no contact with the tenured faculty or scholars holding endowed chairs. While this philosophy can be spelled out verbally in the school's mission statement or pedagogical philosophy, images must do their rhetorical duty by presenting visual metaphors for student-centered teaching at this particular school.

The image of Grecian or Roman pillars, in fact any buildings with traditional-looking Greco-Roman pillars, is also connotative, implying a connection to all the classical Greek pillars we have seen constituting the architecture of traditional universities with ivy-covered halls. The pillars suggest a connection with a traditional academy and a traditional university education, no matter that the 1960s-era campus itself may contain not one single ivy-covered hall decorated with Grecian pillars. The campus Web site will make the case visually.

When they write for the Web and analyze its pages, rhetoricians and compositionists may actually have something to learn from scientists. When scientists write science, they do not communicate their ideas through words alone, and often

> they do not produce linear verbal text; they do not even limit visual forms to the typographical. They do not present and organize information only verbally; they do not construct logical arguments in purely verbal form. They combine, interconnect, and integrate verbal text with mathematical expressions, quantitative graphs, information tables, abstract diagrams, maps, drawings, photographs and a host of unique specialised visual genres seen nowhere else. (Lemke, "Multiplying," 88)

While some of the same rhetorical and design principles that apply to technical communication documents apply to digital rhetoric, Web pages' hypertextual navigability, associative or asyndetic linking, and the possibility of containing visual elements that can move complicate their rhetoric. The texts are no longer sequential but can be. They can be associative but needn't be read that way. Graphic elements and images can be used throughout Web texts for directional purposes while at the same time exhibiting rhetorical characteristics such as metaphor, metonymy, or synecdoche—understandable as such only through analyzing these images in the context of their surrounding words.

> Rhetorics inevitably vary by their substance (here articulated sounds, there image, gesture or whatever) but not necessarily by their form; it is even probable that there exists a single rhetorical *form*, common for instance to dream, literature and image. . . . This rhetoric [of the image] could only be established on the basis of a quite considerable inventory, but it is possible now to foresee that one will find in it some

of the figures formerly identified by the Ancients and the Classics. . . . It is probable indeed that among the metabolas (or figures of the substitution of one signifier for another), it is metonymy which furnishes the image with the greatest number of its connotators, and that among the parataxes (or syntagmatic figures), it is asyndeton which predominates. (Barthes, 49–50)

We can see operating on many Web sites typical uses of metonymy, that is, using something closely associated with another thing to represent the first object. If we say, for instance, "the White House decided to forego a tax refund in favor of a tax increase," the term "White House", a location closely associated with the President, represents him. On some Web sites advertising vacations in the states of California or Florida, we often see clichéd images of oranges or beaches. These objects which are closely associated with both states come to stand for them visually. Asyndeton, the other figure referred to above, is technically a term used to refer to the lack of conjunctions between a series of words, phrases, or clauses. Any connection between them is implied by their being grouped together rather than by the use of any explicit conjunction. If we consider many Web sites—for instance any of the retail sites I mentioned earlier—we see several series of items to click on for further information. Those gathered under a standard topic named something like "news and events" are one such series. The links for further information about recently added items are not conjoined to each other, nor are any of them subordinated to the others. They are simply gathered together minus conjunctions as representations of new items in stock or new events within the retailer's different divisions.

Scholars, certainly, have studied interactions between the word and the image before. W.J.T. Mitchell, in particular, has for decades been grappling with this issue.[11] But the digital, hypertextual nature of the World Wide Web is complicating, or at least shifting, the issue. The social situations that have given rise to and that sustain most of Web culture partly resemble, but mostly differ from those that gave rise to the book.

One big difference is the heavily economic focus, the more or less democratic publishing opportunities, and the prominence of a younger generation (20–30 years of age) of primarily white males as the people who control programming, marketing, and software development. The Web has become primarily a tool to search for information on any subject, a place to play games, and a giant retail space where we may purchase anything we want online.

BACK TO CULTURE

I return now to where I started, to the subject of culture and to ask what we might understand about the culture reflected through various Web pages, a reflection that rhetoric might help us to analyze more completely. The overarching reason, for me at least, to use rhetoric to analyze Web pages so closely and to stress the rhetorical properties of images when reading and constructing Web pages would be to analyze exactly what they reflect about the thinking processes and the culture from which they arise. Take the ever-present, seemingly innocent technique of classification that I mentioned briefly above, the organizing principle of any number of Web pages and search tools. "Categorization is not a matter to be taken lightly" (Lakoff, 5). Basic to any way of thinking in any culture, this inherent, automatic ability to group information helps us to function in our societies. But in cases where institutions, for example,

> make classification for us, we seem to lose some independence that we might conceivably have otherwise had. . . . [I]nstitutions survive by harnessing all information processes to the task of establishing themselves. The instituted community blocks personal curiosity, organizes public memory, and heroically imposes certainty on uncertainty. In marking its own boundaries it affects all lower level thinking, so that persons realize their own identities and classify each other through community affiliation. (M. Douglas, 91, 102)

I recall an old Web page from the Modern Language Association's Web site as a case in point. Items listed under "The MLA at a Glance" showed how this institution has "[harnessed] information processes to the task of establishing [it]self": databases, bibliographies, periodicals, all for the purpose of establishing this group as an imposing, influential institution. The two images chosen to represent the historic nature of the group and its move to modern times were particularly revealing and interesting. The images' lack of parallelism betrayed a move from the more personal to the institutional: somehow, in the move from the 1920 convention to the 1999 convention, these images suggest, the MLA transformed itself from an organization represented by its heavily male, albeit *human*, membership to one that pictured itself in terms of concrete—buildings and skyscrapers. Using rhetorical analysis here would seem to reveal a group that lost sight of its individual members. Clearly, when images constitute the classification, Web designers more easily dropped the kind of critical proofreading guard with which we inspect printed documents. No one recognized or caught the faulty parallelism, the *visual* faulty parallelism. No one realized what an odd suggestion the two mismatched images conveyed.

We understand the world through categories, often finding it difficult to reorganize accepted classification systems in any other way because "to change the very concept of a category is to change not only our concept of the mind, but also our understanding of the world" (Lakoff, 9). Chemists, for example, find bewildering the idea that the periodic system of elements could be organized in any way other than the traditional table they have seen since the day they started studying chemistry. I once made such a suggestion to a good friend, a chemist: offhandedly, I remarked that the periodic table was "just" a classification system, and as such, only one person's organizational idea, only one person's visualization of the way to make visual sense of the elements. Her reaction made me feel like a chemical atheist, better yet, a scientific anarchist bent on overturning centuries of reverently held beliefs. Years later, however, I came across an article by Punyashloke Mishra that contained images of alternate representations of the periodic system of elements drawn up in ways that we have usually never seen. Mishra's article references a volume by Edward Mazurs devoted entirely to showing alternative representations of the periodic system as it was variously conceived over 100 years. Needless to say, switching to these other concepts or reorganizing all visualizations of the elements would necessarily result in changing the fundamental way chemists (and by extension, lay people) understand and organize the elemental world. For this reason, we need to remember that, along with conveying facts and other information, Web pages' images and texts reflect quite a bit about the culture and society producing them.

We can analyze a wide variety of Web pages to note that various clusters have much visual classification in common. Looking at the overarching or global design of many commercial Web page clusters, we recognize that they almost always have somewhere the shape of a directory classifying the information we can expect to find at that site. This mode of classification, likewise, almost always takes precedence over description.

If we look back at retail sites and even humanities-related sites such as the Modern Language Association's that I discussed above, we can see how this tendency to classify and list dominates methods of conveying information on the Web. The index occurs on nearly all opening pages. On some pages it appears as a vertical list usually on the left side of the page. In others it is the equally ubiquitous, but more subtle, narrow horizontal band atop the page. Web pages without such directories or indices are rare. One site, however, that does overcome this nearly universal tendency to offer a classification or index of information immediately belongs to the architectural firm Helmuth, Obata & Kassabaum (http://www.hok.com). But first a little story because my choice of this site is not random. I have been studying it since the mid-1990s. In retrospect, I believe that this site was one of the main influences that drew me into thinking about visual and digital rhetoric and subsequently the importance of digital fusion as well as the rhetorical nature of museum displays.

I became acquainted with the work of Gyo Obata, one of the firm's partners, in a roundabout way—through an exhibit titled "Obata's Yosemite, Obata's Designs" at the Japanese American National Museum from July 9 through October 9, 1994. The exhibit featured the art of Chiura Obata and the designs of his son, Gyo. There I read that because of the impending execution of Executive Order 9066, Chiura Obata wisely removed his son from the University of California, Berkeley, and sent Gyo to continue his studies in architecture at Washington University in St. Louis where he escaped being incarcerated in one of the concentration camps where other Japanese American citizens from the west coast were sent. The exhibit mentioned some of the projects that Helmuth, Obata & Kassabum, now known as HOK, had completed: the Southern Illinois University Edwardsville campus, the National Air and Space Museum, Xerox's Research Center, Levi Strauss' Headquarters, Camden Yards, and Apple's Headquarters. Impressed by this list of architecturally lauded constructions, I searched online for HOK's Web site. What I found was a well-designed, elegant site—especially in the context of Web sites from the mid- to late 1990s—where HOK referred to itself as a visual communication company. Intrigued, I searched through the site and found a page labeled "Design Practice" that, while not using the term "rhetoric", specifically, focused on exactly the kinds of topics rhetoricians concern themselves with when thinking about writing projects. What? Architects using rhetoric and thinking about writing? I was hooked.

The HOK site illustrates exactly what I mean by "digital fusion" and by the digital being rhetorical, cognitive, and cultural. I would argue that this Web site is so elegantly designed not simply because it represents a firm whose work is inherently design-based. Its elegance comes from rhetoric. The HOK site is rhetorically based and rhetorically sound. If rhetoric asks us to be completely aware of our audience whenever we write, HOK's architects and designers put their clients, i.e. their audience, first:

> Though we aim for design excellence on every project, HOK has never wanted to be the "starchitect." We don't wear black capes. Our legacy, from Gyo Obata, is that design is about problem solving, not personal statements. Instead of making icons, we make improvements. Instead of designing buildings that scream, "look at me!" we want to ask our clients, "Did we help you?" (Valentine)

HOK also seems to be critically aware of the variety of audiences for its Web site, not just their clients. Other architects, lay people like me, future clients, students, and those interested in this company's philosophies, architectural and otherwise, can find ample information, often in fused format.

As we are welcomed to this site's opening screen, we see first the words "Ideas Work" followed by images that appear one by one, each slowly fading away before the next one appears, all centered under the motto "Ideas work". Two words. Multiple layers of meaning.

- The firm's *ideas work*—HOK is continually awarded high-profile projects and has won numerous awards
- The buildings that embody the *ideas* encourage *work* within them
- The *ideas* reflected through the work shown on the Web page do the *work* of verbal descriptions, menus listing firms that have hired them, or lists of the wide variety of projects they have completed

Figure 1.1   Carnival UK headquarters. Photo by © Chris Gascoigne. Courtesy: HOK.

Each photo exemplifies these layers. The images work so well rhetorically with their verbal context that this single phrase along with the company's logo and its reputation as one of the world's most respected architectural firms does the work of any number of menus, classification systems, and detailed descriptions. The firm has developed ideas and designs for innumerable businesses and organizations. Photo after photo displays their ideas as they have come to fruition. Their ideas, therefore, work. Their ideas are

Figure 1.2   Office Depot headquarters. Photo by © Barry Grossman. Courtesy: HOK.

also made literally concrete in the actual buildings and work places that are portrayed. Figure 1.1 shows the headquarters of Carnival, UK from outside; we can see four levels of variously colored work areas through the large glass windows.

The ideas also encourage work because the constructions and offices are so pleasant and well designed. Figure 1.2 shows an interior reception area for the Office Depot headquarters in Boca Raton, Florida, with whimsical paper-plane-like banners stretching across the ceiling.

Figure 1.3, an external shot of the Indianapolis International Airport, seems to invite travel. Even more than inviting travel, it also houses the work of travel and the ideas that make travel work smoothly.

Figure 1.3   Indianapolis International Airport. Photo by © Sam Fentress. Courtesy: HOK.

And Figure 1.4 shows an upward shot at a skylight in the Salvador Dali Museum in St. Petersburg, Florida. The skylight captures the idea of Dali's surrealism, while the museum's architecture works to display and support the ideas his work conveys.

The HOK site does not need a menu listing all of the firm's recent projects because we see a visual "list" so to speak of these projects and more as they appear one by one. For this company, visually fusing the firm's characteristics to minimal verbal context for their Web site's audiences is more important than inundating them with indices listing every possible item that a visitor might choose to look up. For those who do want these lists, however, we can easily find them by clicking on "Ideas", "Work", or "HOK".

These important characteristics of keeping visuals balanced with words are conveyed through the company's understanding of imagery-based communication, that hybrid mix of images and text that seems so hard to achieve right now. This company understands that knowledge can be artfully and strategically packaged and suggests as much through the balanced visual rhetoric of its Web site. But this series of photos that I have included here does not approximate the effect and movement of these screens online, nor the ethos, pathos, and logos that they convey visually. The site needs to be viewed online so that the digital fusion can be experienced.

Earlier in this chapter I implied that ethos can be conveyed through digital fusion. The HOK site contains a good example in a timeline. Those

Figure 1.4   Salvador Dali Museum. Photo by © Moris Moreno. Courtesy: HOK.

of us wedded primarily to the word may not realize that a timeline with fused images and texts works just as well as a *curriculum vitae*—or in this case better—to list projects and establish one's qualifications in a particular area. A timeline located under the innocuous label "History + Lore" beneath the HOK logo's menu item "firm profile" shows different company milestones distributed horizontally from 1940 to 2010. Clicking on a particular decade opens a view of thumbnails of projects completed during that time; clicking on a thumbnail opens a photo of the project with information about it. This digitally fused timeline is an example of ethos established both textually and visually through design instead of the usual list of projects we might expect. The site's designers are not bound by thinking in words because they do their thinking in other ways. They are accustomed to having their visuals speak in large part for them. In other words, digital fusion comes naturally.

As far as analyzing a Web site to understand the culture it reflects and the way it might directly or indirectly be arguing for a particular set of cultural values, this site makes such work easier for us because the firm is acutely aware of the cultural tradition architects usually descend from and the way they at HOK, in contrast, hope to influence not simply architecture but also culture and the world in general. Various papers deposited in the site's "Knowledge Center" (again a play on words because the section is a center where papers are deposited but also because knowledge is at the center of what HOK does) reject the traditional notion of architect as "star" (see Valentine) and buildings as hierarchical displays. Instead, a building's shape and interior construction can be created to reinforce vastly different corporate cultures ranging from the hierarchical on one side to the collaborative on the other, as Pamela Light of HOK explains:

If you were to walk into a building lobby and find yourself standing on a marble floor, surrounded by traditional, upright furniture and dark paneling, you wouldn't be surprised to learn you were inside a bank's headquarters. And it's a good bet that the finishes would become higher-end and private offices grow larger as you neared the C-suite.

Those visual clues communicate a formal, hierarchical culture.

Banking companies typically want to send a clear message to clients and employees that they are serious about financial responsibilities.

Now picture a loft space with a polished concrete floor, exposed ceilings, open work spaces, and large, overstuffed furniture in casual meeting areas. Those elements suggest a firm engaged in some type of creative services. That environment hints at a flat organization with an informal culture emphasizing teamwork and an open exchange of ideas. . . .

The characteristics of a workplace—particularly in the public, meeting and food service areas—offer many clues about what type of company resides there.

So perhaps the moral of the story I started a few pages ago is this: we should look for fusion in all the "wrong" places because we can never know what serendipitous paths might open up. But more about poking around in other disciplines' business in Chapter 6.

Students in our composition classes, however, when assigned Web projects, often have difficulty moving beyond an organizational rhetoric of classification and incorporating images in analytic ways that stretch beyond simple visual illustration of the words on their pages because of what they usually see for the most part on the Web. It is not hard to understand why. They have such trouble because of the rhetoric they see constantly reflected from the majority of pages they look at everyday, namely none. A while ago a colleague brought to my attention an entertaining critique of restaurant Web sites that offers a prime example of what happens when Web designers have only design skills but no training in rhetoric, least of all any notion of digital fusion. Audience, rhetorical context, ethos, pathos, logos—all are missing, thus causing a vacuum that led the reviewer to complain:

> The first thing that pops up when you visit the website of the San Francisco restaurant Fleur de Lys is a nearly full-screen animation of celebrity chef Hubert Keller's autograph. That makes sense—when I'm choosing a restaurant, the first thing I want to know is, *Can the chef sign his name?*
>
> Wait a second, though. What does Chef Keller look like? You're not going to bother with this place if the chef doesn't have a good headshot. Good news! After the signature, the site fades into a snappy photo of Keller. Fortunately, he's a looker—think Peter Fonda with Fabio's hair.
>
> After the autograph and headshot, the site transitions to a "main menu," which presents you with links to Keller's other restaurants and his PBS TV show. Tempted though you are, you stay focused and click for the San Francisco restaurant. One bit of advice: If you've got a subwoofer attached to your computer, now's the time to crank it up, because you're in for some auto-playing, royalty-free, ambient techno smooth jazz! As you stifle your urge to get up and dance, you click around in search of information about the restaurant. (The page emits a friendly beep every time you click.) If you spend the better part of your lunch hour scouring the site, you'll eventually find the menu. What you won't find is the price—it takes a Web search to determine that the tasting menu at Fleur de Lys costs $72 a person. . . .
>
> The head-poundingly awful Fleur de Lys site is just one of many in an industry whose collective crimes against Web design are as routine as they are horrific. (Manjoo)

This critique offers a few possible explanations for the general terribleness of restaurant sites, such as an owner's inability to pay for a good designer, restaurateurs wanting to control a Web site and offering an online entertainment experience, Web designers trying to create designs using Flash so that they can charge more for their designs, or designers who don't take the time to explain what most customers would want in a restaurant site. I would argue that it really all comes down to a lack of rhetorical focus and skills.

With our students we should analyze the rhetoric that occurs both verbally and visually on the Web. We could ask when classification, for example, is appropriate and when it is not, when classification occurs visually and when it does not, and what cultural situations might inhibit visual classification: for instance, since classification is a hierarchical structure, we could ask whether women might be less likely to choose it as an organizing principle for images and texts on their Web pages.

Rhetoric as we have known it is everywhere on the Web. To speak and think about *digital* rhetoric as employing both words and images, however, we need not reinvent the rhetorical wheel. We need instead to recognize how science, art, design, and mathematics make meaning, to study the way communication takes place through the use of images and graphics, and to realize that, given whatever larger social cultures we share, we can recognize similar patterns of thinking and then make meaning by considering the degree to which visuals work with their contexts in our rhetorical analysis. We should then be able to instruct our students to recognize such patterns themselves and apply them while writing in the hybrid medium that is today's Web. Recognizing these mental patterns, our students can also begin understanding how such patterns work upon us and at times constrain us. As James Berlin has warned:

> Our business must be to instruct students in signifying practices broadly conceived—to see not only the rhetoric of the college essay, but also the rhetoric of the institution of schooling, of politics, and of the media. . . . We must take as our province the production and reception of semiotic codes, providing students with the heuristics to penetrate these codes and their ideological designs on our formation as subjects. Students must come to see that the languages they are expected to speak, write, and embrace as ways of thinking and acting are never disinterested, always bringing with them strictures on the existent, the good, the possible, and the resulting regimes of power. (93)

Such study is not just a matter of examining Web advertising in terms of media's hold upon us. It goes beyond that to understanding cultural modes of thinking and perception, and finally, to how we view literacy. Big leaps, I know. But, to borrow E.M. Forster's words from a different cultural context, our jobs as scholars of digital rhetoric will be to "only connect" (*Howards End*, Epigraph and 186).

2 Rhetorical Literacy on the World Wide Web

Syntax, Tropes, Schemes, and Figures

The arts of language cannot help having a small but real importance,
whatever it is we have to expound to others: the way in which a thing
is said does affect its intelligibility.

~ Aristotle[1]

Rhetorical constructs such as syntactic organization, tropes, and figures emerge whenever people attempt to convey information, to reason, to describe emotions, to make sense of our world through writing, whether that writing is creative or expository. Think of it this way: only when we work alone do we drop words haphazardly on a page. Or scribble down phrases unattached to clauses. Or hand someone a written page of such disparate verbal elements. We put the words into sentences then put the sentences together in some kind of artful order so that they can make sense to someone other than ourselves, so that they will be intelligible. Or, to use a few similes phrased as questions: do we put the sentences one after the other as if we were dropping each one into separate, paratactically linked boxcars being towed along in a train? If two sentences have similar ideas, do we put them in boxcars with the same color? with parallel logos—two Southern Pacific or three Illinois Central or four Great Northern boxcars? Or do we tape sentences to a hypotactically constructed series of nesting dolls, each doll placed within and subordinated to the larger doll within which it is embedded? Whatever we do with our words and sentences, once we decide to show them to another, we must determine precisely how to package those words, phrases, and sentences so that they make sense to some other reader.

In our post-millennial world, however, we have that further complication, the basis for this book's argument: creative and expository writing no longer and will never again take place only on paper. The written "page" has morphed into text that can take shape both on paper and in digital form, but with digitality comes an increased ability to include the images and graphic elements now integral to writing today. To an extent that they never were for paper texts, images and graphics have become expected, if not necessary parts of those specific texts that we call World Wide Web pages, words and images existing together, or fused in digital contexts. In their fused state on the Web, we must remember, they are also fused rhetorically.

The relative ease of incorporating graphic elements, in whatever form, however, has presented problems for us as rhetorical scholars. Many of us are unaccustomed to thinking of visual elements as being equal to verbal elements when it comes to conveying ideas or information. We can thus easily overlook them in analytic studies. Additionally, when we think of rhetorical elements such as syntax, tropes, and figures of speech, we think primarily of the traditional written text instead of digital screens. Several historical prejudices have caused this skewing. As Eleanor Rosch and Barbara Lloyd explain, "The 'mature western mind' was presumed to be one that, in abstracting knowledge from the idiosyncrasies of particular everyday experiences, employed Aristotelian laws of logic. . . . If other thought processes such as imagery, ostensive definition, reasoning by analogy to particular instances, or the use of metaphors were considered at all, they were usually relegated to lesser beings such as women, children, primitive people, or even to nonhumans" (2). As products of Western culture, we regularly ignore the possibility of being able to reason by way of images, analogies, or metaphors. We are also products of educational systems supporting disciplinary territoriality rather than fostering shared inquiry—a fractured, compartmentalized *paideia*, in other words. Barbara Stafford argues, furthermore, that "in spite of the arrival of what I have termed the 'age of computerism' . . . a distorted hierarchy ranking the importance of reading above that of seeing remains anachronistically in place" (*Good Looking*, 4). Stafford emphatically seconds Rosch and Lloyd's argument above about the mature Western mind when she claims that "in most American university curricula, graphicacy remains subordinate to literacy" (*Good Looking*, 5); we who occupy those universities and who concern ourselves primarily with literacy and verbal texts usually pay scant notice to serious study of graphic elements except when they obviously form part of a writer's canon, as they do, for example, in William Blake's work, or if we happen to be fortunate enough to have some background in technical or professional writing. As a result, we have a hard time distinguishing eloquence in digital language (i.e. text composed of fused visual and verbal elements) and what a close reading of that language reveals. We can see this difficulty displayed in our students' work.

- Some of our students, when using visual elements in their texts, do not incorporate them well—they use images only for decoration or just to illustrate, in the way they see a photograph illustrating a newspaper article. Since later in 2010 through 2011, blogs, which used to be online versions of journals or letters, have been transforming into collections of images and photos with captions only or extremely short entries, suggesting a move away from a conscious use of equally weighted text and images, or even text at all.

- Sometimes, even if students do have extraordinary technical ability, they like to push something that Michele Shauf calls the "Wow!" factor, in other words, using the latest features of JavaScript, Flash, or streaming video, without paying critical attention to the rhetorical underpinnings of their graphic elements (Shauf, 37). This need for "Wow!" is part of the reason why the restaurant Web sites discussed in Chapter 1 of this volume go awry.

Clearly we need to rethink the credence we give to images as well as their ability to simultaneously convey and display rhetorical tropes and figures, especially when they happen to be integral components of digital texts like Web pages. This chapter considers rhetorical arrangement as it is reflected through syntactic order and design patterns on Web page collections as well as on both individual Web pages and within separate sentences and images on those pages. It also examines the use of figures, tropes, and schemes as part of that arrangement.

This chapter has a four-part argument:

1. Syntax and figures of speech which we considered primarily as the property of written text can no longer be attributed only to words, because we can identify them visually in the images and graphic elements that occur combined with text on the Web.
2. Figures of speech appearing visually, whether intentionally constructed or not, can convey either information or misinformation about the cultures that gave rise to those specific instances of metaphor and metonymy, so we had better pay careful attention to the cultural contexts of such figures and recognize them as true rhetorical figures.
3. Sites constructed for people devoted to the study or creation of primarily verbal language appear to reflect an uneasiness with the visual and some difficulty conceiving of the visual in rhetorical ways—that is, ways that aid in transmitting knowledge or furthering any understanding.
4. Sometimes, using visual metaphor or metonymy to focus our attention on Web pages is actually more effective than using words with plain non-figurative illustrations.

CHAPTER ORGANIZATION

First I tackle the subject of digital syntax since syntax for language-arts people seems bound up with words more than other forms of communication. Using the term "syntax" in a digital context, therefore, means we need to understand the concept behind the word so that we might take an idea previously connected mainly to words, and apply it instead to digitally fused constructs like Web pages. Traditionally, syntax referred to the order of words in a sentence. Digitally, however, syntax refers to the order of words and images on Web pages. If we studied patterns of words, phrases, and clauses on a printed page in previous decades, now we scrutinize patterns of words combined with images on digital pages. The primary syntactic patterns I focus on in the first section below are parataxis and hypotaxis.

Next, I discuss rhetorical tropes—metaphor and metonymy mainly, and as a subset of metonymy, synecdoche. I explore the degree to which fused digital texts and images play on the concept put forward by these tropes. However, trying to sort through various explanations of "tropes", "schemes", and "means of persuasion" in order to find an unquestionable, airtight definition, is a bit daunting. I therefore consulted two experts: Sister Miriam Joseph (*Shakespeare's Use of the Arts of Language*) and Richard Lanham (*A Handlist of Rhetorical Terms*) to find workable delineations and clear definitions.

Sister Miriam Joseph explains that rhetoricians from three Renaissance groups (the traditionalists, the Ramists, and the figurists), with the exception of Hoskynes, employed the traditional division of figures into tropes and schemes, and the further division of schemes into those that are grammatical and those that are rhetorical. A trope, such as a metaphor, turns a word's or sentence's significance from its proper meaning to another not so "proper", or more unusual, yet near enough to it so that the unexpected usage increases its force (33). We read poetry in part because we enjoy such unexpected usage. When Seamus Heaney speaks of "the frontier of writing", his unexpected comparison between the mental anxiety and creative peril of setting words on a blank page to the physical anxiety and peril of approaching a border checkpoint with armed guards drives home his point about the feelings associated with writing's psychological difficulty: whether living in Belfast during the Troubles or perhaps, on a much lesser scale, visiting New York City during the time surrounding the tenth anniversary of the 9/11 memorial tributes in New York, Pennsylvania, and Washington, DC, many of us would surely have felt that same unease, that small catching of breath, as armed guards or New York City police peered into cars and taxis stopped at a Manhattan checkpoint, and searched all vans and trucks. Do they think we look suspicious? Will we be pulled over? Or will we get through? Reading the poem, we derive pleasure from understanding the unexpected metaphor. We can derive the same pleasure from viewing rhetorically sophisticated Web sites as we do from deciphering unexpected figurative usage.

Sister Miriam Joseph further explains that grammatical schemes were subdivided into orthographical and syntactical schemes; rhetorical schemes, into figures of words and figures of sentence or thought (33). For Quintilian, says Richard Lanham, "a trope is a change in meaning, a figure is a change in form" (*Handlist*, 155). According to both Joseph and Lanham, however, finding such a clear-cut definition is nearly impossible because of numerous interpretations of "meaning" and "form".[2] I have decided, for the purposes of this chapter, and for expediency's sake, to side with Quintilian, defining a trope as a group of words or a sentence involving a change in meaning, and a figure as involving a change in form; I have organized my discussion accordingly.

The section immediately following, then, examines rhetorical tropes, mainly metaphor and metonymy, but also synecdoche as a subset of metonymy, exploring the degree to which fused digital texts and images play on the conceptual substitutions indicated by these three tropes. Next, I identify and analyze rhetorical figures—those involving repetition or amplification—to examine whether any changes of form or digital patterns emerge and impact our impressions and understanding of the page's or site's information. Throughout this entire discussion I refer to the types of groups or "cultures" in the broadest sense—that created these digital artifacts.

DIGITAL SYNTAX

Syntax or word order, as I have stated, has been easier to analyze in written prose, but much harder in visual compositions. However, if we examine the concept, especially etymologically, and note how various domains handle the concept in their own fields or contexts, then understanding how "syntax" translates within contexts that are digital gets easier.

Any search for the definition of "syntax" in a collegiate or online dictionary will uncover the word's etymological roots in the Greek *syn*, meaning "together", and *tassein*, that is, "to arrange" (see any current edition of Merriam Webster's collegiate dictionary or an online compilation found at www.websters-online-dictionary.org/definition). While we usually think of "syntax" in grammatical contexts, other domains such as computing, aerospace, business, electrical engineering, information retrieval, and mathematics, among others, use this term.[3] Making the jump to a digitized page with syntax consisting of fused images and text does not seem so outlandish, then, because we are working with the concept of arrangement in general, not of word order in particular.

Parataxis in a coordinated prose series, then, emerges as loosely linked words, phrases, or clauses, often using the conjunction "and" inserted between each, while hypotaxis in prose shows up in a subordinated series of clauses as tightly embedded and hierarchically ordered or subordinated thoughts. Richard Lanham gives an example of parataxis without conjunctions: "I came. I saw. I conquered" (*Handlist*, 108). Three separate statements, all of equal weight, no one clause taking precedence or importance over the others, no one clause qualifying another or suggesting an alternative situation. A selection from Sir Thomas Browne's *Hydriotaphia*, or *Urne-Burial* illustrates hypotaxis:

Though if Adam were made out of an extract of the Earth, all parts might challenge a restitution, yet few have returned their bones farre lower than they might receive them; not affecting the graves of Giants, under hilly and heavy coverings, but content with lesse than their owne depth, have wished their bones might lie soft, and the earth be light upon them; Even such as hope to rise again, would not be content with centrall interrment, or so desperately to place their reliques as to lie beyond discovery, and in no way to be seen again; which happy contrivance hath made communication with our forefathers, and left unto our view some parts, which they never beheld themselves. (1–2)

The passage begins with a subordinating conjunction signaling contrasting ideas to follow ("though") as well as cause and effect ("if"), and then another transition preceding a contrasting situation. All of this qualifying and ordering and subordinating occurs within about three lines of text before the first semi-colon. After it we find two relative clauses ("which") casting back to previous phrases and words.

Digitally, parataxis and hypotaxis can appear both in global organization, that is, collections of Web pages—the digital equivalent of an entire essay or chapter—and in the more local syntax—separate sentences or images—of individual pages. Interestingly, company philosophies can be inferred from the global organization of their Web sites. Simply put: hypotaxis = hierarchical, trying to account for and rank every possible situation. Parataxis = unranked, allowing for equal importance and not compelled to subordinate.

Most sites adhere to either the initially obvious hierarchical and exclusive or the unranked and inclusive "type", i.e. either hypotactic or paratactic—unless they are completely unorganized. Viewers of Web pages, however, can become frustrated by designs reflecting a company philosophy if they fail to anticipate such a structure behind a Web site or if such viewers neglect to understand how much a company's philosophy can subsume a Web site's structure. If a structure appears more hypotactic because it is ordered hierarchically, then a viewer wanting to give input sometimes has no recourse. The pages are not open to anyone except those with access to the power structure. Such pages often do not list contact information for those wanting to ask questions or give other input, or make such information difficult to find. Contact information can also be purposely left off such pages, the omission clearly indicating that viewer comments are unwelcome. Paratactically ordered Web pages, however, often invite viewer input because such input does not interfere with a collaborative organizational structure. While paratactic structure, at first glance, can seem more random than intentional, with non-hierarchically ordered links appearing haphazard, such an organization actually offers the viewer a link selection choice.

YouTube is a good example of a site built on parataxis and inviting viewer input. The different videos deposited on this site are not subordinated to one main video. We can and do enter the site in any number of ways. The videos may be linked according to similarity of topic, but none of them depends on another for coherent conveying of ideas. Occasionally we might find videos separated into parts, but this division only occurs because You-Tube previously had a film length time limit for posted videos; any posting exceeding that running time limit had to be divided.

As far as parataxis and choice go, Western culture and a generalized overall culture in the US in particular have been built on a hierarchical system while paying lip service to choice and equality. In reality, we expect to find one person in charge of a course, a college, a city, a state, a company. Organizations built on a hierarchical philosophy—for instance the Microsoft Corporation—have difficulties with parataxis because of company philosophies stressing organizational pyramids with someone at the top dictating organization and policy. Bing, Microsoft's search tool, is a perfect example. During late 2010 and early 2011, Bing TV commercials (see YouTube search: "bing commercials 2010 search overload holidays") poked fun at the supposed randomness of search tools—mainly Google—built on parataxis and the ability to move associatively. About this same time, Microsoft began branding its search engine Bing as a "decision engine", implying that having to make a decision on one's own if confronted with a myriad of findings is troublesome and frazzling, all of which further implies that users of search tools should want to avoid making decisions, much less prioritizing search results, but should prefer instead to leave sorting and deciding to someone else, namely a large corporation. So for one organization, Google, parataxis is natural, choice is "good"; for the other, Microsoft, paratactic choice is not choice but information overload, and thus "bad" because it fills a searcher's brain with Microsoft's opinion of needless information, while hypotaxis—that is, controlled searching—is the wiser choice because no choices are left to chance or to the viewer's own selection process.

CONCEPTION, COGNITION, SITUATION, AND FIGURATIVE EMBODIMENT IN DIGITAL CONSTRUCTIONS

> *The emphasis on finding and describing "knowledge structures" that are somewhat "inside" the individual encourages us to overlook the fact that human cognition is always situated in a complex sociocultural world and cannot be unaffected by it.*
>
> ~ Edwin Hutchins

Theories labeled variously as cognitive rhetoric, situated cognition, embodied cognition, and conceptual metaphor theory figure into my analytic approach in this chapter, that approach being in part to indicate where context and culture bear directly on figurative language and rhetorical choices.[4] If figurative language operates first on the level of cognition, then rhetorical choices—partly consisting of figurative language—must too. As Edwin Hutchins argues above, cognition is always situated in the world. Conceptual metaphor theory, likewise, asserts in part that the community and concepts surrounding the thinker/writer/digital composer constrain the thought process arriving at figurative language:

> Conceptual metaphor theory . . . adopts a constructivist view of language. Far from accepting the mechanistic or algorithmic approach often associated with early cognitive science, conceptual metaphor theorists agree that figurative thought arises from experience. And no experience can be more universal or more influential than our brain-limited, embodied perceptions of front-back, in-out, up-down, source-path-goal; of movement, constraint, energy, fatigue; of pain, pleasure, difficulty, ease. Such perceptions motivate our most familiar metaphors: Life Is a Journey, Problems Are Burdens, Words Are Weapons, Ideas Are Sources Of Light, Morality Is Cleanliness, Desire Is Hunger, and many more. (Eubanks, 7)

Decades ago, Mary Douglas argued that our social environments, institutions in particular, influence our judgments about good and bad, sense and nonsense, and the validity of logical connections, not to mention the way we conceptualize rhetorical constructions such as classification and metaphor. Douglas based her ideas about the individual and society on the theories of French sociologist Emile Durkheim and Polish biologist, M.D., and philosopher Ludwik Fleck. "Both," she says, "were equally emphatic about the social basis of cognition" (11). Douglas invoked Emile Durkheim in her argument that institutions do much of our thinking for us:

> For [Durkheim] the initial error [in thinking about the conflict between individual and society] is to deny the social origins of individual thought. Classifications, logical operations, and guiding metaphors are given to the individual by society. Above all, the sense of a priori rightness of some ideas and the nonsensicality of others are handed out as part of the social environment. (10)

DIGITAL METAPHOR, METONYMY, AND SYNECDOCHE

Born of cognition as much as language, metaphor and metonymy are normally figures of speech that we use in oral and written communication, whether creative or expository. The presence or absence, as well as the use or misuse, of metaphor and metonymy in digital contexts reflects the degree to which literacy scholars and rhetoricians can actually embrace the new digitality with its images, sounds, and words, and then apply their knowledge about literacy, reading, and rhetoric to these digitized texts. Metaphor and metonymy emerge whenever we attempt to convey information, to reason, to describe emotions, to make sense of our world. George Lakoff and Mark Johnson agree that "[metonymy] . . . like metaphor . . . is not just a poetic or rhetorical device. Nor is it just a matter of language. Metonymic concepts (like THE PART FOR THE WHOLE) are part of the ordinary, everyday way we think and act as well as talk" (37). The "everyday way we think": metaphor and metonymy, therefore, are ubiquitous cognitive displays that reveal a writer's mindset, showcase a speaker's originality, and sometimes present a thinker's sense of playfulness: fresh metaphors, unique instances of metonymy, both help us to think about the world in ways we may never before have considered and to delight in the unique transfer of character-istics or traits. Their use cannot be confined to written and verbal rhetoric because as ways of thinking, they operate whenever and wherever people attempt to capture, then communicate, their thoughts.

Because what we see and experience influences our everyday thinking and talking, "rhetorical scholars are responding to changes in rhetorical practice by expanding the data they analyze to include visual symbols. In the last several years, they have used visual imagery as data for the applica-tion, illustration, and explication of various rhetorical constructs" (Foss, "A Rhetorical Schema," 213). Within the broader subject of visual lan-guage, two scholars in particular have supported the rhetorical study of visual elements in texts. Sonja K. Foss argues that "in many . . . areas of the [communications] discipline, visual imagery has received virtually no attention—areas such as language, persuasion, rhetorical theory, rhetorical criticism, and public address" ("Visual Imagery," 85). And Robert Horn has convincingly established that concepts of classical rhetoric can be por-trayed visually (20).

But because metaphor and metonymy have always been primarily verbal constructs for most of us, we have usually been accustomed to identifying these ways of thinking in written or spoken language rather than through images combined with language, or—even rarer—strictly through images. In cases of fused digital composition, then, identifying visual versions of metaphor and metonymy could prove baffling. Visual metaphors, however, surround us and we continually employ them to illustrate concepts. Bathy-metric maps, for instance, illustrate an ordinary use of visual metaphor: we understand changes in the depth of water or altitude of land masses through gradations of color. Any map, as a matter of fact, is a visual metaphor.

Studying visual metaphor and visual metonymy in conjunction with their accompanying texts as they appear on the World Wide Web pro-vides us with a rarely used window on the cultures from which they arise. Like any artifact produced by any culture, Web pages cannot help but reflect their particular cultures and those cultures' practices. (Here I use "culture" in its widest sense to mean any groups or classes of people who have shared practices and understandings.) To reiterate: on one hand, the use or misuse or missed opportunities, in particular, of metaphor and metonymy in digitally fused situations suggests problems for us as scholars of the word if we are unable to embrace the new digitality with all of its components, that is, its images and sounds along with its words, and to apply what we know about rhetoric, reading, and literacy to these digitized texts. On the other hand, however, for those studying the world of digital composition, those occasions when we do stop to examine the figurative language or images in fused compositions can provide a compelling view of the ethos of digital composers.

Richard Lanham, quoting Christine Brooke-Rose, reminds us that metaphor is "any replacement of one word by another, or any identification of one thing, concept or person with any other" (*Handlist*, 101). "The essence of metaphor is understanding and experiencing one kind of thing in terms of another, "according to George Lakoff and Mark Johnson (5), who illustrate two ordinary metaphorical concepts with the phrases "Argument is war" (4) and "Time is money" (7). Metonymy, sometimes considered a subset or special variety of metaphor, occurs when "one word is substituted for another with which it stands in close relationship. . . . e.g., the name of the inventor or possessor, for the invention or possession; the container for that which is contained" (Preminger, Warnke, and Hardison, 499). In the sentence "She likes to read *Shakespeare*," the name of the writer stands in for the entire body of his work. As an example, if we say, "The *White House* decided to raise taxes," the building represents the people who work there. Closely associated with metonymy is synecdoche, "often . . . regarded as a special type of metonymy, wherein the part is substituted for the whole, or sometimes the whole for the part" (Preminger, Warnke, and Hardison, 840). "All hands on deck" or "There are a lot of faces out there in the audience" are two usual examples.

Clearly then, considering figures of speech primarily as the property of written text attributable only to words is *no longer* possible. Figures can be identified in the images and graphic elements that occur combined with text on the Web. If metaphor and metonymy occur visually on the Web, I believe that they serve as more than mere illustrations of the words they accompany: they are crucial components of the rhetoric of Web pages and the arguments that those Web texts make. In addition, they reveal culturally predisposed instances of conceiving of and thinking about ideas, for instance one mentioned by Lakoff and Johnson: the practice in Western culture of using the facial portrait to represent a person.

George Lakoff and Mark Johnson argue that we cannot help but think in metaphoric terms and that we cannot function without these rhetorical constructs: "Metaphor is pervasive in everyday life, not just in language but in thought and action. Our ordinary conceptual system, in terms of which we both think and act, is fundamentally metaphorical in nature" (3). Bob Horn, quoting Lakoff, talks about metaphors helping us to understand unfamiliar concepts in terms of more familiar ones, then says: "We don't really have a choice about using or not using metaphors. Our cognitive abilities are thoroughly enmeshed in metaphors. If we dig down under just about any communication, we will find that something is very often understood in terms of something else" (113).

One example of a Web page constructed without apparent thought given to the rhetorical function of its visuals in relation to each other and to its text occurs on a page called "Learn More about the Modern Language

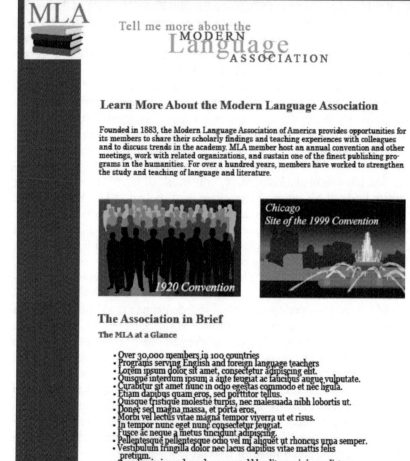

Figure 2.1   1999 MLA Convention Web page diagram.

Association" from the MLA's 1999 Web site discussed earlier in Chapter 1. My assertion merits more analysis. The site is no longer available even in Web page archives, so I hope that my description and reproduction of the content (Figure 2.1: MLA Convention 1999 Web page diagram) are clear enough to help readers visualize the original page. Granted, because this page was created in the late 1990s, its designers were probably thinking more about presenting the appropriate information in a relatively attractive design instead of balancing the page's images and text rhetorically. For this very reason, however, the page is a good example: no one was thinking about digital fusion in the late 1990s.

Prominent on the page next to each other were two identically sized images. On the left was a shot subtitled "1920 Convention". To its right was a photo captioned "Chicago: Site of the 1999 Convention". The 1920 convention shot pictured an old sepia-toned gathering of males. Any viewer would have been hard-pressed to tell whether any women were pictured. If so, they were placed at the very back of the crowd where stood one or two indistinguishable faces with large hats that had not been removed like those of the men standing in the front rows. Women? Perhaps. Nonetheless, the photo works synecdochically to show a part of the association that stands for the entire organization. The photo on the right showed the Chicago skyline with Buckingham Fountain in the lower right foreground.

The pairing of these two photos, their identical sizes and their captions both referring to conferences, indicates in every way that we should consider the photos parallel. And since synecdoche occurs on one side of the parallel structure, we might expect that the other side could also be intended as a synecdoche. What appears, however, is actually faulty visual parallelism that could lead us to some startling conclusions, especially when read in conjunction with the text fused to these images. The MLA in 1920 appears to be represented by people, while the MLA of 79 years later seems to be best represented by concrete skyscrapers, buildings that contain dense numbers of people without letting sight of them appear either on the streets where the buildings are located or in the photos these skyscrapers decorate. We might wonder if the faulty parallelism is actually saying that the MLA of 1920 valued people, while the MLA of 1999 values its corporate identity more than its individual members.

The page is also rhetorically inconsistent. A bulleted list of ten characteristics beneath the images—headed by the line "The MLA at a Glance"—contains facts that are visually and culturally dissonant with the photos just above them. The first point says "Over 30,000 members in 100 countries". The second says "Programs serving English and foreign language teachers". In neither of the photos, however, do we see any members other than white males that all appear, judging by the suits they wear, to be from the US or at the most distant, from all over North America.

The culture reflected on this page is one that has moved from seeing itself represented synecdochically by people (albeit white, Anglo-Saxon males) to one represented metonymically by concrete skyscrapers. The language of the site claims that this association represents many modern languages and members in 100 countries, yet no visual representation of any of this multitude of languages and cultures is offered. Indeed, since women are difficult to see or identify in the photo, the visual rhetoric—that is, the Web pages' figurative visual figures of speech and syntax—leave us with the impression of the MLA as a male-dominated, ethno-centric organization, despite the claims of its text. While on one hand, these disjunctions could simply result from accidents or early Web page creation, on the other, the disjunctions could provide analytic fissures for readers to dig into in hopes of discovering other mismatches that unintentionally reveal an organization's true underlying philosophy. Disjunctions are often important for close readings of many types of texts; hybrid texts with images and words should prove no different. The faulty parallelism of this early site can help us understand how much Web designers should study Web sites for rhetorical as well as design purposes and that their training should include lessons on rhetorical consistency between image and text.

Besides unintentionally exposing discrepancies between lip service and actual corporate values, uses of metaphor and metonymy on Web sites also provide an interesting contrast between high and low culture in the discipline of poetry, one I chose in particular because its practitioners are accustomed to using figurative language in all its variations. While I would not go so far as to claim that images used metaphorically are signs of serious culture, or that graphics used metonymically indicate popular culture, I do see those tendencies in several sets of pages that I will discuss below. Christy Desmet makes the following distinction between the two tropes, a distinction that helps us dig into analyzing these tropes that are difficult enough to unpack when they occur in words, and even more when they occur in images:

> Metaphors are totalizing because they are abstract, suppressing or disavowing differences between the two signs identified with one another. Metaphors therefore expand into allegories; they point away from the ordinary world to the meanings of a higher reality. Metonymy, the trope of association, denies the truth and fitness of these identifications by exposing the conditions of their production, the circumstances under which such associations occur.
>
> In the terms set up by Wertheim (1990) metaphor is a sacred trope, metonymy a secular trope. (58)

Examining the commonplace metaphor "my love is a rose" suppresses the differences between a person's love and a flower, causing us to think about the ways in which the abstract concept of love or caring deeply for another resembles the beauty, delicacy, fragility of a growing organism. The connection evokes thoughts of all this live plant's attributes and physical characteristics—that its life is short, that it has thorns, that it can get moldy from over-nurture, i.e. watering, or dry up from lack of nurture, i.e. sunlight and water.

Metonymy, substituting one word for another closely related to it or substituting effect for cause or vice-versa, occurs in another commonplace phrase that denies the truth or fitness of the equation: "The pen is mightier than the sword." We understand that the pen is a substitute for a writer and that the sword is a substitute for a soldier or by extension an army. The actual fitness or probability of a pen being able to out-duel a sword suggests that in a circumstance under which we would create this association—an uprising, a revolution, a war—a writer could be mightier than a soldier. Today, however, the conditions surrounding the production of these metonymies have changed significantly so that the metonymies may prove incomprehensible for young people who hardly ever use pens to write most documents and for soldiers who no longer use swords. We might as well be saying that the quill is mightier than the arrow or that a finger is mightier than a rock. Considering today's condition of production, we should say instead that the electronic tweet is mightier than the gun.

We can see the difference between sacred and secular tropes operating in three series of Web sites for the Academy of American Poets, the Internet Poetry Archive, and the Cowboy Poets Society. The cultural ethos projected through the Academy of American Poets' series of Web pages is uniformity imposed on a collection of poets, each considered a stellar representative of an elite group, each an embodiment of a level of distinction attained by only a few of the millions of people who have written and are currently writing poems in America. Each page contains a central frame showing the poet's photo—a headshot—surrounded by a brief biographical blurb and exemplifying the culturally determined figurative language mentioned above by Lakoff and Johnson (i.e. facial portraits representing people in western culture). While we would consider such a portrait as a type of metonymy known as synecdoche (where a part of something is used to represent the whole) in the case of the Academy of American Poets' pages, the series of individual portraits work also metaphorically. We recall George Lakoff and Mark Johnson's explanation of metaphorical concepts and argument quoted just above: "The essence of metaphor is understanding and experiencing one kind of thing in terms of another" (5). These images are helping us to understand the Academy of American Poets in terms of the images and poems of those represented on these pages. In other words, the Academy of American Poets equals its poets.

These pages give a sense of a poet as mainly working in isolation, influenced by one or perhaps two contemporaries. We easily understand that the Academy wanted uniform pages and therefore used the same Web page template for each poet. But the problem with such uniformity is, of course, that any sense of wonder or amazement at the poet's unique style, sensibility, use of figurative language, or voice is severely curtailed.

The design of using a poet's portrait as the only metaphoric or metonymic device seems to apply in many Web pages devoted to poetry and poets. The Internet Poetry Archive, like the Academy of American Poets, offers on its splash page the portraits of seven poets, Philip Levine, Seamus Heaney, Czeslaw Milosz, Robert Pinsky, Yusef Komunyakaa, Margaret Walker, and Richard Wilbur. From this page, viewers can click on a portrait and move to that poet's page. The design of these pages makes no imaginative use of graphic elements. It appears as if the thorough concentration on written and spoken language has not encouraged any need to incorporate graphics in a way to underscore the particular use of figurative language unique to each poet.

Even poetry pages devoted to an individual and not sponsored by an organization seem to follow the habit of using a poet's portrait as the primary or sole graphic element on the Web page. The official Gary Soto Web site from the 1990s to early 2007 is a case in point. Except for the fact that it did not include recorded selections that the viewer could click on and hear, this site could very easily have been part of both the Academy of American Poets and the Internet Poetry Archives sites. The seemingly obligatory portrait and ever-present short biography are all that we saw on the old splash page available on the Internet Archive's Wayback Machine (search term: "Garysoto.com"). Since 2008, however, the Soto site has moved away from the simpler focus of the earlier site and presents a more disparate collection of links, from photos of Gary Soto throughout his life, to his most current publications, to information for those who wish to contact him for readings. These links were earlier represented only by words in a horizontal menu at the very bottom of the splash page. The later site, by using graphics for some of the links and splitting its focus between images and texts representing the single words used earlier, seems to end up highlighting the business end of poetry more than the act of creativity. The pages are not rhetorically focused on conveying one single philosophy or idea.

While not presenting as "serious" or literarily elite a site as the ones for the Modern Language Association, the Academy of American Poets, or the Internet Poetry Archive, the Web site for the Cowboy Poets Society presents a contrasting and consistent visual reflection of its culture and prevailing ethos. The site focuses on cowboy poets as entertainers and humorists, down-to-earth blue collar purveyors of a language art that represents a more populist, democratic, inclusive attitude toward the art of poetry than the one we see portrayed by the Academy of American Poets.

The Cowboy Poets Society, by using metonymic graphics, reflects an ethos consistent with the sense of self portrayed by the site's verbal text. The graphics represent items or activities closely related to cowboy life, ones that could stand in for such a life, depending on the context and circumstances. The site, for example, uses section breaks in the form of barbed wire—a tool for helping to fence in livestock, the means by which cowboys make their living. The campfire, more an historical metonymy, reminds viewers of the condition of cowboy labor during a past time when cowboys spent weeks or months living outdoors rounding up cattle and driving them to market then building campfires at night for warmth. The browser originally showed the form of a horse moving across the page leaving traces of its image accompanied by a horseshoe; today's browsers, however, only show a short line of brown and blue horse figures near the left margin of the opening page. At other points throughout the Web page, we see small graphics of the same burning campfire, a boot, and at the bottom of the page, a silhouette of a cowboy riding a bucking bronco. Some of these images could be considered clichés, but therein lie their honesty and their humor. The page designers were not looking for ethereal, unique metaphors that might confuse viewers by causing them to stop and wonder what the graphics represented; instead, the designers chose metonymic graphics that are easily understandable to their particular audience.

If we recall Wertheim's words quoted by Desmet above claiming that the secular trope of metonymy exposes the conditions of production and the circumstances of the association, we can picture the conditions and circumstances of life on the range that caused the association. The metonymic graphics reflect an ethos that does not necessarily aspire to high poetry or to give a dramatic, romanticized notion of the cowboy and his life, nor of the cowboy poet and his (or her) poetry. Visually and verbally, the pages give a more grounded sense of the cowboy and the West than do the large, romantic, melodramatic, mid-1800s canvases of Albert Bierstadt. Lee Clark Mitchell discusses Bierstadt's paintings as melodrama, a mode that he says "consists of a kind of sign language by which values can be arrayed outside of social contexts" (85). Mitchell explains that Bierstadt's grandiose terrain reveals "the ways in which water, rock, trees, clouds, [and] sunlight itself could create a cosmic drama always on the verge of becoming moral and social" (71). In contrast, these Web pages conveying bits and pieces of cowboy life through their secular metonymic graphics appear more appropriate to our postmodern, post-deconstructionist world of the twenty-first century where the cowboy, like the independent farmer, having gradually inherited a diminished position in American cultural sensibility, has all but vanished from American life. Instead of being fixed in a hierarchical social structure, postmodern American life is marked more by anarchy and change. A way of life that families valued and expected to be in place for generations is now threatened and indeterminate.[5] Anne Heath Widmark, in her collection of poems, short biographies, and photos of 12 cowboy poets, laments: "[T]he poets gathered here render the textures of a way of life increasingly endangered by the pressures of modern times. The West, which has been home to generations of ranching families, is under siege as different factions—environmentalists, government agencies, and private landowners—battle over a rapidly diminishing landscape" (14).

While the roots of this particular genre of poetry derive from the folktales and humorists of the nineteenth century, cowboy poetry today reflects serious cultural issues and what seems an ever-present artistic tug between theoretical meditation and concrete representations of those ideas. The title of Widmark's volume mentioned above—*Between Earth and Sky*—portrays these contemporary poets caught between the secular earth and the sacred sky. As text on the back cover states, "Reaching far beyond its cow-country beginnings, the poetry of the cowboy West is awakening a response in mainstream America." Kim R. Stafford, in his foreword, reiterates the division between sacred and secular:

> The American poet William Carlos Williams called for a modern way of writing that featured "no ideas but in things." Don't we have that here? These are not poems of airy philosophy, but of experience rooted to saddle and hoof, glove and rock. (11)

The metonymic properties of a cowboy poets' Web site, if studied seriously, can put us on track to uncover values and tensions that tell us something about ourselves and our culture. We just need to know how to look for it and how to use rhetoric to study it.

Fusion, it turns out, applies to more than word and image. Using rhetorical analysis on the Internet can help us see the connection between the culture producing digital compositions and rhetorical forms themselves. Such documents were probably always available to the public in text form, but access to them was more difficult. Even so, while the Internet has caused more cultures/companies to provide access to more company documents than previously, not much close analysis of these cultures via the fused online documents they produce has occurred. Perhaps the fused "nature" of Web pages can allow us one more tool to analyze particular cultures, especially our own.

3 Classification on the World Wide Web

There is more at stake—epistemologically, politically, and ethically—in the day-to-day work of building classification systems and producing and maintaining standards than in abstract arguments about representation.

~ Geoffrey C. Bowker and Susan Leigh Star

PRELUDE

Early summer, and I am starting to draft this chapter. Today I had a fence built around my backyard. Doing so broke my heart. Enclosure, loss of vision, separation. But then why did I put it there? Truthfully, I grew tired of being the crossroads of my neighborhood, tired of having my grass trampled by boys' feet and mountain bike tires cutting through the yard to the cul de sac behind, tired of having a bird feeder torn down, tired of having my outdoor BBQ grill cover stolen, all actions that my grumpy old geezer's concept of backyard could not handle. So I was left with no recourse but to establish a visible boundary, to classify the plot of ground behind my house as my backyard. I had to acquiesce to and display the social sign for a backyard: a fence. A backyard without a fence in a neighborhood where all other yards are fenced seemed, alas, to suggest that the space filled a different classificatory purpose: it was part of the street, it belonged to everyone, and so on.

Classification is at the basis of language and thought. Without acts of classification no one could relate concepts or words to new concepts or messages, because words and concepts only exist through classification. (Robert Hodge and Guther Kress, 62)

ON CLASSIFICATION

A Web site itself—apart from the information it contains—is a designed classification system, a fundamentally rhetorical system. Of course, whether it is rhetorically *designed* remains to be seen; but more on this subject later. Geoffrey C. Bowker and Susan Leigh Star define classification as "a spatial, temporal, or spatio-temporal segmentation of the world. A 'classification system' is a set of boxes (metaphorical or literal) into which things can be put to then do some kind of work—bureaucratic or knowledge production" (10). By my calculations, a Web site does this work and more because it also fuses:

- a design
- an outline
- a classification system
- rhetorical elements
- its creator's social and cultural contexts

A Web site, then, offers knowledge that is informative, but behind the informative facts and details, a site produces knowledge about its sponsoring person or organization—that is, all the individual items classified therein, items that when considered together paint a picture of that entity and also reflect knowledge about where the entity situates itself socially, politically, and culturally, and whether it does so consciously or inadvertently.

Richard Lanham makes the case that rhetorical figures are evolutionary strategies that developed in order to help the brain with memory, computation, and iterative searching (*Handlist*). So too with classification systems—included within "memory"—which falls under one of the five parts of rhetoric, along with invention, arrangement, style, and delivery (*Handlist*, 165). Classification has many rhetorical names: *divisio, partitio, propositio*.

- *Divisio* (also called distribution, merismus, dinumeratio): "Dividing the whole into its parts" (*Handlist*, 59), or "Division into kinds or classes" (*Handlist*, 60).
- *Partitio* (also division or diaeresis): "[D]ivision; logical division into parts" (*Handlist*, 110).
- *Propositio*: "Sometimes *propositio* is used simply as a figure, rather than the part of an oration, to indicate a brief proleptic summary 'which compriseth in few words the sum of that matter, whereof we presently intend to speak' (Peacham)" (*Handlist*, 122).

Whatever the name, classification is both rhetorical and a part of rhetoric.

In their introduction to *Cognition and Categorization*, editors Eleanor Rosch and Barbara Lloyd gather essays arguing that "the segmentation of the world [is not] essentially arbitrary" (2). And in her chapter "Principles of Categorization", Rosch, furthermore, asserts:

[1] [T]he task of category systems is to provide maximum information with the least cognitive effort; . . . [2] the perceived world comes as structured information rather than as arbitrary or unpredictable attributes. Thus maximum information with the least cognitive effort is achieved if categories map the perceived world structure as closely as possible. (28)

Other scholars whose research serves as the foundation for my inquiry in this chapter are James Elkins ("Problems of Classification" in *The Domain of Images*), George Lakoff ("The Importance of Classification" in *Women, Fire, and Dangerous Things: What Categories Reveal about the Mind*), Geoffrey C. Bowker along with Susan Leigh Star (*Sorting Things Out: Classification and Its Consequences*), and Susan Leigh Star ("Grounded Classification"). Bowker and Star contend that "as a culture we have not yet developed conventions of classification for the Web that bear much moral or habitual conviction in daily practice" (8). Because building classification systems has many more far-reaching consequences than just putting objects into groups or representing these groups in charts and images, we should ask ourselves what such conventions might then imply for those of us conducting Web studies. Bowker and Star contend that classification actually impacts epistemology, politics, and ethics (10). If we cannot escape the ever-growing, innumerable categories and classification systems proliferating digitally on the Web, will consequences eventually arise that we need to envision today lest they catch us unaware tomorrow?

More than 16 years ago, one of the earlier essays examining classification in connection with technology, specifically computer software, began by quoting George Lakoff: "Categorization is not a matter to be taken lightly." The essay's author was Gail Hawisher, and both Lakoff's and Hawisher's thoughts about the importance of classification and categories remain significant to our world of new media. All authors above, Hodge and Kress, Buchanan, Lakoff, and Hawisher, stress that classifying is situated at the base of thought. To me, this foundational character means that we must analyze the shapes and components of classification as they appear on the Web and we must recognize their fused nature as both a designed shape and a textual classificatory grouping.

Certainly, one of the most ubiquitous techniques we see on Web pages everywhere we look is classification. Search engines, online retail, university sites—all rely on classifying their information, products, or services so that they will be easily accessible to their viewers. The manner in which Web sites break down their subject's identity, the way they group and thus classify what they display, offers a window into the culture as well as the individual or institution creating that classification. Analyzing classification systems, moreover, offers insight into the ways the sponsoring institutions want to control their identities and how we perceive them. I agree with Bowker and Star's claim cited above that our culture has yet to develop classification conventions for the Web that results in any deep-seated, serious, or regular use in everyday life (8). But part of the reason, I would argue, is that we have literally been looking at the Web in the wrong way: we search for pieces of information, we admire easy-to-use navigation, or we notice a pleasing design. We tend to want a handle on the way an entire site has been constructed, so we look at the pages, the links within the site, and the links pointing outward to other sites. This general habit of looking could result from the Web's origin as a hypertext document and earlier types of hypertext. In what might seem a bit of a paradox, to explain further I need to digress briefly by looking backward and reviewing those types.

FROM HYPERTEXT STRUCTURE TO THE WEB'S STRUCTURE

Text is linear and so too are its organizational structures. We can draw up outlines of essays we plan to write, we can create lists of points we want to make, we could ask students to outline famous essays so they can see the logical progression of an argument and the types of evidence an author presents to buttress various claims. Visually, we may create tree diagrams in linguistics to picture relations between ideas, but no one organizes an essay as a tree diagram. While these textual and visual structures may still be possible with some hybrid texts on the Web, most Web sites would make such a linear or tree construction difficult. Certainly we also used to see "outlines" of hypertext, ones attempting to map the pages of a hypertext document and their links. Stuart Moulthrop does exactly so in his chapter "Reading from the Map: Metonymy and Metaphor in the Fiction of Forking Paths". On page 127, we see a figure that is a conglomeration of linked boxes representing pages of the hypertext under study and the direction in which a reader could move while reading (see Figure 3.1). Moulthrop's diagram shows how the links in this story connect. The directions in which one might move are hardly linear.

The different "pages" relate to any numbers of others, not just the one before or the one after. A reader could start on a page in the middle of the collection, for example, then could connect to one of the first pages as well as a few three fourths of the way through, depending on the various

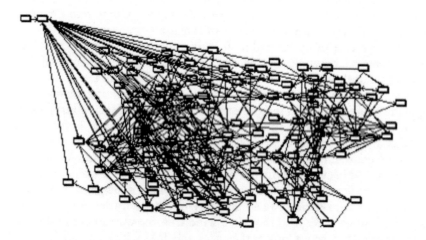

Figure 3.1   Storyspace map of "Forking Paths" hypertext. © Stuart Moulthrop.

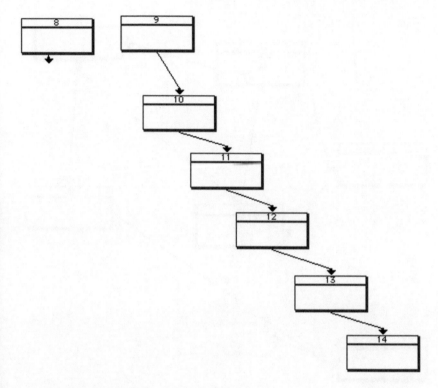

Figure 3.2 Exploratory hypertext map.

story lines the reader wanted to follow. Attempting to distinguish between early uses of hypertexts, Michael Joyce labels these uses "exploratory" and "constructive". Exploratory use, he explains briefly, is "a delivery or pre-sentational technology . . . [that can] encourage and enable an audience . . . to control the transformation of a body of information to meet its needs and interests" (11). Joyce points to Hypercard as an example (Figure 3.2 [my construction]).

Those of us who can recall Hypercard remember that it worked a bit like a Rolodex. While one could start anywhere, the movement was either forward or backward, but not side to side. In constructive use, however, Joyce states, "hypertext becomes an invention or analytic tool" (11). Joyce points to Storyspace, Eastgate System's hypertext software, as an example here (Figure 3.3 [my construction]).

Within Storyspace, a writer can create pages of text that link to other pages in any direction; writers can also embed text within a page. That embedded text could link to any other page, not just the one in which it is embedded. The movement here is more akin to the non-prescribed move-ment we usually follow on today's Web sites.

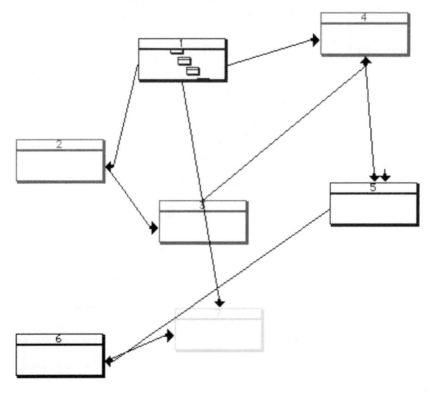

Figure 3.3   Constructive hypertext map.

The shapes of earlier hypertexts are important for helping us understand why we might have inherited a way of reading and designing today's Web sites with an eye to navigating rather than planning the rhetorical shape of the information contained therein. However, visualizing the shape of an individual page—rather than writing down a traditional outline of the information it contains—might be more productive in understanding how placement of material on a page, both verbal and visual, could be called classification. Richard Lanham's famous analytic distinction between looking "at" prose to discern its syntactic form rather than looking "through" it for information or to discover a meaning, deep or otherwise, applies in this case.[1] If we step back from a Web page before getting caught up in its information, sketch or assign shapes to its different chunks of information, then label parts of this sketch according to the type of information or the types of images it contains, we can begin to grasp two ideas:

1) the ways the site designers classified the information that they felt was crucial for us in order that we understand the subject being represented, and then

Figure 3.4 Web page diagram showing primary and secondary classifications.

2) the ways the designers prioritized this information and assigned associated images with appropriate placement, size, and color within what we can now begin to recognize as an overall classification system.

We can look at the diagram I sketch in Figure 3.4 above modeled loosely on an actual site. Diagramming or visualizing the shape allows us to look "at" the structure rather than "through" it for content. We see a typical top of a Web page that contains both images and text identifying whatever the page is portraying, in this case a writing program's logo and name. The page also gives us information about where the portrayal falls in the wider outside world of Web sites—in other words, how we should classify its topic: a writing program, a business, a service, an individual, an educational institution, a search tool; the top of the page gives us all of this primary categorical information at a glance so that we can place the site squarely within the larger system of similar objects, people, organizations, or tools. The next menus displayed either further down on the first page or with a smaller font are meant to be secondary classification levels for understanding internal parts of the program being portrayed. The primary menu shows the principle elements that the site's creator felt best represented the program. But if the site has additional menus, they are inserted as subordinate, secondary, horizontal menus, or alternately, vertical menus on either the left or right side of the first page. The subordinate menus break the classification down further or provide additional context. In the case of this figure, the left menu contains links to local, state, and national organizations that bear on the type of information being displayed. Since this figure is based on a university writing program's site, the secondary menu lists links to the department, college, university, state, and national organizations that influenced the site's content. This menu shows that the program considers itself embedded in multiple contexts and believes that such a context adds to its credibility. Classification thus serves to support the program's ethos.

An additional secondary menu lists the program director's welcome, contact information for all program administrators and staff, and housekeeping information for instructors about syllabi requirements and exam dates, all of which further help the viewer infer the ethos displayed through the site's elements.

Hypertext, we remember, was the early form of the structure we now call the World Wide Web. Its most recent incarnation, Web 3.0, handles more visual elements and is more structurally complex than hypertext as a stand-alone, non-networked application could be. In Figure 3.5, we see more of the contextual classification I discussed regarding Figure 3.4. Because this next figure also reflects an educational institution, the diagram of the site depicted must show that it belongs within the larger classification system where it belongs: university Web sites. Next, below the main classification system shown in the horizontal menu, the site includes images of three people. In this case, the actual figures displayed ranged in age from approximately 25 to 45, there are two females and one male, and they belong to different races. The figures also display representatives from both the faculty and graduate students in the program. Rhetorically, the site draws on the technique of parallel structure, suggesting indirectly the equality of the figures portrayed rather than a hierarchy valuing only the program's professors. The site's construction—its fused text and images—shows a decidedly social constructionist pedagogical philosophy and program foundation.

My third example (Figure 3.6) shows a less obvious classification. The site has several rotating images of projects that a design/architectural firm has completed. The images represent a classification system that breaks down the types of projects the company specializes in and undertakes. Instead of using a text list, however, the company chooses a visual classification. This

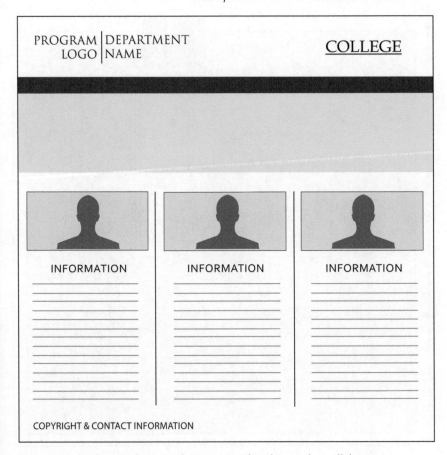

Figure 3.5 Web page diagram showing visual and textual parallel structure.

figure actually shows an outline of the HOK site that I discussed in Chapter 1. While the images might first seem to be a random collection, further analysis reveals that each image displays a different type of architectural assignment, from interior office design to building design to airport design to museum design and more.

This site is unique because it relies on images without much surrounding text except for the company logo and motto at the top of the rotating series of photos. The motto is particularly potent, though, and its singularity causes us to stop, then examine the phrase because it has several layers of meaning:

Ideas Work 1: First, this company's employees get ideas that work for their clients. Then, as the architects and designers provide such clients with a service, all of the people involved begin to see how those ideas are taking shape and are thus "working".

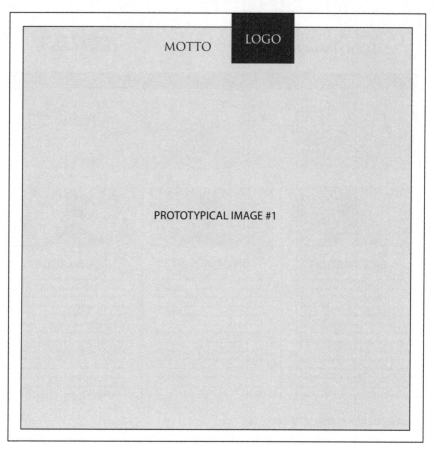

Figure 3.6   Web page diagram showing fused image, logo, and motto.

Ideas Work 2: The ideas that create a place to work help the employees to perform their jobs or their "work" better. In this second meaning of the phrase "ideas work", we understand that because the architects' and designers' ideas work, employees find their work environment more pleasant and efficient, and can therefore "work" better.

Ideas Work 3: Yet a third meaning of the phrase exists: the ideas that any company produces as its principle "work" provide a working intellectual thread between the architectural company's employees, its clients, and all the products the company has designed. The over-all impression the motto and the images leave us with is one in which the production of ideas and the reality of work are closely integrated and celebrated.

SEEING CLASSIFICATION

Over the past several decades, many scholars have studied the epistemological, political, social, cultural, and rhetorical significance of classification. Carol Snyder points to the work of Michel Foucault during the 1960s and 70s (C. Snyder, see especially her note 2 on 216). George Lakoff, Robert Hodge and Gunther Kress, James J. Sosnoski, Jack Goody, Geoffrey Bowker and Susan Leigh Star, Jeff Rice, and Amy Kimme Hea ("Destabilizing") are just a few of the others who discuss the importance and implications of categorizing during the 1980s, 1990s, and 2000s.

Despite being so deeply embedded in human thinking and activity, the results of classification can easily and often do go unnoticed. Like ideologies and ancient artifacts, embedded classifications are hard to unearth enough to be seen and then analyzed. I recall staring at the periodic table of elements several years back while co-teaching in a learning community that linked an environmental chemistry class to my first-year composition course. I remarked to my co-instructor offhandedly that the periodic table is just one person's idea about a way to sort out and picture the elements. Then I asked the unaskable: whether there might be another way to classify them. My chemist colleague, actually a good friend, reacted as if I had spoken heretically. I meekly retracted my question. After all, I am no chemist. Several years later, as I mentioned in Chapter 1 of this volume, I did discover that there are actually dozens of ways to classify and sort out the elements, but just not the traditionally accepted way. Edward G. Mazurs has authored an entire volume on the subject: *Graphic Representations of the Periodic System During One Hundred Years*. Out of all these many representations, one person's idea, one classification system, became a set of groupings set in stone, a chart that no one notices or questions—an example of ideology at its best.

My argument continues to be that we need to consider Web pages as classification systems precisely so that we can purposely unearth the classifications then analyze their social significance and the impact they have on our day-to-day actions in this regard. I am asking us to look at Web pages in a number of ways, first as classification systems, and then second to see these classification systems in two different ways, one, by looking at the categories displayed as fusing both textual and visual components, and two by looking "at" introductory pages and their relation to the subsequent pages in their group rather than "through" them for the meaning of their content. Just as syntax—sentence shape—reveals much about the thinking processes that string words together in particular order with particular coordination or subordination, the syntax of a Web page reveals choice nuggets of information about its creator's mindset. True, a classification system is a design on the Web with all the attendant importance of a design, and much previous scholarship has dealt with Web page design:

Design is what all forms of production for use have in common. It provides the intelligence, the thought or idea—of course, one of the meanings of the term *design* is a thought or plan—that organizes all levels of production, whether in graphic design, engineering and industrial design, architecture, or the largest integrated systems found in urban planning. (Buchanan, 108)

A Web page, however, is also a classification system. And because we have been unaccustomed to considering Web pages as such, we have not been asking the same types of questions we would were we to see a traditionally constructed system of categories in text. We have literally not been seeing or recognizing them, and we have not been seeing their visual elements as crucial parts of those systems. Classification on the Web involves fused categories that display themselves visually as much as textually.

ANALYZING CLASSIFICATION

Because each page on the Web both reflects and encapsulates rhetoric and ideology, my concern here is more to encourage the kind of rhetorical analysis that would lead us to uncovering the ideological contexts converging in a Web page and that would lead us to understanding what we ourselves are reflecting through images as well as text when we create Web pages. In doing so, we can better understand how we are affecting our audiences.

Carol Snyder quotes Stephen Jay Gould's similar take on classification: "Classifications both reflect and direct our thinking" (211). Snyder's essay contains a thorough discussion analyzing how "classifications have the power to dispose their objects" (212). Snyder argues that our students—and I might include us, their teachers—hardly ever notice classifications as human interpretations of items and groups, so she offers a scheme to use in helping students to think more critically about classifications instead of unquestioningly accepting their categories as irrefutable facts. Briefly, Snyder's exercise asks students to do the following:

1. Identify the object of the classification.
2. Identify what the classification excludes.
3. Identify the human subjects who devise or use the classification.
4. Locate the classification in time.
5. Locate the classification in space. (212–214)

Elaborating on her fifth point, Snyder urges students to consider all social or institutional practices giving rise to the particular system. I would suggest that attention to culture, politics, caste or class, economics, and geography should be added to this list.

To show how we might use Snyder's guidelines to analyze a Web page's categories rhetorically, I have selected two sites that are already classifications—Google and Bing—Internet search engines. Other sites belong to the classification of Internet search engines—Yahoo and Jeeves, for example—but I selected these two because, side by side, they help to illustrate how rhetorical analysis can help unearth ideological contexts, especially for our students.

1. Identify the object of classification.

As I mentioned above, Web users employ Internet search tools like Google and Bing to find information varying from the mundane (a fast food menu) to the complex (directions for fixing a leaky faucet) to the serious (cataract surgery procedures). Of course our students know that both sites are search tools, and these students probably all have their favorite tool. But I doubt that they have thought critically about the rhetorical reasons for the sites' appearances and the way rhetorical motives impinge upon any user's search choices.

2. Identify what the classification excludes.

A first response to this directive might be to assume that since a search engine has any digital information at hand, it excludes nothing. But we need to look at the structure displayed, not the possibility of any search's content. Richard Lanham pops up here, reminding us to look "[a]t, not through". Looking *at* Google and Bing, then, we notice that to streamline the search process in a specific area, both sites have menus directing visitors to images and videos, for example, or shopping and maps. Closer examination does show that both sites excluded overt links to advertisers and something I would call "advertising clutter". However, both sites do include links labeled "advertising programs" (Google) and "advertise" (Bing). The most obvious *ex*clusion on the Google page is an image, and what may distinguish Bing from Google at first glance is its *in*clusion of an image. Bing's images change daily, but the site maintains an archive of past images. In a way, Bing's splash page appears more appealing than Google's stark white splash page. However, Google does contain a link at the bottom-left part of its splash page that will let a viewer "change background image". If we pursue this one small difference between excluded and included images, we find crucial information about the next of Snyder's points.

3. Identify the human subjects who devise ~~[or use]~~ the classification.

For my purposes, I am splitting Snyder's third point as originally written and concentrating first on the human subjects who devised these particular classification systems: employees of the Microsoft Corporation, Bing's parent company, and employees of Google. Microsoft has decided to choose the image for us; Google lets us choose whether 1) we want to see a background photo while entering a search term, and 2) we want that image to come from our own photos on our own computer, a Picassa Web photo account, a public gallery of other users' photos, or finally an editorial selection from various artists. If we conduct a fused analysis of the Bing site and ask how the photo reflects the rhetorical goals of the site, we realize that several of the images come from travel destinations and that the photos are in effect ads for the destinations. Each image also has little hidden windows that pop up during a mouse-over and each gives us some esoteric information about the location or item. As a rhetorician, I have one big question: what does this image have to do with the goal of a search site, which I assume is to help a visitor find information quickly? In the case of Bing, the photo can distract us because let's face it, who can resist looking at travel information and who can resist looking for those little pop-up windows once we know they're there? So the technicians and designers who created this classification system are subtly including other elements into the classification pictured: advertising and travel. Those who created Google's splash page appearance are indicating that the search itself is the most important action and that they don't want to distract us.

4. *Identify the human subjects who [devise or] use the classification system.*
   Many Google users have been employing Google for a long time. They may thus simply use it automatically almost as a default tool. Or, as I hinted above, they may be people who agree with the site's creators that they don't want to be distracted in their searches since searches themselves can provide enough extraneous material to tempt us away from our original tasks without the site's creators providing any additional distractions.
   Since Bing went online in 2009, those who use it may have been Microsoft customers who choose to use Microsoft products. They could have been attracted by a completely new tool or by television commercials, especially those stating that users won't have to sift through confusing amounts of information themselves because Bing will choose the most important items for them. In a comparison between Google and Bing, our choices seem to be: either have Microsoft's people select my information for me, or browse on my own through the thousands of offerings that Google unearths—albeit that the material is ordered in Google's own particular way—and select the information myself.
   Basically, however, if we compare search results from Google and Bing side by side, the lists of items are pretty much the same. This similarity leads us to ask whether or not the search tools are fundamentally interchangeable, and if so, what we might learn about the reasons why users choose one over the other and to what degree their choices are caused by the designers' and company' motives.

5. *Locate the classification in time.*
   The difference in time between the dates when Google and Bing first came online (1998 vs. 2009) may have to do, partially, with the difference

in the sites' appearances. Google came online at a time before Web 2.0 hit, when visual elements were not as widespread as they are now in the second decade of the 2000s. Today, however, Web designers are more likely to include images, whether or not those images pertain to the site's rhetorical purpose or goal.

6. *Locate the classification's culture.*

Point 6 is mine, not Snyder's. I added it in order to provide an interesting window on the two classification systems/search tools being examined. Both arise from a distinct corporate culture, and the sites' appearances and categories embody two very different corporate philosophies. While Bing appears to focus on searching, the daily photo on its splash page does distract somewhat from the search and may cause us to click on the hidden links or to find out more about traveling to the site pictured. The news links at the bottom of the page may entice us to find out more about "Lohan in Jail" (the attention-grabber on one of the days I examined the site). The fact that Bing has advertised itself as a cure for "decision overload" (for an example, see: http:// http://www.youtube.com/watch?v=dx9Cmp6qQzY), in other words, a site that makes our decisions or choices for us so that we don't have to think on our own, while humorous as a catch phrase, is disturbing on an intellectual level: early Bing commercials like this one suggest that average users, given numerous search results with numerous decisions to make about which to read, will turn into blithering idiots capable only of free association without any ability to assert intellectual control. Furthermore, while the entertainment and travel links are more subtle than ads we might see on other sites—online newspapers for instance—they are still ads and reflect a corporate culture that is hierarchical, in that the company chooses what we see, and focused on economics. Those ads pay the company's bills. We all know that Microsoft made its name in computers and software first before its search engine went online. In fact, a quick look at the Microsoft Corporation's company information finds that its "mission and values are to help people and businesses throughout the world realize their full potential" (http://www.microsoft.com/about/en/us/default.aspx), so a focus on business, even in their search tool, is unsurprising.

Google, on the other hand, came into being *as* a search engine and has a ten-point philosophy directly reflected on its Web site. A few key points are:

- Focus on the user and all else will follow
- Democracy on the Web works
- You can make money without doing evil (http://www.google.com/about/corporate/company/tenthings.html)

Google's separate philosophy regarding user experience also has ten principles. Among the full descriptions of each, the following statements stand out because we can see them reflected directly on the Google splash page:

- A well-designed Google product . . . doesn't try to impress with whiz-bang technology or visual style—thought it might have both
- Delight the eye without distracting the mind (http://www.google.com/intl/en/about/corporate/company/ux.html)

The distinction between the sites is the difference between a business-centered site versus a user-centered site. Epistemologically, this is the same as the difference between a teacher-centered versus a student-centered pedagogy, the first one holding that knowledge originates with the teacher who contains the information and doles it out to students, and the second maintaining that knowledge arises from students interacting with each other while thinking through problems, then creating their own knowledge through these interactions. We need to ask ourselves whether knowledge belongs to the corporation that can process it first and then give the user this pre-digested information, or whether knowledge is created by the user who can interact with the search tool to find her own path and thus her own knowledge.

ANALYTIC CONSEQUENCES

Classification or categorization clearly has far-reaching consequences. The seemingly simple act of putting items in groups can and has caused great celebrations or heated discussions in some disciplines. The sciences, in particular, come to mind. Scientific reputations can be built on the discovery of a new species, field, and a lifetime's worth of research can follow. The humanities, specifically the field of English literature, have had problems when it comes down to agreeing about a classification, where the categories involved in canon formation have led to serious problems of exclusion and ensuing canon and anthology wars: scholars squabble over the groupings and representative authors selected for major literary anthologies. Less obvious to us, perhaps, is the possibility that including or excluding items in a classification can reveal less serious consequences and sometimes less transparent motives like validating or denying the worth of the item to the whole system. Either adding or omitting an item could also reveal a desire to shift a paradigm or a refusal to change a worldview.

Many of us have experienced frustration while trying to find information on some Web sites because the categories we expect to find before reaching the site differ greatly from the ones we actually see once we arrive. We feel a sort of cognitive disjunction at first, possibly because the classification scheme we have been acculturated to expect has completely different categories from the ones created by the site designers. It could be that we come from different sub-cultures that classify, identify, and work in radically different ways. As an academic, I tend to visit more academic Web sites. I have also helped to design a few academic sites. My brain expects a site to be

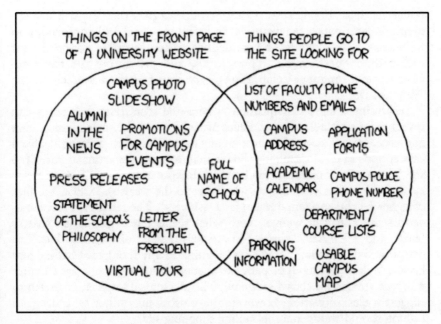

Figure 3.7   Site users' expectations of university Web sites. © Randall Munroe.

classified in a certain way; my expectations, then, are not the same as some-one with either a strong design or business background. Education, design, and commerce have different rhetorical purposes and approach audiences in different ways—that is, if they even consider "audience". We can see this disjunction, literally, in a 2010 cartoon that Randall Munroe published on his Web site "xkcd" (http://imgs.xkcd.com/comics/university_website. png). The cartoon (see Figure 3.7) shows a Venn diagram of the differences between what site users expect to see and what site designers give them.

In one insightful drawing, Munroe encapsulates the differences between the rhetorical approaches of two groups who are not actually thinking much about rhetoric when they design or when they look for information. Many reporters for online venues have discussed this cartoon, among them Steve Kolowich writing for the online news source *Inside Higher Ed*. What these discussions reveal is a clash of opinions about what categories a university site should contain, what the classification system should look like, and what discussions about rhetorical purpose take place: exactly none. Instead, as Kolowich states, "some colleges' home pages are saturated with features that do not so much reflect guesses at what visitors need, but what various campus interests want" (http://www.insidehighered.com/ news/2010/08/04/ websites). Internal politics, then, rather than decisions about rhetorical focus, audience, and purpose, drive many Web constructions.

Even so, perhaps my expectations for academic sites have been sub-consciously molded by the business purposes that overtake the rhetorical concerns of academic sites. Craig Stroupe argues that English departments in particular, for example, in being practical and conforming to university requirements and guidelines, place business concerns first rather than "performing, representing, and promoting the meaning-constituting, language-celebrating *practices* of English studies on the Web" (611).

Analyzing a site's classification system and identifying categories can reveal quite a bit about the audience aimed for and the social class of that audience. Images selected to accompany categories often portray idealized conceptions of class members; the Neiman Marcus department store Web site (www.neimanmarcus.com) contains images of high-end fashion models and the names of designers who cater to the wealthy. In fact, the first category on the horizontal menu is "Designers". The remaining menu categories are aimed at women, with what seems like a gratuitous "Men's Shop" and "NM Kids" thrown in towards the end of the menu bar. The categorical designation "NM Kids" eliminates any thought of babies, and leads to a divergent analytic path extraneous to this argument (see Chapter 4 in this volume for that discussion). The ideological implications seem to suggest a clear direction, however: site visitors unfamiliar with designer fashion should choose another online shopping site.

Even the specific words chosen to label categories can reveal something about the site's creator and targeted audience. Many university Web sites, for example, use the word "athletics" as one of the categories a visitor could explore. Clicking on the word leads to the usual list of teams at the university, sometimes first divided according to gender. UCLA, an exception, uses the word "sports" rather than "athletics". If we think about the levels of diction reflected by the two terms, however, "athletics" comes from an elevated level of academic diction, while "sports" is a term more commonly used everyday by everyone. We turn to the sports section of the newspaper, after all, not the athletics section. And we don't watch "athletics" on TV. Use of the word "sports" on the UCLA splash page is consistent with the university's identity, stated on the splash pages of past years. UCLA defines and represents itself as a public university serving all the people of the state, not just the rich, the famous, the well educated or the children of alumni. One of its recurrent mottos is "UCLA is owned by the people of California. All 38 million." The motto appears from time to time on the splash page of the current site (www.ucla.edu) and is occasionally displayed on some of its previous pages, September 25, 2008 for instance (see the Wayback Machine: waybackmachine.org). The level of diction chosen for the site aims to include all social classes within that 38 million.

When we study classification and its labels on the Internet, we can discover quite a bit about whether the rhetorical action of designing a Web site includes patterns and choices that support the message conveyed through a site's words and images.

BUILDING VS. BEING FOISTED UPON (OR THE REST OF THE STORY WITH APOLOGIES TO PAUL HARVEY)[2]

Up to this point I have been discussing Web site builders primarily from the angle of individual builders only, without paying much attention to those builders' contexts—

- those constructing a simple classification system within a site or
- those designing an entire Web site as a complex classification system to house the many pieces of information to be conveyed so that users have the most efficient access to that information

—people, in other words, who like to make objects. But the cognitive act of puzzling out exactly where to place information is not the sole activity involved in creating a Web site for an organization itself classified as part of a larger overall system. That act dictates that the builder be aware of other rhetorical considerations and pressures.

I thus offer readers a small experiment to try like I did as I was reflecting upon the subject of classification and exploring what exactly gets included in most college Web sites: clicking first on the opening pages of the following schools all in a row and keeping them all onscreen like a fanned-out hand of cards, or, if one's screen is large enough, spacing them out so most of the splash pages can be viewed together: Brown University (www.brown.edu), Columbia University (www.columbia.edu), Cornell University (www.cornell.edu), Dartmouth College (www. dartmouth.edu), Harvard University (www.harvard.edu), the University of Pennsylvania (www.penn.edu), Princeton University (www.princeton.edu), and Yale University (www.yale.edu).

What we see in this array pretty much covers all of the items Randall Munroe lists on both sides of his Venn diagram shown in Figure 3.7 above. We also see every topic we come to expect on an Ivy League school's Web site menu: academics, admissions, research, campus life, about . . . , alumni, visitors, athletics, libraries, and so on. Along with these menu items we might also find a photo slideshow depicting individual students, groups of students, notable faculty members, the most picturesque campus views of the season, attention-grabbing scientific work that can be portrayed in a single image like an extreme close-up of an insect's eyes, an athletic event, or a single athlete or student scholar who exemplifies a spirit or quality that administrators feel best represents what the school offers and who therefore also draws positive attention to the school. The menu items fused with text, the selected graphics, and the photographic images all work together to establish a particular cachet, the quality and prestige that accompany the name of that university, the (invisible) ethos that administrators, alumni, and current students subconsciously expect to be established through all these elements.

The second part of the experiment comes next—clicking on the opening Web site pages of the next group of schools, and all in a row just like the first series: Sierra College (www.sierracollege.edu), American River College (www.arc.losrios.edu), Meramec College (www.stlcc.edu/mc/), Harold Washington College (www.ccc.edu/colleges/Washington/), Shelton State College (www.sheltonstate.edu), Lorain County Community College (www.lorainccc.edu), Bristol Community College (www.bristolcc.edu), Tidewater Community College (www.tcc.edu), and Yakima Valley Community College (www.yvcc.edu). Here we see more of the items listed on the right side of the Munroe diagram, items Munroe labels as "what students want to see". The items here are more likely to be: degree and certificate programs, financial aid, students services, online services, centers, support services, transferring, Saturday flexible learning, business/industry, community services, and continuing education. Elements on these sites establish a pragmatic value along with a contextualized local appeal.

If the first series of Web pages was decidedly lush and picturesque, this series is decidedly not. We see fewer images, fewer videos, fewer displays of famous faculty, fewer images of campus buildings and lush scenery—not that the schools in this second series lack famous faculty or lush, picturesque scenery. Such displays, rather, may not serve the same important purpose that they do for the first group. Using some of the points listed in my modification of Carol Snyder's chart covered earlier in this chapter, as well as points discussed in more detail in the following chapter's Figure 4.1, we can begin to understand that different political and ideological agendas may actually be what lie behind what at first appear to be superficial visual differences. Such differences serve more to emphasize varying ways in which the Web sites perform rhetorically. And in a way, while the differences do point to unique missions, they also suggest a disruption of the classification system in which their organizations have automatically been included: levels of higher education.

So it turns out that building a Web page, classifying information to be posted, and choosing which visuals best represent an organization's focus and mission are really only the first part of the story. The rest of the story involves having to work with and accept the stratified confines of whatever group within which one happens to be classified. Classificatory confines include many more elements or pressures than we can control individually, or to be more precise, those seemingly abstract but all too concrete realities like what step of the classification we fall into, what social, cultural, and political strictures come into play because of being placed into that group, or in this case, what we cannot escape because of having that educational "class" foisted upon us.

Now while we all like to think that we as individuals can move between classes, such movement is in actuality not easy for most people, much less for a large organization like a college. In this example, an "Institution", the educational system of the US, operates almost as a separate entity that colors the way different classes within that system perceive themselves and each other. Mary Douglas, as we have seen earlier in Chapter 1 of this volume, has argued that as members of a classification system created by a community, we gain an identity and perceive others through our affiliations within this system. Douglas, however, warns us:

> But individual persons do not control the classifying. It is a cognitive process that involves them in the same way as they are involved in the strategies and payoffs of the economic scene or in the constitution of language. Individual persons make choices within the classifications. (102)

We do not control the classification system. We operate within our particular classification level. Whether we like it or not, realize it or not, accept it or not, we all function within classification systems determined by our political and cultural contexts. Context determines our ability to function. What we see on the Web pages of different classes within the educational system, then, reflects the values within that class, those conscious preferences and subconscious pressures that mark the community college as being different from and occupying a different class from an Ivy League college.

We have an educational class system in place in the US, whether we like it or not. The class system, furthermore, extends well beyond those of us directly involved in education, those of us who know what strong teaching goes on in levels other than those with the highest status: the class system itself dictates how much money gets funneled to the hierarchically privileged groups, whether by alumni, fund-raising campaigns, or the government, and also through self-selected or familially influenced student enrollment—students with money will choose to pay tuition at more prestigious schools; less money ends up being appropriated to the other group by state and local government, and also through financially strapped students choosing the least expensive educational alternative available to them. We also usually never hear of these schools conducting major fund-raising campaigns over a period of years like the first group does.[3] As Donna M. Desrochers and Jane V. Wellman report:

> Although the recession technically was declared over in mid-2009, sustained economic growth has yet to return, and the negative consequences on state budgets in particular won't play out until 2012 or 2013 when the state fiscal troughs will be at their lowest levels, and the federal stimulus funds will have been spent. . . . The immediate effect of the recession was most evident at public community colleges. Spending per student fell in 2009, fueled by a combination of enrollment growth and revenue losses. As a result, community colleges fell further behind other institutions—public, non-profit, and for-profit—in their ability to serve growing populations of students with resources adequate to ensure access, attainment, and quality. (5)

In a subtle way, the recession of the mid-2000s has reinforced the educational class system more than we realize, by stripping away financial resources and aid from those students who need them the most.[4] The Desrocher/Wellman report was published in 2011. Their prediction that we would not be able to see the consequences of negative state budgets until 2012–2013 has become a reality. In California, community college tuition increased, effective May 2013, in order to offset state budget shortfalls. Course offerings were cut, faculty laid off, hiring frozen, and course sizes increased. As a result, enrollment declined, and some colleges proposed a differential tuition plan based on courses most in demand and a student's ability to pay—in other words, students who are wealthier would pay higher tuition.[5]

ANALYTIC FOCAL POINTS

Earlier in this chapter I mentioned certain points that I will use again to analyze the community college Web sites as a group so that we might understand their constraints and their qualities as a separate step within the educational hierarchy:

- Identify the object of the classification.
- Identify what the classification excludes.
- Identify the human subjects who devise the classification.
- Locate the classification in time.
- Locate the classification's culture.

And a few points I borrow from the chapter following this one:

- Rhetorical situation
  - Overt subject / underlying or hidden subject
  - Assumed audience
  - Persuasive purpose
  - Occasion (what was the reason for creating the Web site?)
- Epideictic rhetorical situation
  - Is this Web site being used to create or reinforce any particular values associated with a particular community?
  - Is this Web site's audience being asked to reconsider any particular beliefs and/or values?
- What ethos is being projected from this Web site?
  - How do you perceive the writer's character from what she or he is saying?

We can "identify the object of classification" as community colleges in the US. These colleges represent different geographic regions; some belong to districts comprised of several colleges, others are single-district colleges. No matter their geographic location, however, they consistently display similar missions: to serve their immediate communities and to offer those who wish for one a quality education whether it be to fulfill their lower division course requirements inexpensively with the purpose of transferring later to a four-year institution, to enroll in vocational certificate programs that will equip them with the necessary background for gaining employment in fields such as medical technicians or restaurateurs among many others, or to take courses for personal enrichment such as learning to play an instrument, picking up computer skills, or writing for popular magazines. We can begin to see part of the reason for the appearance of the Web pages—these colleges are focused on drawing students from their communities, not from across the country, and for reasons that would lead their pages to state: "Start Here . . . Go Anywhere", "Your High Quality, Affordable Choice", "ARC, a Springboard to Many Options". The St. Louis Community College district pages advertise that their colleges are engaged in "Expanding Minds. Changing Lives." Another college's Web page contains visuals and testimonials from students about teaching quality, affordability, and support. The mission of these colleges, basically, is to give everyone a fighting chance at education, especially those who cannot afford the cost of an elite, Ivy League, or state flagship institution.[6]

The next point is to "identify what the classification excludes." Web sites for community colleges are nothing if not pragmatic. These pages generally focus on support services, finances, academic calendars, and other types of information listed on the right side of Randall Munroe's Venn diagram in Figure 3.7: application forms, campus address, campus maps, course lists, and parking information. Web sites for schools in this classification generally exclude those visual appeals that Ivy League or flagship universities must—reasons to attend their university as opposed to any other across the country. So this point is where the lushness begins to come into play: those picturesque images showing park-like grounds, architecturally impressive buildings, and the latest research being conducted by award-winning science professors—none of this shows up. Additionally, because so many students who enroll in community colleges are first-generation college attendees, the college Web pages do not showcase students or families who have attended that particular school for several generations.

I have combined the next point, "identifying the human subjects who devise the classification," with "locating the classification in time" because for this situation, the origins of community colleges, those points are inseparable. Community colleges—formerly known as junior colleges until the 1970s (Cohen and Brawer, 4)—arose because of social needs and pressures, and in particular because of prevailing social movements. These ideological foundations lie behind the devising of this particular step of the educational classification system in the US today and come from its location in time. As Cohen and Brawer explain:

The ideas permeating higher education early in the century fostered the development of these new colleges across the country. . . . Social institutions of practical value to society were being formed. This was the era of the Chautauqua, the settlement house, the Populists. And in the colleges, the question, "What knowledge is of most worth?" was rarely asked; the more likely question was, "What knowledge yields the greatest tangible benefit to individuals or to society?" (1–2)

Practical value and tangible benefits: for the community college, value and benefits lie in the area of gainful employment so that its students can have productive lives and give back to that same community. A tangible benefit is "success", a word used on many community college Web sites like Sacramento City College and Glendale Community College to indicate practical value. American River College's Web site had an entire paragraph on its first page explaining the success the college could help with:

ARC is a premier learning community that transforms and enriches people's lives. Here, you can be part of a diverse and exciting group of people, learning in an atmosphere of mutual respect and trust, joining many others who have gone on to successful careers in all areas of endeavor. (January 19, 2012)

Shelton State Community College features a student specializing in Culinary Arts and hoping for a job as a chef, and another working in the area of office administration with a specialty in bookkeeping and accounting specifically to further her professional career (March 12, 2012). Meramec Community College mentions its Center for Visual Excellence housing the latest in computers, operating systems, and software, designed especially to serve students "training for careers in emerging visual arts areas". And Forest Park Community College showcases itself as the "leading provider of health technology training" as well as "the premier trainer for the hospitality industry in St. Louis" (March 12, 2012). Study at these colleges is directly linked to practical value rather than theoretical value or cachet and is also embedded in local context. The St. Louis metropolitan area is renowned for its medical care and highly ranked medical facilities such as Barnes-Jewish Hospital, St. Luke's Hospital, St. Louis University Hospital, Missouri Baptist Medical Center, and St. John's Medical Center. So it makes pragmatic sense that one of its local community colleges specializes in training future employees for health care and its related technological needs.

Locate the classification in space, that is, within the space of the classification's culture: if we place the class—community colleges—within the culture of higher education, and find out how much money gets allocated to community colleges, we can see that budgets are handed down to those community colleges that are publicly funded, and that those budgets seem to impact the appearances of their Web sites mainly because the urgency of creating a Web site as an idealized space is less pressing for community colleges. Strictly speaking, they are drawing upon a local rather than national community and see themselves as stepping stones for students wanting to better their economic status by learning a trade, upgrading their skills, or earning college credits that will help them earn promotions in their current employment.

A rhetorical situation involves analyzing the overt subject of a piece along with the underlying subject, determining the piece's assumed audience, its persuasive purpose, and the occasion for the piece. The overt subject of community college Web sites is the particular college, the assumed audience is community members, and the occasion is those members' interest in taking courses. Studying this group of sites, however, leads us to realize that the underlying subject is not simply the college but also what the college signifies: opportunity—a chance at education for those who might not have envisioned themselves as college material, an opportunity for first-generation college attendees, a second chance for those whose high school efforts were less than stellar, an opportunity for self-respect through a practical career, a chance to retrain for a different career path, an opportunity to undergo technology training for specific types of companies, and a chance to become successful without incurring a massive educational debt. The persuasive purpose of the sites, then, is to help people in the community to see themselves as college material and then to believe they can gain a college education. The student becomes the main focus rather than the name of the prestigious college. The driving force is pragmatic rather than idealistic.

An epideictic rhetorical situation involves creating or reinforcing any particular values associated with the participating community, and in some cases, an audience finds itself being asked to reconsider beliefs and/or values. Close fused analysis of college Web sites as different groups within a classification system reveals the different values associated with each group within the system and the varying financial situations that come along with being on those different steps of the educational ladder. The question of "value" itself can come into question: what is the true value of a degree from an Ivy League university; what is the true value of a degree from a community college; what do community colleges value most; what do Ivy League colleges value? Epistemology may also figure into differences in value: what do these different types of institutions value as the origins of knowledge they offer? Is the "expert" a practitioner who has been involved, practically, in a field or profession, or is the "expert" someone with the highest degree possible for the subject matter? Close fused analysis of college Web sites as different groups within a classification reveals not only the different values associated with each group, but the unequal financial distribution that comes along with being on different steps of the educational ladder. Those bodies who provide funding base their value on and reinforce these values based on hierarchical rungs of the ladder rather than pragmatic results. How many young people with a B.A. or B.S. degree are looking for jobs compared with people graduating with an A.A. degree from a community college and entering a profession, or whose goals for their time at a community college were to transfer to a four-year institution?

Finally, fused analysis of the ethos being projected from community college sites shows that the "writer's character" changes subtly between those universities occupying the top of the educational hierarchy to the community colleges classified as being lower. While the elite universities focus on themselves and what facilities, faculty, or funding they have at their disposal, the community colleges generally tend to focus more on the student and the community. If they focus on facilities, faculty, or funding, they show these elements in service of their students and their community. The community colleges' Web sites display attitudes and characters dedicated to service. And as we have seen above, these Web pages show a consistent emphasis through visuals and text on movement, success, and opportunity. As Tidewater Community College's site states confidently: "From here, go anywhere."

These colleges really turn the educational classification system on its head by ignoring traditional university values that pit colleges against each other in terms of endowments, Nobel-prize-winning faculty, and a prestigious name by showing on their sites that they value their students above all, and will help them gain a productive place in their community.

4 Rhetoric, Context, and Culture on the World Wide Web

Analyzing the Internet's Virtual Mall

Because images are conventional, they must be explained by refer-ences to culture, not to nature.

~ Linda M. Scott

Calling the World Wide Web "the information superhighway" now verges on being an outdated cliché in this, the second decade of the twenty-first century. Labeling the Internet a digital super mall in the world of Web 2.0 or 3.0 might be more appropriate. Today's highly commercialized Web contains everything we find in a physical shopping mall and more, some-times even tailored to our very own personal preferences. Amazon.com tracks what we view then shows us products considered by other custom-ers with similar online "window shopping" habits. It personalizes recom-mendations each time we visit the site and allows us to keep wish lists that it uses to build other recommendations. iTunes, likewise, makes specific recommendations based on our buying habits or its "genius" tool that can analyze what we already own in our personal libraries. It suggests music, movies, and television shows we might want to rent or purchase. Let's be honest: when faced with a drive to any mall during which we fight traffic all the way and use up precious gallons of too-expensive gas, most of us would rather sit at our home computers and shop online. Without a doubt, digital media on the Internet inundate us, our children, and our students hourly as we all conduct research, purchase items, download music, play games, and generally live our lives online, Facebook or not.

Parents and educators have been aware for some time now that the con-tent of Internet "texts" needs constant monitoring for young children and teenagers because graphics could turn out to be *too* "graphic". Images themselves, however, are not the only part of the Internet that we should monitor. We need to study the accompanying text, yes. But as I have been arguing throughout this book, the fusion itself between images and text also merits closer attention and deeper analysis.

Digitally fused texts on the Internet do not arise from neutral situations to offer content that is uninfluenced by context. These days nearly every social situation gives rise to Web texts and every social group needs them: during the spontaneous fall 2011 March on Wall Street, for example, its organizers immediately created a site for regular news updates (occupywallst.org). Innumerable specific social and cultural situations like this one give rise to digital pages, then—a proliferation needing careful contextual study and reflection. But in order to analyze Web texts effectively, we must push beyond what Ananda Mitra and Elisha Cohen call "the more 'reductionist' content analysis" (181). Using the word "text" broadly to include both written words and "associated multimedia images", the authors argue that

> the image is the result of specific conditions of production that can determine the way the text [including both image and word] becomes meaningful in the public sphere. The objective of critical textual analysis is to move beyond an analysis of the volume of text and its content to the level of understanding the effectivity of the text and what it says of the community of people who produce and consume texts. (181)

Mitra and Cohen's particular critical approach relies on semiotics and structuralism, but when these scholars insist that we analyze the Web in the context of its producers and consumers, we need to pay attention to them. Foregrounding the rhetoric of digitally fused texts is one way to do so. Countless numbers of Web sites whose designs are often motivated by commercial interests may provide material for careful rhetorical study. Because they capture students' eyes and minds, the sites consciously and subconsciously reinforce particular values through their rhetorical displays while also reflecting additional information about the people and cultures that produce them.

Those of us engaged in such study and careful analysis also need to consider whether Web texts, their continued use, and lately their increasingly sophisticated construction are introducing new systems of evaluation that influence Web sites' rhetoric since Web page construction must now provide more than a simple offering of information, or more than commercial success and increased retail sales. We all know that sites need to avoid dead-ends, bottlenecks, slow-loading pages, and basically any navigational problem that would cause viewers to abandon a page and then a site. A poor Web design—poor, that is, in that it loses viewers and thus business—not only fails to anticipate what an audience wants, but also that an audience must be able to find it easily and quickly. As Josh Keller explains in an April 2011 article in the *Chronicle of Higher Education*, an analytic process for Web sites that has been more familiar to the commercial world than the realm of higher education is increasingly being implemented: Web analytics help explain the principle way to "sell" a school, or in terms more palatable to educators, to attract students trying to decide what college or university to attend. In other words, Web sites are the principle vehicle for higher education's commercial success. Now in order to be successful, university Web sites must reach beyond clean, attractive designs or adequate content; sites must be easy to use, in the full sense of the word "use": links to major information or application forms must work flawlessly, avoid bottlenecks, and bypass sections with content irrelevant to the prospective student. Web site construction today must therefore involve gathering data through Web analytics programs, mining the data properly, understanding the data, and then translating that understanding into Web pages that are highly effective in their rhetorically fused presentation. Keller mentions, in particular, the rhetorical values of clarity, focus, and audience awareness. Site developers must have a clear idea of the site's purpose. That is, they must be skilled in rhetorical and textual analysis, but with a contemporary twist: their rhetorical skills must be transferrable to digital documents. We teach our students about audience, but now it seems that for Web designers, analyzing audience is extremely complex:

> College Web sites must do much more than get prospective students to apply; they must speak to many audiences at once. John Drevs, manager of Web services at Loyola University Chicago, calls the quintet of main university audiences—students, prospective students, faculty, staff, and alumni—the "five-headed monster." It is, he says, difficult to create general Web pages that have the right information for five different groups. . . .
>
> So Loyola Chicago has stopped trying so hard. Instead, the university is building software to identify in advance which audience group a visitor falls into. (Keller, A10)

Keller's article interviews other Web managers who offer additional support for my argument in this volume that the practice of textual analysis needs refreshing and a concerted application in our age of the ubiquitous, digital, visually loaded World Wide Web text.

This chapter examines the rhetoric of businesses and corporations as conveyed through the words and images displayed on their company Web sites in order to analyze the effects of different rhetorical strategies as well as the degree to which those effects mirror the companies' qualities and philosophies. Our students need stronger critical skills than the ones they apply to advertising ploys and appeals found in other media. We all need techniques that will help us to determine what sites are more open than others about using rhetorical strategies that display their motives clearly. By analyzing sites that display clear company philosophies and by analyzing the use of visuals, including visual rhetorical devices—that is, figures of speech such as metaphor, metonymy, and synecdoche portrayed visually—and the visual syntax of complete Web sites, we can better judge whether businesses and organizations present a consistent appearance on the digital "street" and, furthermore, whether these sites reflect an understanding of a local audience as well as the global audience present on the World Wide Web. Applying traditional rhetorical tools to analyzing fused visual/verbal sites will help us all begin to develop visually literate and culturally attuned analytic skills that will serve us as citizens and employees in our lives both in and beyond our classrooms. In some cases I will argue that certain sites, in their visual appeals to their intended audiences, might seem to reflect only an elitist, exclusionary attitude within the executive culture of the sponsoring organizations. Closer inspection of the entire site, however, reveals a more complex position. But before I talk further about analysis, I want to mention the concept of "remediation" as Jay Bolter and Richard Grusin define the term. Bolter and Grusin argue that media never exist in isolation, that they refashion, reconstitute themselves to meet new challenges, that they are always "re-mediated":

> No medium today, and certainly no single media event, seems to do its cultural work in isolation from other media, any more than it works in isolation from other social and economic forces. What is new about new media comes from the particular ways in which they refashion older media and *the ways in which older media refashion themselves to answer the challenges of new media.* (15; my emphasis)

Taking Bolter and Grusin's statement a bit further, I add that our analytic tools also need to refashion themselves in order to answer the analytic challenges of new, "remediated" media. Finally, as a point of departure for supporting this claim and to offer a concrete example of such a refashioning—but as this refashioning applies to the act of analyzing—I point to Jack Selzer's essay "Rhetorical Analysis: Understanding How Texts Persuade Readers". Selzer offers a detailed list of rhetorical tools that have not previously been applied to new media. I argue, therefore, that not only new media themselves, but also the very process of analyzing them, can be an act of "remediation". In their application, rhetorical tools can help our students and us to dig more deeply into today's fused, mediated texts. Selzer's piece is an excellent reminder of the various levels—from global to local—on which such analysis takes place, of the plethora of rhetorical tools we have at our disposal when conducting such analysis, and of the relative ease of conducting such a normally difficult process once we understand the degree of awareness involved in such a study.

ANALYTICAL TACTICS

> *This is a study of method, not content.*
> ~ Robert Venturi, Denise Scott Brown, and Steven Izenour

Although close rhetorical analysis is an art fast vanishing, Jack Selzer reminds us not only how rich and rewarding such analysis can be; he also stresses its importance when we encounter documents designed especially to persuade us:

But especially if . . . pieces of writing have a persuasive intent, especially if (in other words) they have designs on your beliefs and attitudes (and nearly all writing does have that purpose, to some extent), the activity known as rhetorical analysis can offer you additional perspective and understanding. (279)

Adding to Venturi, Scott, and Izenour's words above by combining them with Selzer's, I would say that this entire book is a study of method, not content, a study for the purpose of perspective and understanding. Selzer's words focus on printed texts but also apply to digital compositions: Web sites are, in fact, necessary to include because these digital compositions are all designed to persuade us or—in less subtle terms—shape our opinions, about everything and anything, where to shop, what colleges to attend, what cutting-edge technological innovation we need to pre-order.

While young people use technology every day, my students have been unaccustomed to considering that Web sites have a singular, persuasive purpose even though these same students understand that non-digital texts such as printed academic essays are written to persuade. Encountering this bafflement and knowing about Selzer's work, I devised the tool below based on his essay, hoping to help my students who were encountering close rhetorical analysis for the first time, and in this case, an analytic rhetorical assignment made even more difficult, in their minds, because I was asking them to study digital texts. None of them had ever been asked to examine Web sites critically before, much less to analyze them rhetorically.

This exercise directs students to consider more general, global qualities first, such as appearance/presentation, and ease of use, before moving on to rhetorical elements. Because of students' unfamiliarity with and lack of experience practicing close rhetorical analysis, such an exercise might best be conducted as a staged process, first as a discussion including the entire class—one during which students can test their abilities and ask about terms they find confusing, next in smaller groups all working independently yet tackling the same site so that the groups can compare their different insights at the end of the exercise, then individually on self-selected sites, with an actual analytic paper or project due as the final product.

Before launching into a detailed explanation of the chart, I want to note that: 1) interestingly, the appearance of some sites seems to draw on the standard appearance of the media genre that they descend from. This form of media ancestry, or in Bolter/Grusin terms, "remediation", may need to be explained to students because they are more unfamiliar with print media than we might realize (how many, I wonder, actually sit down today and read any part of the Sunday paper besides the comics?); and 2) I am using only the Web addresses of these sites—their URLs—because I have realized over a period of several months that the sites' structural formats remain the same overall even though pieces of text and images change slightly depending on the seasons of the year or the companies' weekly retail emphases.

The Saks Fifth Avenue site (www.saksfifthavenue.com), then, in its stream-lined, minimalist appearance, contains the same design outline month after month while also drawing on the layout format of the department store brochure or catalog. The Wal-Mart site (www.walmart.com) on the other hand, presents a busier look more closely resembling its newspaper insert that appears every Sunday tucked in with all the other sales inserts from grocery stores, restaurants, and fast food drive-throughs. The actual design structure of these Web pages alone is remediation at work.

Now back to the chart. Asking students to evaluate a site's overall appear-ance as if it were an actual presentation given before a class and includ-ing additional instructions directing them to label what they are about to analyze elicits more thoughtful critiques than simply telling them to judge according to the vague term "appearance" and coping during class discus-sions with the purely subjective reactions such superficial study might call forth. So, for instance, instead of just saying they "like" or "dislike" a site's appearance the way they would judge each other's daily fashion choices that rely on a trend or an individual's fashion taste, having to consider appear-ance as a presentation can prompt them in their judgment to realize a site's effect on a wider audience than themselves: the graphics, images, logos, and other design elements that populate a Web site need to make sense given the site's topic/subject and depending upon the site's audience. I would hope that their evaluative focus shifts from self to audience. Most of our students have given presentations at some point in their academic lives. They under-stand that a successful delivery automatically involves not only self but also an "other", an audience. They are more likely to think about how a site's words and images play to an audience within the overall context of similar presentations they have made and seen. Cryptic, obscure references, or in this case, images, can confuse a Web site visitor enough to cause that visitor to leave. For this reason, ironic images or images that are inside jokes tend to drive away all but the rarer visitors who consider themselves part of the inside group. Collections of images, the content of the collection, and even what might be missing from image clusters are all important to consider. If sites picture employees and management, these images make a statement different from a site that pictures only management, or even a site with no people pictured at all, such as the Amazon.com site.

Fonts should match images on several levels—formality, site purpose, and intended audience. But again, focusing on an overall presentation made to an audience should cause students to stop and think before proclaiming a font to be "great" because "I like it," "it's different," or "it's cute." A "cute" font usually does not belong on a formal site unless the font has a rhetorical purpose. John Trimbur, in fact, sees "writing not as a derivative of speech at all but instead as a typographical and rhetorical system of sign making" (191). Evaluating what previously fell under the designation "typeface", but is now covered by the term "font", can take a more analytic turn if students realize that many histories and classifications of typeface (see for example

RHETORICAL ANALYSIS CHART: DIGITAL MEDIA

Overall Appearance (digital presentation)
    Graphics
    Font appropriateness (level of formality) and size
Overall Usability
    Textual clarity, readability (no unintelligible acronyms)
    Navigability (broken links?) (links that do not make logical sense?)
    Links that lead to irrelevant information
Context (Does this Web site fit into a group of similar Web sites?)
    Was it written in response to any other Web site?
    Is there a particular event that caused the Web site's creation?
    In other words, what can you gather are the surrounding circumstances for this Web site?
Rhetorical Situation
    Overt subject / underlying or hidden subject
    Assumed audience
    Persuasive purpose
    Occasion (What was the reason for creating the Web site?)
Epideictic Rhetorical Situation
    Is this Web site being used to create or reinforce any particular values associated with a
        particular community?
    Is this Web site's audience begin asked to reconsider any particular beliefs and/or values?
What ethos is being projected from this Web site?
    How do you preceive the writer's character from what she or he is saying?
What pathos can you identify?
    What emotion is the Web site projecting?
What logos can you discern?
    Is there any particular intellectual reasoning that you can discover?
    Do any link appear illogical?
    Do any pages contain irrelevant information or graphics?
What would you say about elocutio, the Web site's overall sylistic maneuvers?
    Does the Web site just seem thrown together without any thought to the way images and
        text complement each other?
    Do you notice any particularly clumsy areas of writing?
    Can you identify the writer's voice, and does it work with what the Web site is trying to
        accomplish?
What grade would you give this Web site and why?

Figure 4.1   Rhetorical analysis chart for digital media.

Lawson or McLean), typeface rules (Keedy), and even work studying the impact and design possibilities of punctuation (Solomon) exist.

Adding to or subtracting from a Web site's credibility and persuasive power is its usability—that is, how hard viewers have to work within the site to find the information they need. The text must be readable both in its appearance and in its diction: font size readable by all ages including older folks like myself who cannot read 8-point font online, text that avoids insider acronyms and jargon, and text that is clearly written. Usability also involves the way the designers classify the information on the site—that is, what items they put in the menus and whether the terms they use for these items make sense to users. The rhetorical message given to users who cannot find terms for the information they need is that the designers are more concerned about themselves than about their audiences. In other words, the designers have no rhetorical background or training.

After considering general factors, we can shift our focus to rhetoric and the way it shapes the features and content of these digitally fused sites. One point to consider early on in an analytic exercise is the site's context (see below for a more extensive discussion). Web sites, as I have been arguing, are never just free-floating creations lacking connections to similar pages and surrounding cultures. Site owners often want their online representations defined and created in relation to other sites so that the owners distinguish themselves from others in a similar group—like colleges and universities do—or in direct response to another site like the aforementioned Bing search site and tool created as a competitor to the more well-known (at least when it was first introduced) search engine Google. Additionally, scrutinizing a site's context goes beyond identifying its rhetorical situation because we must ask not just where the digital text is situated, but what the specific rhetorical occasion was, and whether the overt subject matter of the site is accompanied by a hidden subject or underlying motive.

The Bing site discussed earlier in Chapter 2 presents itself as an alternative search tool. By labeling itself in television commercials and on the site as a "decision engine" as opposed to a search engine—the usual term associated with sites that conduct searches—it sets itself in opposition to "search" engines. The underlying subject is that searching is random and unorganized and that people would/should prefer that someone or something else make their decisions for them. The indirect suggestion, finally, is that users should prefer a hierarchically arranged list of the most important results prepared by someone/something else.

Selzer's chapter explains epideictic rhetorical situations, so I include epideictic rhetoric as a point on my chart because asking whether or not an epideictic situation exists pushes the point of rhetorical situation just a bit deeper. If we return to the Bing site and ask ourselves whether it is trying to reinforce particular values associated with any community, we can begin to see that the hierarchically organized business model with its focus on retail consumption is the underlying value. Continuing along this vein, we can say that college and university sites reinforce the value of pursuing a higher education, retail sites reinforce the value associated with our type of economy—that we should buy what we want, not just what we need—and technology sites reinforce the belief that newer is better, or newest is best. Getting students to understand that written text reflects a writer's values, that it does not just present neutral facts, is difficult enough; but persuading them that graphics and images do the same thing is harder still. If students can understand the influence wielded by both text and image, however, getting them to understand that fused texts are doubly reflective may follow.

The next three items, "ethos", "pathos", and "logos", are ones with which our students are more familiar if coverage of these items takes place during their first-year college expository writing courses. Students can judge whether a site's presentation lends it credibility (ethos) or not, whether a site projects or attempts to depict or elicit any emotion (pathos), and whether the whole presentation appears logical (logos) in terms of complementary text and graphics, links within the site, and appropriate rather than irrelevant or confusing content.

Before the final act of grading, however, "elocutio"—judging a site's stylistic maneuvers—comes into play. More obvious items to look at regarding elocutio are the site's consistency from page to page and between internally linked pages. Students need to determine whether pages are eloquent in that the writing is clear and both text and images sustain a consistent tone. While voice is somewhat harder to discern with fused texts than prose alone, it is still possible to project a voice through digitally fused prose and graphics. In other ways, however, elocutio is a bit more difficult to analyze. Selzer discusses the difficulties in his chapter, and he is "only" talking about sentences. How much more difficult a task do we have, then, if we are studying fused text where not every item we study is a sentence with particular syntax or clauses that can be parallel or subordinate, or metaphors and other figures of speech that can cast an idea in a particular light?

And finally, after judging all of these elements, students should grade the site, then be prepared to support their reasoning. Selzer's chapter contains a richer, much more encompassing study of rhetorical analysis than my brief exercise indicates. But for our students the points discussed here will be enough to start them off.

CONTEXTUAL ANALYSIS

These days, analysts of new media insist on a situated, contextual approach to digital and technological analysis.

- Sonja Foss urges us to evaluate visual communicative functions in relation to the culture producing them.
- Marita Sturken and Douglas Thomas believe we must attend to historical context and rhetorical effects when analyzing technology in relation to society.
- Lee Brasseur believes that literacy for technical communicators involves all sensory experiences and understanding how a variety of literacies—and by extension, cultures—interpret semiotic language.

- Jay Bolter and David Grusin, as we have seen above, insist on culture as a given basis for any media's work.
- Linda Scott, discussing images, believes that creating, seeing, and understanding cannot function without a relation to culture.
- Amy Kimme Hea ("Riding") believes that Web research should account for the influence of cultural narratives and should involve situated, rather than universal, research practices; she argues that articulation theory provides the best means for such practices.

These scholars all agree that we must give the same attention to critiques of the organizations funding these Web sites as we might to more markedly persuasive texts. That is, we should conduct the same intense analysis focusing on the cultures giving rise to various organizations as we might to a study of the documents authored by a group that holds a particular political position with which we may take issue.

If we agree that analysis needs to be contextual, to account for the culture encompassing a site, then we must also decide what we mean by "culture", a word whose definition literally ranges from the sublime to the nearly ridiculous. Clifford Geertz, for one, has pointed out the difficulties in trying to define such a slippery term from an anthropological viewpoint (4–5). Edward Said, a literary and cultural critic, defines culture more narrowly in terms of high culture—generally uplifting practices that we might associate with a more elevated social position within a stratified culture:

> As I use the word, "culture" means two things in particular. First of all it means all those practices, like the arts of description, communication, and representation, that have relative autonomy from the economic, social, and political realm and that often exist in aesthetic forms, one of whose principal aims is pleasure. (xii) . . .
>
> Second, and almost imperceptibly, culture is a concept that includes a refining and elevating element, each society's reservoir of the best that has been known and thought, as Matthew Arnold put it in the 1860s. Arnold believed that culture palliates, if it does not altogether neutralize, the ravages of a modern, aggressive, mercantile, and brutalizing urban existence. (xiii)

For my purpose, analyzing Web sites on the Internet, I understand the term "culture" as being more akin to a sub-culture or popular culture—any group sharing an outlook or common practices—and less to do with being refined or elevated above others.

Casting a wide net in an attempt to define popular culture, John Storey states first that "popular culture is simply culture which is widely favored or well liked by many people" (4). He continues by explaining it is "the culture which is left over after we have decided what is high culture (5), . . . mass-produced commercial high culture, whereas high culture is the result of an individual act of creation (5), . . . 'mass culture' (6), . . . the culture which originated from the people (7), . . . one which draws on the political analysis of . . . Antonio Gramsci (8), . . . [and culture] informed by recent thinking around the debate on post-modernism" (9).

As we think about the different cultures reflected in the Internet, we should not confine ourselves to focusing only on large groups having to do with nations, races, ethnicities, or religions. Smaller cultural groups abound. How much do multimediated texts as well as other media shape a culture and its perception of itself? Cultures dictate how we see ourselves but in turn, we can gain insight into the ways those cultures WANT us to see them and they ways they see themselves.

Said's study of the early novel suggests in part how novels distribute narratives about culture and thus notions of how cultures wanted to see themselves and others, occasionally leading to stereotyping and imperialistic attitudes:

> Since my [Said's] exclusive focus here is on the modern Western empires of the nineteenth and twentieth centuries, I have looked especially at cultural forms like the novel, which I believe were immensely important in the formation of imperial attitudes, references, and experiences. I do not mean that only the novel was important, but that I consider it *the* aesthetic object whose connection to the expanding societies of Britain and France is particularly interesting to study. (xii)

While I would never make similar claims about the Internet, I do want to suggest that heavily consumed media—like novels in their day—shape attitudes about self, others, and cultures. The 2011 Arab Spring uprisings show that concepts about different types of cultures other than monarchies or dictatorships can be spread through fused digital texts conveying democratic ideals in contrast to more oppressive practices and that these texts can cause people to begin seriously questioning their existing, traditional, cultural narratives.

BEYOND THE SPLASH PAGE

Deeper, fused Web site analysis encompassing both the images and associated texts distributed across an entire site can show the extent to which Web creators focus and organize their projects. I chose to examine the Web site for Neiman Marcus, selected randomly along with a few others about a year before I began to write this chapter. I thought that the audience for this book might not be the same audience for the Neiman Marcus Web site and that readers might be coming to the site more or less cold and unbiased. This site's overall design structure or outline, as I mentioned earlier about the Saks Fifth Avenue and Wal-Mart sites, remains consistent even though the photographic images on the opening splash page change regularly. So the difficulty of analyzing the site then presenting that analysis via print like this, especially an analysis of a constantly changing digital site, is somewhat mitigated.

The site was not simply created to sell clothing. Unlike a shopper bound by a physical location such as the shoe department of a large retail store, a digital shopper can experience the full epideictic rhetorical treatment in addition to being able to purchase a pair of shoes: besides helping retail sales, the Neiman Marcus site was also created to reinforce, positively, the value of expensive exclusivity associated with a retailer selling an image of itself as a high-end, well-rounded organization with roots in its founding community, consideration for its customers, employees, and shareholders, and an awareness that as a company it should give back in some way to others less fortunate than its targeted base of the top 2% of households in the country (see below). If we think about the difference between shopping in a nineteenth century marketplace or reading about such a location in a nineteenth century novel, we can begin to grasp the fact that someone's consciousness intervenes between the viewer/shopper and what is displayed on the company Web site. In the case of reading about a marketplace in a novel, we have the novelist's consciousness intervening between a shopping experience and the actual marketplace. In this current chapter's example, the Web designing "consciousness" is well aware of the context and the surrounding circumstances of its particular retailer, and thus the site includes a few items important to that context. In doing so, the site also cannot help but reflect, indirectly, particular idiosyncrasies sometimes associated with the notion of "Texas" and being "Texans". Furthermore, while the company strives to draw on its Texas roots, we can sense it working against a perceived stigma attached to Texas money as belonging to the nouveau riche, a stigma attached less to east coast money that is older and inherited through many more generations. Thus the site makes an effort to establish that:

- This retailer has existed for over 100 years.
- It was founded in Dallas, Texas.
- It draws on characteristics of the west: legends and tall tales.
- It capitalizes on uniqueness, especially being a non-east-coast retailer in contrast to the majority of larger department stores founded along the eastern seaboard.

The site's overall appearance, its presentation, makes sense given this retailer's chosen audience, households earning the top 2% of income for the entire US, and its corporate mission focusing on "merchandise, customer service and marketing", with the goal of being "the best luxury and fashion retailer" (http://neimanmarcuscareers.com/story/mission.shtml). This retailer's specific focus on exclusive fashion dictates the intentional choice of photos showing models who look like and pose like those strutting the runways of top fashion designers. The site is highly usable as we would expect from a professional group; all links work and lead to relevant information. The list of links on the horizontal menus at both the top and bottom of the page reflect the priorities of this company. The very first menu item on the left, "Designers", is consistent with the group's mission, then continues on to items for women first, then men, children, and the home. The very last item is "Sale", apparently not a high priority topic.

The menu at the bottom of the splash page is also consistent with the mission focusing on service—in this case, "Investor Relations". On one of the days I happened to check this site, shortly after the disastrous spring 2011 tornadoes in Tuscaloosa, Alabama, and Joplin, Missouri, a small notice showed up with the words "Support disaster relief" followed by the logo and name of the American Red Cross—indicating that while this group focuses on that top 2% of households, they hope their customers and online visitors will help those recently devastated by the storms.

Another item recurring for at least a year on each iteration of the Neiman Marcus Web site was a photo of a shoe. Granted, the shoe was an enticement to win a $5,000 shopping spree from the well-known shoe designer Manolo Blahnik. To someone like me, who only buys shoes on sale for under $50 if possible, and only neutrally colored black, brown, or navy shoes at that, the significance of the shoe escapes me, unless the shoe is not just a shoe, but a metaphor playing on the old cliché of being "well-heeled", not only nicely dressed but extremely wealthy. Certainly, being bare-footed can often signal poverty and wearing shoes run-down at the heel suggests being less than middle class. Imelda Marcos' collection of expensive shoes, on the other hand, signified excessive decadence. A shoe could also represent romantic, fairy-tale escapism: the scenario played out in the story of Cinderella losing her glass slipper but the Prince using it to find her. Some shoes become synonymous with locations of the country, like cowboy boots are for Texas, hiking boots for the Pacific Northwest, or flip-flops for southern California. Shoes can be signs of status—not just designer shoes, but athletic shoes. Air Jordans were once the must-have shoe for teenage males, because everyone wanted to be Just Like Mike. Shoes, then, are metaphors for a number of values: wealth, athleticism, rugged outdoorsmanship, practicality, and social responsibility (Toms Shoes). The year-long shoe display on the Neiman Marcus site could have just been a shoe display. Or it could have been a display calculated to influence viewers subconsciously and rhetorically through some of a shoe's metaphoric associations.

LOGOS: INVITATION TO A LIFESTYLE

I never enrolled in a marketing class during my entire college career. The closest I have ever come to studying retailing occurred when I held a part-time summer job at a department store after my junior year in college. I can only guess, then, at what a Marketing 101 class would cover: topics like how to make customers want a company's products, key marketing concepts such as pricing, service, manufacturing operations, marketing plans, strategies, and customer needs. But as I look around the Web at different retail sites, what strikes me over and over is that the most interesting sites in terms of digital fusion are not simply trying to sell a product. They are trying to sell a lifestyle or even more, a psychological, emotional attitude, a state of mind, if you will. While retailers want functionality in a site because an efficiently working site helps customers order their products easily—or if not place orders, inform the public about what products are available—need, pure pragmatism, or logic do not usually sell products over the long run. The more intriguing Web sites sell a particular lifestyle to create a need and perhaps build customer loyalty that can sustain their organization through decades.

Needing to buy sound, though. How strange is that? Even stranger still is the degree to which we seem to need sound enveloping us constantly today, and to what lengths we go in order to keep from spending hours without sound. The Bose Corporation, a manufacturer of sound systems for buildings, planes, and automobiles, as well as noise reduction equipment for groups like the military, has retail stores in higher end shopping malls across the US and Canada, and worldwide from Argentina through Hong Kong to New Zealand. Its customers extend far beyond those who visit their physical shops in a mall or their online shops on the Web in order to purchase speakers or home theater equipment. Not solely confined to the music, automotive, and aviation industries as one might first think, Bose itself explains that it custom-designs sound systems for places like: auditoriums, hotels, performance centers, places of worship, restaurants, retail, schools, stadiums, and other venues the company might not yet have imagined (http://www.bose.com/controller?url=/professional/index.jsp). As for the company's actual products, Bose's Web site tell us on its "Company History" page under the link "About Bose" that

> [t]oday, you can find Bose wherever quality sound is important. From the Olympic games to the Sistine Chapel. From NASA space shuttles to the Japan National Theatre. In the home and on the road, from large outdoor arenas to intimate neighborhood stores, restaurants and clubs, you can hear the realism of the most respected name in sound—Bose.

One certainly needn't be affiliated with the Sistine Chapel to have good equipment from Bose or any other sound system company. But those who are accustomed to a slightly better quality of living than the average lower or working class citizen can aspire to, probably do—in other words, those who can afford to add "style" to their lives instead of just scratching out a living. Richard Lanham puts it this way: "A flourishing industry caters to people interested in high-level musical reproduction, the so-called high-end audio world. People in this world become extremely conscious of recording techniques, the basic rules of acoustics, listening-room design, the nature of human hearing. As a result, the act of listening becomes acutely self-conscious. People become connoisseurs of sound" (*Economics*, 143–144).

While having better sound around us is not exactly frivolous or exclusive as the word "lifestyle" might connote—a word, by the way, that Bose actually uses to name its line of home sound systems—the Bose Corporation Web site chooses to focus on the professionalism and research that make such better sound. In fact, Bose's motto, "Better sound through research", is written in as the "title" within the opening lines of their splash page's html source code. This phrase, then, appears not at the extreme top of that page, but at the top of the entire window of whatever browser the viewer happens to use—above the space for the company's URL. The motto, its location on the corporation's main page, its company philosophy, "Research fuels technology, and superior technology leads to superior performance," and, finally, historical information about the company itself, all indicate that the motto itself is the focus for the entire suite of pages. Overall, it serves to establish the company's ethos and logos while building support for the site's thesis or argument that Bose's intellectual research and energy provide superior products for its customers.

The digital fusion we find within the Bose Corporation's pages displays text and images highlighting logos as rhetorical invention more than any other type of invention technique, and Bose uses logos to establish its ethos. Such a move is not especially surprising since Bose was founded in 1964 by a professor of engineering, Dr. Amar G. Bose, who taught at the Massachusetts Institute of Technology. Bose's pages exemplify the way in which logos can be applied hypertextually in a digital age: the company argues rationally for the exceptional quality of its products and works on proving its case by showing us how much brain power goes into developing these products. Bose uses the term "intellectual assets" on a page titled "About Bose". We see references to "innovative thinking" on its "Learning Center" page, and the videos and diagrams embedded within the text illustrate topics such as "Direct/Reflecting technology" or the way sound reflects off of flat surfaces in concert halls before we actually hear it. Establishing logos in a digital age, we see, is no longer only a matter of linear thinking and words.

Now I could be wrong, but I find very little appeal to emotion on these pages; instead of putting a customer in the mood to buy a product through appealing photos of that product or sounds to set a mood, we find rational evidence in the place of photos or sound. The usual tactics we might find in relation to pathos are pretty much missing. Logos on these pages is, instead, the road to pathos. A viewer of the Bose Web site might find curious the fact that the Web 2.0 pages of a major corporation devoted primarily to sound delivery contain no sound. But if we think about this omission carefully, that choice becomes logical, especially when we read a few sentences about the reasons why Amar Bose founded his company: as a graduate student shopping for and then purchasing sound equipment, he "was disappointed to find that speakers with impressive technical specifications failed to reproduce the realism of a live performance" ("A History of Bose"). Including sound clips on its Web site to be heard under uncontrollable audio circumstances—that is on devices ranging from smart phones to tablet devices to laptops or even to the highest end CPUs—offers no guarantee of or control over sound quality. Such a move would be anathema to a company and CEO concerned with the best quality of sound possible.

For an ordinary shopper like me, someone with no background in engineering or passion for sound equipment, the presentation on Bose's Web site is not only rhetorically compelling but highly educational. And while I'm sure that the same information exists on paper in the form of glossy brochures available to any potential customer who walks into a Bose store, the information is even more widely available on the Web. I have walked into a Bose store exactly once in my life, hesitating at other times admittedly because I felt intimidated. Such a roadblock disappears on the Web and the opportunity for education is increased—the latter especially becoming a compelling enticement for someone, again like me, working in the field of education. Logos leads to pathos.

BEYOND LIFESTYLE

To tell the truth, though, if I think about products that sell a lifestyle, I think first about cars, automobile names that used to suggest images of a different type of life while I was young: Porsche, Ferrari, BMW, Mercedes. Maybe convertibles of whatever make or model. But definitely not a station wagon, my family's car while I was a teenager, and what I had to drive if I wanted to borrow the car. These exotic, foreign names became metaphors for living a better life, moving out of the working class, having money. Such symbolism should not surprise anyone living in the US since cars in this country have been marketed this way for decades.

What happens, though, if the particular car that a corporation is trying to sell is not an exotic import from Italy or Germany? What happens if that car is manufactured in one of the cities in the US that kept sinking during the economic downturn of the mid-2000s and hit rock bottom? What happens if that place is Detroit, a city that Julia M. Klein calls "what is arguably this country's most economically aggrieved city" at that? The Chrysler Group faced just such a dilemma, but began a marketing campaign that we find encapsulated on their site (www.chrysler.com) as of May 2012. The site operates in a rhetorically sophisticated way in its fused digital presentation and provides us with an example of ethos, pathos, and logos displayed in a way that can only be accomplished with a fused, digital text. The company directly challenges the traditional concept of "lifestyle" conveyed by foreign imports in one of its slogans: "Imported from Detroit". It also tries to recall the greatness prevalent during the heyday of automobile manufacturing in the mid-1900s by picking up on Detroit's nickname as the Motor City. But the Chrysler Group is decidedly not dwelling in the past; all the dynamics of the fused site work toward a new ethos connected to those three words, "The Motor City". Text, images, videos, sound—all contribute to shaping viewers' attitudes about themselves, the city of Detroit, its people, and its place in American culture.

* * * * *

I chose this Web site more or less randomly, like I did the Neiman Marcus site, partly because I had hardly any notion about the company at all when I began, and what I did have led me to a preconceived expectation that I would not be struck one way or the other when viewing it. Happily, as was the case with the Neiman Marcus site, I was greatly mistaken. What I found there helped me to see the company in a new light and also to understand even further, myself, new digitally fused ways of presenting ethos, pathos, and logos in our multiply mediated age. My second reason for choosing this site boiled down to the simple fact that I found the Chrysler slogan— "Imported from Detroit"—intriguing in its television commercials and the commercials themselves, I must confess, quite thought provoking.

For some reason we usually discuss the proofs for invention—ethos, pathos, and logos—in that order. Here, however, I am reversing it. I want to talk about logos first. The rational appeal/argument behind the Chrysler site is embedded in the second part of its motto: "This is the Motor City. And This is What We Do" (see Figure 4.2).

One of the site's links connected thematically to this motto reads "This is Chrysler." Clicking on it opens a page with a menu of items: overview, history, imported from Detroit, collections, commercials. Chrysler's history about its story provides the rationale: in existence for so long, the company knows what it's doing. And if history can serve as proof for an argument, we get "History" with a capital "H" on these pages.

What we first see is a timeline with dates between 1920 to 2000+. Beneath the timeline is a small window where a viewer can scroll through dates important to the automaker's history. Chrysler's site designers seem to understand that huge blocks of uninterrupted text on a Web site are off-putting; the choice, therefore, to place such text in a small box with a sidebar for scrolling is not only good design sense, but a commendable rhetorical strategy: the designers are aware of their audience and understand how blocks of text on a Web site differ from straight text, or uninterrupted paragraphs within a codex book: such blocks would make most Web readers move to another part of the site, stop reading, or leave the site entirely.

Placed off to the right of this relatively brief historical recap is a small image with the words "View the Full Chrysler History" linked to an

THIS IS THE MOTOR CITY.
AND THIS IS WHAT WE DO.

A company redefining the level of luxury that every American deserves.
The beating heart of a city in resurgence. Proving grounds for the belief that hard work pays off.

THIS IS WHO WE ARE. THIS IS CHRYSLER.

SEE OUR STORY

IMPORTED
FROM
DETROIT

VISIT IMPORTED FROM DETROIT

IMPORTED FROM DETROIT

IMPORTED FROM DETROIT™
New Merchandise Now Available

additional, more expansive, historical recap. Clicking on the image reveals a new page with an expandable timeline from 1800 to the "Future" with thumbnail-size photos that, when clicked on, open to individual pages covering the item—each one includes additional information, videos, and photo galleries. Photos within those galleries are part of a slideshow, and they all contain explanations of what they are, for instance, an old employee identification card with the explanation, "The locomotive engineers' traveling card dated July 14, 1909 for 'H. Chrysler,' Walter's father, certifying his 30 years of experience on steam engines." This same reliance on history undergirds the company's display of the Chrysler 300, listed under the menu title "Iconic Vehicles", a model that has existed since the 1950s. Each word of the display's title connotes history—"A Legendary Pedigree—and so does the blurb accompanying the model:

> The story of the Chrysler 300 visits the rich design heritage inaugurated by Virgil Exner's "Forward Look" philosophy of the early 1950s. The racing 300 series, Letter Series and Sport series will be highlighted to define their roles in the evolution of the 300 up to today's current award-winning models. Engineering, style and performance have always been trademark qualities of the 300 series and you will be introduced to these elements which, refined over time, became iconic characteristics making up the ongoing legacy of the Chrysler 300. (http://www.chryslerhistory.com/IconicVehicles/Content.aspx?topic=The-Chrysler-300)

The page devoted to the Chrysler 300 contains a video, one that keeps mentioning its "legendary heritage" and intersperses photos of the current model with early 1950s models. This example of digitally fused logos displays at its best that same rational type of appeal visible on the Bose Web site.

The Chrysler site, however, is not just a model of visual logos. Pathos figures in an especially important way. Not just marketing a product, the Web site is also "marketing"—for lack of a better word—an attitude and emotion: hope. This appeal is not hidden or indirect. It serves as the focus or argument of the entire site. If this were a strictly text-based scholarly essay, the appeal would be the thesis statement. Clicking on the centrally placed main menu tab, "This is Chrysler," leads to a page titled "This is the Motor City. And This is What We Do." In a smaller font below this argument we find the equivalent of an essay map, a statement explaining in brief what subjects a traditional essay would present in order to prove its thesis or argument: "A company redefining the level of luxury that every American deserves. The beating heart of a city in resurgence. Proving grounds for the belief that hard work pays off. This is who we are. This is Chrysler."

If we know anything even remotely about Detroit as a city during the last three decades or so, we understand that it has been and still is a city in crisis.[2] Scott Martelle explains:

Powerful forces built Detroit into one of the nation's, and the world's, great industrial centers and cities. Similarly, powerful forces have led to its collapse. The result is a national problem, not a local one, both from a moral and a financial standpoint. The long-term stability and viability of a society depends on its cohesion. Hundreds of thousands of people living in close proximity to each other who have lost a sense of connection with the broader society is a political crisis in the making. Less dramatically, unless the cycle of poverty in Detroit and other urban cores is broken, future generations become recipients of government spending rather than contributors to the common weal. On a more humane level, it is morally reprehensible to look away while so many fellow citizens live in misery, and without hope. (245–246)[1]

A thorough, fused study of the Chrysler Group's site reveals that the company is highly aware of the audience for its site: people wherever they may be in the world who are interested in the company and its products, and also the people of Detroit. So the site suddenly becomes one that is attempting to address this problem indirectly by offering employment and hope. Richard Lanham explains that pathos involves "putting the audience in an appropriate mood, by playing on its feelings" (*Handlist*, 166). The site is trying to instill in all of its audiences a sense of restoration, rejuvenation, and hope. And it does so by choosing to showcase people and occasions outside of the corporation: sports figures, popular music, local music and musicians, all to foster pride in a city. They illustrate the motto "Imported from Detroit".[2] Among the people chosen for each commercial vignette we find not simply those who hail from Detroit, and not simply internationally or nationally acclaimed figures. Those chosen display an attitude or spirit consistent with the one articulated in the sub-heading or essay map, if you will, quoted above.

- The musician and movie star will.i.am, while internationally renowned enough to be asked to perform at Queen Elizabeth's Diamond Jubilee celebration in Buckingham Palace on June 4, 2012, was born in east Los Angeles and raised in Boyle Heights, infamous for past decades and still now as one of the toughest, grittiest neighborhoods in Los Angeles, and like Detroit, home in successive decades since the 1920s to the city's cultural outsiders—Japanese Americans, African Americans, and currently Mexican Americans.
- John Varvatos, a fashion designer acclaimed worldwide, was born in Detroit. His vignette stresses his "blue collar attitude" in the world of fashion. The phrase "Show where you're going without forgetting where you're from" figures prominently in this piece.
- Ndomukong Suh, a defensive tackle for the Detroit Lions football team, was a 2009 finalist for the Heisman Trophy when he played for the University of Nebraska, won numerous awards, and was selected second overall in the 2010 National Football League draft. Known

for his aggressive playing style, Suh is shown returning to his blue collar neighborhood to visit his mother; the above-mentioned tag phrase used in the John Varvatos vignette is also the signature phrase for Suh's. The Detroit Lions, out of all the city's sports teams, represent the struggle of the city as an organization rising from the ashes: the Lions team was known for decades as one of the NFL's worst, but has in the last few years been poised to make a comeback.

- Eminem, the rapper, made the movie *8 Mile*, the name of a well-known, historic road in Detroit that separates the city from its suburbs and that has come in more recent times to signify the racial and cultural divide that contributed to Detroit's collapse.

- The work of Edgar Albert Guest (1881–1959), Michigan's only poet laureate, is read as background to a slideshow of images of Detroit.

- Alissa Czisny, while a slightly lesser known figure than will.i.am, shows up exemplifying a characteristic the Web site wants to emphasize: "Perseverance". This young figure skater from Detroit who competed for World Championship titles and won the 2010–2011 Grand Prix Final championship yet failed to make the Olympic team was selected to be the main figure in the Chrysler video. She speaks about literally having "the courage to get up after you've fallen". An effort that figure skaters make thousands of times during a career thus becomes a metaphor for what the city of Detroit is attempting. She talks specifically about her belief that the commercial she is a part of inspires optimism and hope. "Detroit is coming back," she says. "Threads of hope are there."

- Pastor Larry Callahan of Grace Tabernacle Ministries Worldwide is shown directing his traveling "Selected of God" choir. Pastor Callahan speaks proudly of Detroit as a place of "reconstruction, hope, and life", with music everywhere in the city signifying life, healing, and breakthroughs. "Detroit always bounces back," he says, and firmly believes that Detroit will return and affect the globe again. In the background we hear the choir singing the refrain "I'm on my way to better days."

- Musicians in the Juliets, a local pop music group, speak about the vibrancy, optimism, soul, and imagination they feel in Detroit and their loyalty to a city of history, culture, and passion, one they feel is on its way back to prominence. Detroit, they argue, has the best pop, rhythm and blues, punk, and rock 'n' roll. Their vignette features their own music which, like the music of the Grace Tabernacle Ministries Choir, fuses with the vignette's related text, videos, and photos to reinforce emotions of rejuvenation and hope.

Others we find here are a Detroit law enforcement officer, and a state championship high school hockey player and coach.

Both logos and pathos, then, as constructed on the Chrysler Web site, serve as backdrop for establishing the company's ethos, its character, and thus its credibility. Sister Miriam Joseph referring to Aristotle's *Rhetoric* explains ethos in simple terms as "the confidence which the personal good-ness of the speaker inspires in the hearers, their belief in his good sense, good moral character, and good will" (274).

Earlier I mentioned that I would examine ethos, pathos, and logos in an order reversed from what we usually see. My reasoning was that ethos depends heavily on the ways in which logos and pathos are conveyed. As Sister Miriam Joseph explains:

> Ethos is the persuasion exerted upon the minds and hearts of the audi-ence by the personal character of the speaker, causing them to believe in his sincerity, his truth, his ability, his good will toward them. Both *logos and pathos promote ethos* [my emphasis], for people more readily believe and trust a speaker who reasons clearly and cogently and who creates in them a friendly and sympathetic attitude toward himself and what he has to say. (272)[3]

But ethos, really? It's even more complicated: establishing character for any person must involve context. And it's doubly or even triply complicated if ethos involves the Web with its capacity for non-verbal communica-tion or performance conveyed through images and sound. Edmund Leach explains: "Just as verbal communication in man is dependent upon context, including elements of non-verbal context, so also 'non-verbal communi-cation' in man takes place within a context which includes language. . . . Just as [man's] verbal performance takes place within a matrix of verbal competence, so also his non-verbal performance takes place within a wider matrix of cultural competence or cultural convention (315). Establishing an entire automobile company's ethos in the twenty-first century, then, after the context of the country's economic downturn of the first decade ratch-ets the difficulty up to another level. Chrysler's Web site reveals what the company believes constitutes character for Chrysler and what it feels not only supports its ethos in the second decade of the twenty-first century but provides a multivocal, multimediated illustration of that ethos.

While it is a given that a commercial site will display its products, the links to actual vehicles and purchasing tools on this site are located, interestingly, on the periphery of the Chrysler site's main menu. Occupy-ing a central position on that menu is the tab labeled "This is Chrysler," leading to the page focusing on Chrysler's history. Embedded within this page is that other important link discussed just above, "Imported from Detroit". These connections are absolutely crucial for establishing Chrysler's character today: its history, its origins, its people, its music, its sports. Nothing is randomly chosen; all represent blue collar origins, Midwestern values, humility, hard work, dedication to accomplishing goals despite previous failures.

With global viewership made possible through the Web today, the rhe-torical consideration of a Web site's audience assumes a more nuanced com-plexity beyond simply asking a writer to address an essay to the specific people who will read it. The question now becomes: how wide a range of viewers must Web constructors realize their appeals will reach? The traditionally white male audience for automobile sales, the audience of the 1950s, is no longer viable. Chrysler's Web site indicates that the company understands in particular how its audience must be different, and for continued growth, must appeal rhetorically to a wider audience in terms of generations, race and ethnicity, sex, current and future earning ability, and social class. But we can also see that it does not forsake its origins and the citizens of Detroit themselves, a theme running throughout the site.

As Scott Martelle emphasizes, "Despite the current devastation, Detroit remains a place of tremendous resilience, with generations carving out lives and livelihoods alongside—and often outside—the roller coaster of the auto industry" (xv). The Chrysler site provides some of that "alongside— and often outside" of itself, a move that might be calculated by its marketing experts, but one that we should also credit as commendable. Today we find it so easy to be suspicious of and cynical about marketing; if we think of marketing in terms of rhetorical pathos, however, we might understand that at its best and at its most human, it is an attempt to appeal to feelings other than a base desire to possess material objects. In the case of the city of Detroit, those feelings of resilience, if not already present, desperately need to be kindled and then sustained. The opportunities for digitally fused presentations afforded by today's multimediated Web allow a rhetorical canvas never before possible with the codex book or with any single medium. Chrysler's entire focus on history would have been so much less compelling without the range of digital tools used by its Web designers, designers who seem to be completely aware of the power of rhetoric. Chrysler has thus taken full advantage of the new range of rhetorically persuasive appeals enabled by today's digitally fused Web capability.

Pressing analytically on all the components brought together in a multimediated Web site can help us—for worse or better—understand the display's message more clearly: we could discover selfish, distasteful, or underhanded manipulative motives behind those messages. But we may also discover less self-serving motives, ones more focused on helping others in a community. Close analytic reading guards against taking a first impression at face value or holding false assumptions. It keeps us honest. Warning literary scholars against the more recent lure of the new historicism, especially the recent few decades' dangerous trend toward completely historicizing literary study, Jane Gallop argues that teaching students to analyze texts closely and carefully represents "a real alternative to the banking model" of education,[4] and "our most effective antiauthoritarian pedagogy". Gallop continues:

> [S]tudents [have] to encounter the text directly and produce their own knowledge; closer reading [means] they [cannot] just apply knowledge produced elsewhere, not just parrot back what the teacher or textbook [has] told them. I fear that the demise of close reading as a

classroom method will leave us with students who learn cultural history by rote and then apply it to texts. I fear this will mean the loss of one of the most widespread and successful examples of a nonbanking pedagogy. . . . It is precisely my opposition to timeless universals that makes me value close reading. I would argue that close reading poses an ongoing threat to easy, reductive generalization, that it is a method for resisting and calling into question our inevitable tendency to bring things together in smug, overarching conclusions. I would argue that close reading may in fact be the best antidote we have to the timeless and the universal. (185)

Although meant strictly for literary study and teaching literature, Gallop's words apply easily to rhetorical study and instructing students to apply the full range of rhetoric while analyzing suites of Web pages.

Analyzing Web pages closely can reveal motives, values, and cultural ties. Discrepancies can mirror unspoken or unwritten tensions, and considering a Web site in totality can help us realize when the site presents its organization in a light different from one we might have anticipated prior to such an examination. Web sites are cultural snapshots like the drawings on the cave walls at Lascaux in France that record and are records of cultures. Talking about their architectural analysis of Las Vegas, Robert Venturi, Denise Scott Brown, and Steven Izenour explain that studying any one of the many architectural variables "in isolation from the others is a respectable scientific and humanistic activity, so long as all are resynthesized in design" (6). Cautioning readers who analyze separate pieces of an architectural creation, then, the authors remind all of us next about the step needed after separate analysis—resynthesizing those separately analyzed pieces together within the total design of whatever construction to which they belong, a caution and reminder we should apply when studying all the different modes present in a Web site.

Venturi, Brown, and Izenour emphasize additionally that their study is not a critique of the values that surface while studying Las Vegas's architecture in the 1960s. I make the same disclaimer here. By pointing to the values that different sites highlight, I am not critiquing, questioning, disapproving, or approving these or any values. I simply believe that such close examination can teach us something about ourselves, and that this knowledge is worth gaining. As humanists, we can look to Web sites to provide us with more information about what makes us and our different yet fellow humans tick, or in other words, to give us the kind of perspective and understanding that Jack Selzer feels we can all gain from such close rhetorical study:

> [R]hetorical analysis can itself be part of the unending conversation that Kenneth Burke celebrated—a way of learning and teaching within a community. (303)

5 Rhetorical Delivery, Digital Performance, and Media Fusion on Web 2.0

Delivery has been much studied in our own time, but not by students of rhetoric. The behavioral biologists and psychologists call it "nonverbal communication" and have added immeasurably to our knowledge of this kind of human expressivity. . . . As the use of animation continues to grow in electronic communication, and as the icon/alphabet ratio in everyday communication continues to tilt from word to image, Delivery may find itself returned to its traditional eminence.

~ Richard Lanham

Web 2.0's multimediated possibilities allow more rhetoricians today besides those involved primarily with spoken discourse to employ and analyze delivery, a previously often ignored rhetorical canon. For decades, as Richard Lanham notes above, delivery, or rhetorical performance, has been a minor concern to rhetoricians—if one at all—except to those involved with oral communications.[1] Delivery has also been missing from composition textbooks discussing effective writing strategies such as invention, arrangement, or style. Part of the reason for this absence? Kathleen Welch explains: "In our own century, the canons' enormous and largely unacknowledged power has occurred in the reliance of writing pedagogy on textbooks that truncate the five canons from five to three, so that invention, arrangement (form), and style repeatedly colonize the last two—memory and delivery—and then eradicate them" (Welch, "Reconfiguring," 18).

Web 2.0, however, by allowing sound, thus speech and music, to be embedded in a document along with images and text, resurrects the canon of delivery because it adds a performative aspect to Web information, especially information presented through suites of electronic "pages" on Web sites. In the past, yes, we could have witnessed a speaker in person giving a presentation while music was playing in the background and images were being projected onto a screen behind that speaker. We would have considered such a scenario to be a performance, though, and we would have been able to critique that performance. Academics in the field of communications would have been able to study such a performance in terms of all the rhetorical canons. Today those who have been accustomed to studying strictly text—where delivery and performance have minimal impact on the written word—must now reconsider electronic, digital texts as equally capable of delivery and must grant to such digital texts all the rhetorical possibilities such text can include:

- Not only visual aspects of images, photos, and videos studied by art critics, art historians, and artists,
- not just words studied by literary scholars,
- not just the argument, focus, and development studied by compositionists and rhetoricians,
- not just a rhetorical performance studied by forensics experts, musicians, and sound specialists,

but all of these together as digital media elements become fused in the world of Web 2.0. We must pay more attention to all in order to understand what we can do and how well those working in all these areas are accomplishing a strong rhetorical delivery and performance. Now, beyond just critiquing design or the inclusion of sound, we need to consider how well items like sound and design fit the rhetorical purpose and focus of a site. Now we need to consider how the sound and design fit with ethos and the audience being focused on. We need to understand the degree to which the site's primary creator has considered its cultural context within which the site will exist. The old aspects of delivery like facial expressions, tone of voice, gestures, sound volume, and fluctuations in posture or movement while speaking may have given way to the new aspects of delivery made possible by Web 2.0, or quite possibly still exist but have remained hidden, their digital forms disguising their unrecognizability.

"Delivery" has traditionally referred to those non-verbal cues such as facial expressions, dress, stance, body movement, intonation, or voice modulation that help speakers present information convincingly. Robert N. Gaines, in a brief online introduction, separates oral rhetorical delivery into two categories consisting of "The Speaker's Delivery Resources" and "Delivery Outcomes". His explanation of a speaker's delivery outlines the following cues:

- Pronunciation—consisting of articulation and dialect
- Accent—referring to "the stress placed on individual syllables of words"
- Emphasis
- Pauses or Stops
- Pace
- Volume
- Tone
- Gesture (http://www.arsrhetorica.net/gaines/delivery.html)

Ray Nadeau explains that the *Rhetorica ad Herennium* "divides delivery into vocal qualities and bodily movement" (57). This text follows outlines for voice and tone established by the Greeks and then

> very briefly suggests gestures appropriate to each one. For the sustained debate tone, for example, all you need is an occasional quick gesture of the arm, a mobile countenance, and a knowing glance. For the broken debate tone, you must use a very quick gesture of the arm, pace up and down, stamp the right foot, and have a look of intense concentration. For the pathetic tone within the classification of tone of amplification, the writer [of the *ad Herennium*] says: "slap one's thigh, beat one's head; and with a sad and disturbed facial striation goes a sometime calm and composed gesticulation." (57)

Today we need to analyze then decide whether studying delivery simply means that we are trying to fit new digital elements into old methods, or whether these digital elements are really just variations on traditional techniques eventually recognizable as such if we analyze them closely enough to understand (the concept behind the quality). I would argue that "intonation" on a Web site where no "speaker" is present can still be achieved through methods other than a voice; in addition, a speaker's dress or costume may have a digital equivalent to fabric if we think less literally. Many design elements such as background color, texture, font style, arrangements of text in relation to images, and placement of information on a Web page could be the digital equivalent of design elements added to a speaker/performer's costume: fabric color and texture, length, periodicity, finishing touches such as lace, buttons, hats, scarves, gloves, and so on.

Ironically, while the field of composition and rhetoric all but ignored delivery in previous decades, recent attention has greatly proliferated, making difficult both our grasp of the ways in which this canon operates today and our understanding of how to theorize it for a digital age. Several studies, in fact, within the last decade (DeVoss and Porter; Yancey; Prior *et al*; Brooke; Porter; and McCorkle) have echoed each other in their calls for scholars to reconceive and redefine the rhetorical canons, most notably delivery, in order to account for changes now taking place because of technology. However, two different—but not necessarily competing—definitions of "delivery" seem to be operating within these areas, complicating the matter even further: 1) delivery as it was understood in classical times, that is, associated with the personal tools a speaker in the midst of an oral presentation had available to him—such as those described by Gaines and Nadeau above—and 2) delivery as the technological (used in its broadest sense) tool used to transfer an object from one place to another.

Nonetheless, we find among the variety of topics being addressed, defined, and discussed with regard to rhetorical delivery:

- Delivering and administering instruction throughout an educational institution (Yancey; Porter)
- Methods of distributing or "delivering" curriculum within an individual classroom (Weiser; Neff; Rutz; Redd)
- Web site design as enabling pedagogical delivery to both physical and online classes (Bodmer)
- The ways delivery shapes and is shaped by the physicality of the inhabitants within the spaces where rhetoric is delivered, or in other words, the "materiality and physicality of rhetorical acts—in this case the body language of instructors and students operating in the architectural space of a four-walled composition classroom" (Taylor, 128)
- The ethical dimensions of delivery in a digital age (Dragga; DeVoss and Porter)
- The remediation of "delivery" in an age of technology and digital writing in order to account for "distinctive rhetorical dynamics of Internet-based communication" focusing on production, delivery as *techne* or art, resulting in a theoretical framework for digital delivery (Porter), as well as recomposition, and rhetorical velocity (Ridolfo and DeVoss)
- Secondary orality and delivery as related to television (Welch)

Sometimes within the groupings above, authors take their essays in additional directions. DeVoss and Porter's article, while discussing ethics, approaches digital delivery as it touches on filesharing, copyright, and intellectual property rather than the canon of delivery specifically. Sam Dragga, while pointing out that reviving the canon of delivery confers new rhetorical power yet creates new ethical obligations, shows in detail that ethical delivery covers subjects such as "proportional display, minimal design variation, minimal graphic dimensions and clear and detailed labeling" (81); his essay applies more to technical documentation rather than Web displays, but to extend his ideas to considering the ethical delivery of Web suites is not an unreasonable or far stretch of the imagination.

Still other researchers add different dimensions to the subject of delivery. Ben McCorkle studies historical recovery "to tease out a cross historical narrative based upon a theoretical rereading of rhetorical history" (8). Paul Prior, Janine Solberg, Patrick Berry, Hannah Bellwoar, Bill Chewning, Karen J. Lunsford, Liz Rohan, Kevin Roozen, Mary P. Sheridan-Rabideau, Jody Shipka, Derek Van Ittersum, and Joyce Walker study rhetorical delivery reconceived as remediation, invoking Bolter and Grusin, McLuhan, and Latour, then arguing that "it makes more sense to begin remapping rhetorical activity, to trace distribution and remediation, than to attempt to retrofit this ancient tool to do varieties of work it was never designed to address" (http://kairos.technorhetoric.net/11.3/binder.html?topoi/prior-et-al/index.html). Jay Bolter discusses hypertext as a new mode of delivery, arguing that as such it redefines the other rhetorical canons. His essay includes a thought-provoking discussion of hyperbaton and hypertextual arrangement. Finally, he believes that hypertext and discontinuity of voice constitute a part of delivery. For John Frederick Reynolds, "Rethinking delivery simply requires that one see equivalencies between oral, written, and electronic *pronuntiatio* and *actio*—analogies between voice/gesture and layout/typography, for example—something that composition specialists focused on and studying technical and computer-assisted writing have been doing with considerable ease for some time now" ("Memory," 4).

My chapter here adds to this list of approaches. Rather than questions of ethics, composition instruction delivery, or the production of digital delivery, however, it rethinks and analyzes delivery solely as the digital act that takes place on a Web site, in other words, not teaching writing or producing anything. To "borrow" and flip James Porter's language focusing on digital "production", I focus here instead on digital "consumption". Earlier in this book's introduction to Chapter 5, I used the metaphor of a delivery truck driver. Here I am extending that metaphor to explain that the final end of "consumption" involving delivery needs

1) an appropriately designed and appealing product that someone wants to order,
2) an efficient delivery driver who can reach a final destination, and
3) a customer or consumer who accepts the delivery.

In this age of Web 2.0, people writing digital text for the Web include other "delivery" cues to make convincing and clear points. Digital delivery today fuses images, video clips, and sound with texts, so it merits our critical attention and study as such. I would argue that digital delivery on the Web is also akin to a theatrical or musical performance meant to be seen, heard, or experientially "consumed" by an audience.[2] Instead of an individual, unaccompanied solo performance on a single instrument like a violin or cello, the digital performances we experience through a Web site are more comparable to orchestral performances. We witness sections for strings, woodwinds, brass, and so on, plus, depending on the musical score, other occasional instruments like kettledrums or xylophones; a string section consists of various numbers of violins, violas, cellos, basses. In the same way the "visual" components of a Web site performance could consist of various numbers of photographic images, graphic icons, and designs, videos, charts, or graphs, the sound section can contain spoken narrative without an image, like a voice-over, background sound or music, or entire musical pieces.

Additionally for all these elements of a digital performance, the least of which is verbal, we can draw on rhetoric to help us with our analytic endeavors and to help us understand the point of the whole performance, the equivalent of a conductor's interpretation of an orchestral score:

The amalgam of precepts, exercises, models, and clichés that we call classical rhetoric nevertheless endures. It may pass in or out of fashion, becoming more or less prominent in the theory and practice of art, but it invariably remains too useful to ignore. For artists, rhetoric may suggest ways to compose and to perform; for audiences, ways to respond; and for critics, ways to understand the phenomena of composition and performance. At the very least, rhetoric provides a vocabulary for making communication explicable—and not just verbal communication. (Beghin and Goldberg, 2)

The sheer amount of non-verbal communication taking place on most Web sites, when we stop to think about it, is monumental. If we can use rhetoric to help us analytically, however, and if we can understand a site comprehensively, holding in our minds all elements involved in its performance, we will better understand the whole.

To study communication is, in many ways, analogous to the old Indian fable about the blind men and the elephant. One man feels its leg and thinks the elephant is like a tree; one man touches its trunk and believes it is like a snake; and another man grabs its tusk and declares it is like a spear. Each offers a partial description of the animal but fails to grasp how the parts make up a whole. Communication is like the elephant if only for its sheer magnitude. Everything we do cooperatively in society (and often alone as well) implicates us in some communicative act, whether it is something obvious like a speech or something more subtle like a glance or a conspicuous silence. To try to offer a single, comprehensive description of communication often seems an insurmountable challenge. (Crick, Pecchioni, and Butcher, v)

In fact, while we can locate, identify, and "see" a speaker in most performances, rhetorical or otherwise, we can only—in any rhetorical delivery on a Web site—experience the performance itself, because it shows us no physical speaker, only traces of that deliverer/creator conveyed through sounds, words, and images, all of whose rhetorical properties lead us to understand how that creator intended to influence us. Analyzing such sites by keeping always in mind the media fusion evident before us can help us to identify and place that speaker with regard to his or her values and culture, a placement that is really the reason for studying Web sites in the first place.

I do need to add a few words about prior departmental separations and academic divisions that make studying delivery in a digital age so difficult. The complications of connecting rhetoric with performance studies and even further, delivery, are outlined clearly in Stephen Olbrys Gencarella and Phaedra C. Pezzullo's introduction to their volume *Readings on Rhetoric and Performance*: "When departments of communication studies, theater, English literature, anthropology, and folklore emerged in the early twentieth century, attention to various aspects of rhetoric and performance tended to be divvied up. This is one reason why no single discipline or department today may claim exclusive ownership of the intersection between rhetorical studies and performance studies, and why interdisciplinary collaboration is so fruitful for creating synergy between the two" (2). Gencarella and Pezzullo also warn us:

> Despite the appeal many scholars have identified in recognizing the ways rhetoric and performance intersect . . . there are those who do perceive risks. Part of what is at stake in the entanglement between rhetoric and performance is the different histories, theories, and practices each can bring to bear. Some scholars in performance studies, for example, express concern at rhetoric's legacy as an instrumental tool (that is, used to persuade X audience to do Y) or at the cause-and-effect value that some rhetoricians—though certainly not all—use as a standard for judgment and evaluation of which practices are worthwhile to enact or to study. The concern is that such a linear approach to evaluation may miss the value of performances that are whimsical, unpredictable, and/or marginalized because of the ideas expressed, the identities of those involved, and more. Conversely, we have witnessed a concern in discussion among some rhetorical scholars that performance studies may be satisfied at times with playful and/or detailed descriptions, without making the move to a more explicit critique of unjust power relations. The worry is that whimsical, ambivalent, or marginal acts may be too readily dismissed by the status quo and, therefore, not make a difference. (3)

While studying digital delivery, therefore, and the rhetorical performances that we see operating on Web sites, we need to bring together for study all the theories and practices now claimed by those different departments. Remaining isolated in separate departments, refusing to draw from each others' theories, and continuing to reinforce borders instead of "creating synergy" will end in intellectual stagnation rather than the growth of all.

* * * * *

Performance—that is, delivery—is the ultimate test of rhetorical theory.
~ Tom Beghin and Sander M. Goldberg

While trying to recall memorable performances I have witnessed, my mind, for some reason, turns first to live musical performances—solo instrumental concerts, then maybe to one or two unforgettable poetry readings. Next it turns to recorded performances, including speeches, and finally to outstanding athletic performances. We all have such memories of different events performed in a range of categories. But pinpointing what made them memorable is more difficult, that is, identifying specific qualities making them so. Once identified, however, we should also be able to translate these qualities, if need be, to their digital equivalents, involving yet more analysis. We must do so if we want 1) to consider a Web site as being capable of giving a digital performance, and then 2) to analyze exactly how its elements work, or don't work, in order to make a Web site's digital performance rhetorically effective.

ATHLETIC RHETORICAL PERFORMANCE

I must admit that I was surprised at my mind's turn to sports. While games and athletic competitions are certainly performances, I have never stopped to think of them being related to rhetoric or to rhetorical delivery. Deborah Hawhee, however, might argue that such a turn is only natural if we think back to the early Greeks. She has written extensively on this subject in her volume *Bodily Arts: Rhetoric and Athletics in Ancient Greece*, particularly in Chapter 7: "The Visible Spoken: Rhetoric, Athletics, and the Circulation of Honor". Explaining such relations, Hawhee makes especially clear the connections between these early rhetoricians, their athletic festivals, and the whole concept of rhetoric; she also draws our attention to a line of rhetoricians who have previously studied rhetoric, athletics, and festivals, among them scholars like Richard Enos, W.K.C. Guthrie, John Poulakos, and Scott Consigny (164). Pointing to the *Panegyricus* written by Isocrates, Hawhee emphasizes Isocrates' idea that

> the festival produced a gathering of onlookers to witness "contests not alone of speed and strength, but of eloquence and wisdom and of all the other arts". . . . These gatherings, with all their variegated activities, social connections, participants, and spectators, thus occasioned a furious celebration of and—by extension—circulation of honor. The ancient festival, that is, constituted a space of visibility that showcased honor (*timē*) precisely by facilitating its exchange. Exchange of honor, as Isocrates makes clear, happened through athletic and rhetorical displays. Isocrates therefore articulates a critical connection between athletics and rhetoric: they both occasion gathering and witnessing. (165)

An athletic spectacle enables visual displays of abstract values, qualities that appear through the event itself and all of the participating athletes' endeavors. Hawhee elaborates: "Within the festival context, athletics and rhetoric inhabit distinctive modalities of appearance: athletics resides more in the realm of the visual, while rhetoric, of course, deals with words. But the curious moments are when the two come together; when what is seen enters into a relation with what is said. As distinct modalities of appearance, rhetoric and athletics help sketch out the complicated relations between 'forms' and 'words'—the visible and the articulable" (163). What is therefore important for us in identifying the rhetorical within the athletic and thus the performative qualities that can also be used to analyze digital performances is that "festivals as networks of spectacles shaped rhetoric as an art of performance, one that is immediately bound up with the articulation and circulation of honor (*timē*), virtue (*aretē*), and fame (*kleos*)" (165), or to paraphrase, because of athletic events, certain performative qualities we now identify as rhetorical exist. They include honor, virtue, and fame, not as isolated abstract qualities but as concrete, visually identifiable qualities forming an inextricable cultural, social connection, the "gathering and witnessing" mentioned just above, between an audience and a performer whether that performer be an athlete, an orator, or a musician.

MUSICAL RHETORICAL PERFORMANCE

Honor, virtue, fame, and the cultural/social connection between audience and performer can be identified in musical performances as well as athletic ones. Rather than a festival during which honor is displayed, these performances exhibit something closer to an orator's rhetorical display during a convincing argument. Discussing performance—or delivery—in relation to Haydn's Keyboard Sonata, Tom Beghin asserts 1) that the training for orators in Quintilian's day "unites all categories of oratory" (131) and 2) that the stages of oratory, *inventio, dispositio, elocutio*, and *memoria*, culminate in good delivery. He continues: "On this continuum, the notion of a 'text' is neither a goal nor a point of departure; it is an intermediate stage between invention and delivery. Delivery is of the 'ideas' rather than the words; conversely, the purpose of inventing ideas is not to have them reflected in elegant prose, but for them to be orally effective; in judicial oratory, being 'effective' means winning one's case" (132). The deliverer wins the case when the audience responds in the ways the composer desired because the performer successfully integrates the composer's ideas with his or her own understanding of the complex totality of ideas conveyed. Beghin allows: "[T]hat Haydn's interests as a composer were first and foremost in the performance of his texts may be corroborated by many statements about his desire to create certain effects and to provoke certain reactions from his audience" (143). In cases of some composers who have left no documentation of their intentions, the musical scores themselves contain a record of intentions, perhaps the best record. During a discussion about Bach's cello suites, the internationally renowned cellist Anner Bylsma answers a question about "authenticity" and true performances by saying:

[L]et's say 'true' playing is the way that Bach would have liked it. This will cover many approaches. I wouldn't want us all to play exactly the same way. . . . I don't think this discussion will get us anywhere, since Bach isn't here to defend himself. But I must say that it's very hard for me to agree with what I used to do, and with what most cellists do today. . . . [I try to] look at what the manuscripts actually say, instead of trying to guess what Bach may or may not have meant, or assume that Mrs. Bach didn't play a string instrument and therefore threw in meaningless slurs. Taking a fresh look at the manuscripts has given me so many new ways of thinking about the bow arm that, at the moment, I'm kind of a zealot. Next year I may be different, but, for now, I'm trying to play exactly what's written, which is very difficult, both technically and musically. (quoted in Janof, 2)

To complicate the analysis of musical performances even further, we sometimes also need to include the particular musical instrument used so that we are actually analyzing the interplay between the musician, the instrument, and the composer's intentions—to determine the success of the rhetorical delivery.

One example of all the above takes place in Anner Bylsma's 1992 recording of Johann Sebastian Bach's *Suites for Unaccompanied Cello*. For this performance, Bylsma was allowed the use of an antique cello, the *Servais* Stradivarius, owned by the Smithsonian's National Museum of American History. In the notes accompanying the 1992 digital recording, Kenneth Slowick gives details about the unusual stringing and tuning of the *Servais* cello, then concludes: "[T]he resulting performance is one of the most beautiful and convincing examples of Baroque string playing on disc. The purist's discomfort at this apparent anomaly will disappear upon hearing the extraordinarily beautiful and unquestionably 'Baroque' sounds Mr. Bylsma coaxes from the Servais. 'Playing this instrument,' he has often remarked, 'I am bounded not by any shortcomings in my equipment, but only by the limits of my imagination'" (7). The performance becomes more "convincing" because this particular instrument's sound contributes to the composer's complete idea being delivered through it via the performer.

With music, then, the sound created in a performance—whether by a conductor directing an orchestra or a solo musician playing a single instrument—is rhetorical in that the musical "idea" of the composer, conductor, or performer, is convincing. The "idea", to emphasize Tom Beghin's words above, is what we need to think about, and is a concept that can be conveyed in ways besides just text. To take this idea one step further and apply it to the fused texts created for the Internet, we need to remember that sounds embedded in Web pages, whether spoken sound, songs, or instrumental music in linked videos or in embedded musical clips, all contribute to the rhetoric of a Web site just as much as its words and images.

DIGITAL PERFORMANCE AND SOCIAL IMPACT:
THE ELOQUENCE OF EXIGENCE

One final quality needs our attention before we move forward with the subject of digital rhetorical delivery and performance: we should try to determine what it is, exactly, that distinguishes a rhetorical effort from being just simply a piece of communication. Nathan Crick, Loretta Pecchioni, and Joni Butcher remind us about basic rhetorical concepts that students of rhetorical, performance, and communication theory learn early on in their academic careers:

> The *meaning* of rhetorical discourse is located not in words but in practice. Because rhetoric is oriented toward social action, the *practical* meaning of rhetoric is determined by the effects it has on audiences and their subsequent decisions and attitudes. There is, of course, also a textual meaning located in the discourse itself that we can interpret much as we would do with a poem or a tract of philosophy. Much of what is called *rhetorical criticism* engages in this aspect of interpretation that is detached from questions of practical effect. However, the final judgment of any rhetorical act is ultimately how it impacts the social world in which we live. Without starting with this practical meaning, rhetoric becomes indistinguishable from any other form of communication. (161)

A rhetorical act impacting our social world: important words, these.

Those Web sites containing more memorable rhetorical performances, eloquent performances, I would argue, have impacted our social world in a way consistent with their particular focus. Furthermore, if we ask what might be involved in analyzing a compelling rhetorical performance given digitally, we need to account for a Web site's non-verbal as well as verbal communication and whether or not the total performance does in fact make an impact on that "social world in which we live". While we might think that such sites would then need overt political or social content, this need not be the case if we consider the widest meaning of the term "social": having to do with a particular group or wider community. For some of these sites, the effort to impact the world might not be immediately obvious, especially if we turn to a Web site to buy a particular product well before we make an actual purchase, if we want to research the company's previous projects, or if we feel compelled to study a company's past performances before we decide to hire it. Finally, if we identify the underlying purpose of the performance and ask which performative elements are best suited to help achieve that end, or if we can pinpoint the site's rhetorical exigence, we can begin to identify how digital non-verbal communication comes together to address a pressing situation, that is, the idea prompting the performance and shaping the delivery. Often the exigence involves variations on those aforementioned qualities such as honor, virtue, and fame mentioned above in relation to athletic performances. It all comes down to being involved with and impacting a particular community, a social group.

Now while the possibility of non-verbal digital "gestures" exists, we might ask how they would be conveyed to achieve a welcome, for example, to distance viewers (whether intentionally or not), to create drama, or to achieve an understated effect. In reality, there could be no standard template for examining effective rhetorical delivery because the examination depends on the site's exigence and social purpose; non-verbal elements needed for a highly dramatic performance, for example, would differ greatly from a performance intended to be understated. However, general directions to take for such analysis might include the following:

- Inward: first, what we can learn about the speaker/agent/performer, then second, how and why this knowledge is important rhetorically and socially.
- Outward: what we can assume about the intended consequences of the performance, given the rhetorical exigence that prompted it.

Some of the exigent circumstances that have given rise to memorable digital performances on Web sites are a dying city's need for resurrection, our world's need for sustainability, the importance of staying ahead in the competitive world of technology, and the importance of making education relevant to minority students then retaining them in higher education. Two of the four sites I discuss below have shown up in other chapters of this book; here, however, they are also apropos because the social impact they are working towards provides an additional layer to their Web sites. Studying sites with an eye to fusion and rhetoric can help us dig below the surface of a site and keep us from making snap judgments, that is, seeing only the most obvious and superficial of its elements, or stereotyping a site and dismissing it instead of understanding its complexity.

What exactly is involved in analyzing a compelling rhetorical performance given digitally? One point would be to refrain from judging a site as "good" or "bad" only because of its design or navigability, but instead to understand whether the performance's purpose, its "idea", was achieved. The second would be to identify the underlying purpose and to judge whether the site's performative elements are well suited for that idea and help to make it clear. For me, the most rhetorically eloquent Web sites are the ones that understand the fusion possible between various media and use all, not simply for the sake of "using", but to convey a singular point of view—a thesis really—about their products or their services, and to show how that product or service and the company itself connects to a larger community.

1) Chrysler: Performing from Hope to Action

Back in Chapter 4 I discussed a portion of the Chrysler Group's Web site in terms of the pathos, logos, and ethos it projects and argued that these rhetorical elements worked together to inspire hope in viewers, especially viewers connected to Detroit. When we examine the site closely while trying to assess its entire orchestrated digital performance, however, a larger picture begins emerging: the Chrysler Group's concerted effort to address a rhetorically exigent social situation much larger than the company itself—the urban collapse that has blighted parts of many cities throughout the country. By focusing on Detroit and the recent near death of a city that, in its heyday, was one of this country's most vibrant urban centers, then showcasing that city's effort to revive itself, the site's performance is a study in self-help for other troubled cities. Over and above its inspirational yet abstract motto's effort to provide hope for this city, then, the site reveals Chrysler's subtle determination to point to the groups that support and serve the larger community of Detroit, a showcase that allows viewers to discover places where they might provide monetary and physical support through donating and volunteering. While trying to restore its pride and vibrancy as a city by including practical ways to ward off the exigence of its collapse, then, Chrysler's site goes beyond inspiration to the next step: making visible and bringing together some of those who can help. The rhetorical performance here is a clear example of Crick, Pecchioni, and Butcher's key already quoted above to distinguishing rhetorical discourse from other communication: "[T]he meaning of rhetorical discourse is located not in words but in practice" (161).

At the time I began writing this chapter in 2012, the opening splash page displayed the company's most recent models, as do most automobile manufacturers' pages. That page is now one of two rotating splash pages. Most important to note, however, is that the setting or backdrop for these Chryslers both then and now appears to be either a factory, a warehouse, or a barn—a location suggesting blue collar employees or farmers, people who use their hands to make a living, people who decidedly do not spend their working lives pushing paper behind a desk. What used to be the central menu item, "This is Chrysler," has now been moved to a menu for Chrysler enthusiasts at the bottom of the page but the link remains the same (www.chrysler.com/en/this-is-chrysler)—although the central menu item has become Chrysler's motto, "Imported from Detroit". Chrysler's rhetorical performance on the portion of its site showcasing its new models stems from its desire to use its digital space to do as much as it can today to pay tribute to Detroit and her people, and by extension, to recognize a group not usually celebrated: the working class across America. The digital performance is designed in part to make us think about Detroit's past, present, and future, using history to help make the present more hopeful and the future better for both Detroit and cities like Detroit that have nearly failed due to lack of vision and planning for a future. The other part of the performance, however, focuses on practice and action.

The main menu, as I described in Chapter 4, contains five links to click on. Four out the five concern items we would expect, for instance, a place to find out more about the various Chrysler models, or a place for Chrysler owners to register for news and information such as owners' manuals. What used to be the central item on the menu, however, the one previously labeled "This is Chrysler," reveals the most about Chrysler's awareness of its urban context and the exigency of that context in terms of Detroit's near collapse. Linked or not, once we arrive at the page itself, its heading reads "This is the Motor City. And This is What We Do." Part of the sub-heading directly below reads: "The beating heart of a city in resurgence. Proving grounds for the belief that hard work pays off" (www.chrysler.com/en/this-is-chrysler/). Directly below the headings, we find three rectangular boxes:

- on the left, "Imported from Detroit" that links to the Carhartt clothing company that has collaborated with Chrysler to use that slogan for a special line of clothing,
- in the middle a rectangle with the words "See Our Story" superimposed over an archival photograph of one of the early Chrysler models, and
- on the right the words "Imported from Detroit" repeated, previously linked to a page that connected us with a list of charities that support the Chrysler Group, musical and choral groups from Detroit, partners who hold benefits for some of the charities, and Chrysler commercials that feature people from Detroit, some of which were:
  - Boys and Girls Clubs of Southeastern Michigan (www.bgcsm.org)
  - Habitat for Humanity Detroit (www.habitatdetroit.org)
  - Marshall Mathers Foundation (www.excellencefordetroit.org/tag/marshallmathers-foundation/)
  - Think Detroit PAL (www.thinkdetroitpal.org)
  - John Varvatos (http://www.johnvarvatos.com/stuart_house.aspx)

These groups are now mentioned on a page titled "Community Support Overview" (see below), but they still appear on the Carhartt Company page that I will examine next.

Imported from Detroit Merchandise and Carhartt

The rectangle on the left titled "Imported from Detroit: New Merchandise Now Available" leads us to the Carhartt Company's page (http://www.ifdstore.com/ welcome.asp). It specifically addresses the need to rebuild Detroit and to pay tribute to blue collar workers across the country. The company has teamed up with Chrysler to use its slogan "Imported from Detroit" both written out and shortened to "IFD" on a line of Carhartt clothing and other items such as bags, posters, and postcards. The page displays the same group of Detroit charities previously depicted on the Chrysler page leading to a page with fused text and an image of blue collar workers wearing Carhartt clothing that is also a slideshow presentation of individual clothing items, some modeled by the same workers, with background music titled "Rehab" by an artist named Action Davis. (http:// www.carhartt.com/webapp/wcs/stores/servlet/CategoryDisplay?storeId=1 0051&catalogId=10101& langId=-1& categoryId=63111). The page is no longer linked to Chrysler but still exists, and the connection between Carhartt and Chrysler is still emphasized. The text reads:

> Re-Building a city is hard work. With a fist full of motor city pride, Chrysler and Carhartt have teamed up to make clothing for this monumental task. It was designed in Detroit, Made in America and built for the people who aren't afraid to get their hands dirty.

Carhartt has designed an IFD logo that transforms the Chrysler's logo, a set of sleek wings with the name "Chrysler" embedded between the wings. The "Imported from Detroit" logo uses the two wings, but replaces the name with a clenched fist. While the company explains above that the fist represents "a fist full of motor city pride", it has visual connotations of unity and power, recalling emblems of several workers' unions around the world, a raised fist sometimes used by the Black Panthers Organization, and the raised fists of the two track and field athletes, Tommie Smith and John Carlos, on the medal podium during the 1968 Summer Olympics—an image still remembered 44 years later during the 2012 London Olympics.[3] The logo's fusion of text and image, while simple in design, represents a wealth of history and determination to succeed against all odds, a powerful representation of the exigent situation that the fused rhetorics, first of the Chrysler Group and then of its partner, the Carhartt clothing company, are working to address. The logo's power comes directly from the digital fusion; either the visuals or text alone would not contain the literal and connotative power of the two combined.

Imported from Detroit

While the link on the left took us to Carhartt, the link on the right, also labeled "Imported from Detroit", leads us to a page where we previously found links to several of Chrysler's television commercials discussed in Chapter 4. Today we see a group of images referring to recent commercials. Two in particular have sub-headings that continue to display qualities and attitudes crucial to the city being revived. The previous 2012 page listed such traits such as "attitude", "see it through", "dedication", "perseverance", and "homecoming", while the more recent pages have images with the following text:

- "Halftime in America: This country can't be knocked out with one punch. We get right back up again, and when we do, the world is going to hear the roar of our engines."
- Videos: "The People of Detroit show what makes this city so inspiring." (www.importedfromdetroit.com/)

Clicking on the image portraying individual videos takes us to a page where traits similar to the former 2012 video page are listed: "perseverance", "dedication", "lose yourself", "Loon [a music video by the Juliets]", "the Juliets", and "voices [featuring Pastor Larry Callahan and his choir]". While some videos are commercials trying to sell cars, they are also working to give examples of, and thereby legitimize and applaud, traits associated with the character of Detroit's working class. They are simultaneously trying to develop more pride in that group of people.

The page also pictures the logos of organizations that support the Chrysler Group's focus on Detroit's exigent situation. All groups are clearly working towards supporting Detroit's citizens and rehabilitating the city's infrastructure. Two groups should be familiar to most viewers: 1) Habitat for Humanity, which operates in cities and towns across America by partnering with local residents to help them build homes and improve their living situations; 2) Boys and Girls Club organizations, also found in cities and towns across the country, work in various ways to support local youth. The other groups represented on Chrysler's page, however, are specific to the city of Detroit and focus on its children, the literal and figurative representatives of the city's future. The groups indicate the degree to which Chrysler wants viewers to focus on those working in the present to improve the city's future.

Think Detroit PAL

While we find Police Athletics Leagues in many cities, like Boys and Girls Clubs and Habitat for Humanity, Detroit's group merged with a group called "Think Detroit" and combined their mission.

> Detroit PAL is a non-profit organization positively impacting the lives of nearly 10,000 children each year through athletic, and leadership development programs. Formed through a merger of Think Detroit and the Detroit Police Athletic League in 2006, Think Detroit PAL has roots dating back to 1970. (http://www.thinkdetroitpal.org/about/index.asp)

The organization works specifically on developing character and attitudes for Detroit's future citizenry, building on diversity by inviting and supporting children from a variety of ethnic, racial, and class backgrounds so that they develop friendships with each other; and to understand how to resolve conflicts with others they might first superficially perceive as different from themselves. It operates after-school and summer athletics programs, believing that children working and playing sports together will help to build camaraderie, tolerance, and acceptance of others in ways that only those who participate on sports teams can understand.

Marshall Mathers Foundation/Excellence for Detroit

Marshall Mathers' name is familiar to those who follow hip-hop, rappers, and contemporary music in general. Marshal Bruce Mathers III, also and more famously known as Eminem, founded an organization to work with at-risk children in the greater Detroit area. The foundation contributes to organizations like "Excellence for Detroit" that include the Mathers Foundation's mission on its own site.

> The Marshall Mathers Foundation's mission is to provide funds for organizations working with at-risk youth in southeast Michigan and throughout the U.S. The Foundation has given financial support to Gleaners Community Food Bank, Coats for Kids campaign in Detroit, Common Ground Sanctuary, a crisis intervention agency, the American Red Cross National Disaster Relief Fund and the Hip-Hop Summit Action Network, Ninemillion.org, as well as many others. (www. excellencefordetroit. org/tag/marshall-mathers-foundation/)

As the foundation's site explains about itself,

> Excellence for Detroit prepares high-achieving students from the City of Detroit for success in college and in the twenty-first century workplace. We focus on three key areas of comprehensive college preparation for students approaching graduation: college counseling, core academic skills, and college entrance exam prep. Our approach is centered on intensive workshops and one-on-one mentoring sessions led by high-achieving college graduates and professionals in the Detroit area. (http://www.excellencefordetroit.org/mission/)

John Varvatos: Stuart House Benefit

A previous link in this series connected viewers to a site advertising a 2012 benefit for Stuart House. While that link no longer exists, John Varvatos, a spokesman and designer for Chrysler, still hosts this benefit. 2013's description:

> Presented by Chrysler, co-chaired by Jennifer Garner and Ben Affleck, with an amazing kids' tent created by Hasbro, and featuring a live concert by Steven Tyler, and Joe Perry of Aerosmith, with special guest, Slash—the event was a spectacular success. Over 1,500 people came

together to enjoy good food, shop, participate in live and silent auctions and listen to a spectacular musical performance. The event shines light on the issue of child sexual abuse and the work of Stuart House, the Rape Treatment Center's internationally recognized model program created to meet the special needs of child victims. (http://therapefoundation.org/events-news/)

Varvatos is a Detroit native often featured in Chrysler's commercial campaigns; his particular 2012 "Imported from Detroit" commercial featured the following trait: "Attitude". Born in Detroit, Varvatos has achieved national recognition as a top menswear designer. And like the Carhartt clothing company's "Imported from Detroit" collection, Varvatos is closely associated with the recognition and celebration of blue collar workers. The final line in the short commercial featuring a video of him driving a Chrysler and a voice-over celebrating his achievements stated: "[T]hat's what a blue collar attitude can do in a white collar world."

Stuart House, a program located in southern California at the Santa Monica-UCLA Medical Center,

is an internationally recognized, model program created by the Rape Treatment Center to serve the special needs of sexually abused children and their families. Stuart House is also an exemplary public/private partnership. It was designed to solve problems in the child protection system that often revictimize young victims. (http://therapefoundation.org/programs/stuart-house/)

Varvatos' sponsorship of a group outside Detroit moves the entire rhetorical delivery of Chrysler's site beyond their primary local focus on Detroit. Here we should once again remember Crick, Pecchioni, and Butcher's words quoted earlier in this chapter: "[T]he final judgment of any rhetorical act is ultimately how it impacts the social world in which we live" (161). By linking a native of Detroit like Varvatos to a national group and another city, Chrysler is reminding us that Detroit's problematic situation belongs not simply to itself but also to other cities and by implication, the entire nation. Detroit and its citizens ultimately care about their city's context—the social world in which they live.

On its current Web site (as of May 2013) Chrysler has actually made more visible than before its links to and support of many Detroit-area organizations. In 2012 those first supportive indications were simply the small images mentioned above of various groups' logos. Now the site has an entire series of pages under the heading "Community Support Overview" that makes explicit the actions it is taking: "Chrysler Group LLC recognizes that part of being a good corporate citizen is actively working to make a positive, lasting impact on the communities where we operate. This includes investing in our facilities and creating jobs; providing financial support to charitable organizations and initiatives; and supporting our neighbors and communities through volunteerism" (http://www.chryslergroupllc.com/community/Pages/Overview.aspx). The page calls our attention to the Chrysler Foundation (established to administer the company's charitable work) and presents a bulleted breakdown of key areas where it focuses its attention and awards: Education, Military, Multicultural/ Diversity, and Youth Development. After this list, the site again stresses volunteerism, now showcasing by name several of those organizations discussed previously, the ones connected only through Chrysler's display of their logos:

> The spirit of volunteerism is part of the culture at Chrysler, one in which employees are encouraged to become involved in their communities and in issues outside the walls of our plants and offices. In response, employees have collected and delivered food for community food banks, beautified neighborhoods, donated generously at company-organized blood drives, participated in charity walks and runs, supported Habitat for Humanity, United Way and more. In addition, Chrysler Group executives lend their time and talents by serving on boards of various community institutions and organizations.

Finally, under a more recent section titled "Global Diversity", the company lists places where it has been given special mention and awards because of the groups it supports both within and outside of the company. Among these are:

- 2011 Readers' Choice: A Top 50 employer—*Workplace Diversity* magazine
- Recognized as a "Top Supporter" of engineering programs of historically black colleges and universities
- 2012 Reader's Choice: A Top 50 Employer—*Woman Engineer* magazine
- 2012: Best Places to Work for LGBT Equality
- 2012: Diversity Inc.'s Top 50 Companies for Diversity
- Named one of the 100 Best Companies for Working Mothers by *Working Mother* magazine 13 times
- Named on *Hispanic Business* magazine's annual Diversity Elite 60 list every year since 2009 (http://www.chryslergroupllc.com/company/Pages/GlobalDiversity.aspx)

All groups described above used a fused rhetorical display to help focus viewers on Detroit's exigent situation. While the more jaded among visitors to the Chrysler site might consider these links to outside organizations merely Chrysler's attempt to look more contemporarily humanitarian, I would argue that studying the fused rhetoric of Chrysler's page in connection with its links to people and charitable organizations beyond itself reveals a deeper involvement with Detroit and its people as well as an ethical concern that carries far beyond than just a company updating an image of the out-dated Chrysler of previous generations that nearly went financially bank-rupt. The company realizes that today it must focus not just on physical infrastructure, but psychological infrastructure—rebuilding and rehabili-tating damaged and ignored children as well as supporting and employing previous social outsiders. Chrysler works to draw non-Detroiters in and to make clear, although indirectly, that the company is refuting the lack of concern and the elitism of those who think Detroit should just be left on its own during its slide into bankruptcy.

2) Helmuth Obata & Kassabaum: Performing Sustainability

I wonder whether today's architects look back to the "good old days" when "all" their professional ancestors had to worry about was designing buildings that met local building codes and avoided collapsing. Oh yes, and perhaps being relatively innovative in their architectural designs. But change comes with time. In the second decade of the twenty-first century and beyond, the exigent situation for architects will still be to design the most eye-catching buildings or bridges. While architects still and always will need to design buildings that won't collapse, however, today's archi-tectural exigency demands that they also attend closely to sustainability and the environment. Architects, then, who may want to use materials that might no longer be readily available, must face hard choices about the financial implications and design elitism implied by including such materials in their designs. Most important, they must—if they consider themselves ethical—consider what kind of environmental footprints their constructions will leave today and in the centuries to come: if, after 100 or 200 years, their constructions are razed to make way for the future, they must grapple with that future now by making every effort to predict all possible environmental problems their work today might possibly leave for their fellow architects and engineers to come.

In the two or so years between the time when I wrote in Chapter 1 about the architectural firm Helmuth Obata & Kassabaum (these days more strictly known as HOK) and now, the HOK Web site has undergone a significant transformation that makes even clearer how much HOK as a company understands its part in an environmentally exigent situation with which it, at least, believes architects and their clients must concern them-selves. The fact of rhetorical performance is at the forefront of this con-cern since it is precisely HOK's ethical, environmentally aware, spectacular rhetorical performance that focuses its viewers' attention on the qualities the company believes necessary for addressing this exigency. The perfor-mance—for me, at least—is not only captivating but compelling, making me want to pause on this site, then stop completely, read through all the text, study the photos, and watch the embedded videos. The performance has been designed to make us think about the future and the idea of using architecture to inspire local residents and global visitors with the concepts of possibility and change, but most of all to uplift the human condition. Finally, the performance illustrates the different ways we will need to think in that future. The links on today's HOK site emphasize sustainability, collaboration, client success, values, and service. The media fusion works to make the entire site rhetorically persuasive.

One of the most recent photographs in a series of five, one that happened to be onscreen the day I returned to the HOK site, and one that compelled my using the word "spectacular" just above, is an aerial night shot of Baku's Flame Towers. The photo made me stop, literally, in awe. The cliché rang true for me then: the photo took my breath away. I must confess that I don't get far out into the world much less to Azerbaijan, but I had never seen towers shaped like these or lit like these at night. Viewers can see the Towers as one single image among a rotating slideshow reached by clicking on the red "arrow" on the page's right side and can find additional information about the Towers on a separate Web page with ten photos (http://www.hok.com/ design/service/architecture/baku-flame-towers/). Barry Hughes, principle HOK architect involved with the towers, explains in words what the sight of the Flame Towers signifies: a "remarkable symbol" that resulted from an "incredibly direct series of ideas"—the fused, rhetorical experience giving viewers a sense of past, present, and future of the people of Azerbaijan:

> If you go back to the region around Azerbaijan, the Zoroastrians populated this entire area. They worshipped the flame. Allied to that, one of the things that's propelling the economy forward in Azerbaijan today is natural gas. It does start with that single germ, that one gestural sketch that says, "this is the idea."
>
> (Hughes' words can be read as a pop-up on the Flame Towers' individual slide and also heard in the CNN video http://www.cnn.com/ video/data/2.0/video/world/2012/09/26/great-buldings-architecture-barry-hughes.cnn.html)

HOK's Web site in early 2013 varies slightly from the earlier HOK site discussed in Chapter 1. Its design today is less minimalist. Brought to the forefront in this revision, instead of only visuals, are symbols and words that lead us to explanations of the company's sustaining values. These values were always present on HOK's earlier site, but a viewer had to search harder to find them. Now we are seeing catch words on the opening splash page and the values are highlighted. We can thus see that today HOK considers itself as much more than simply an architectural firm. The final item on the splash page's main horizontal menu is a deceptively simple word, "About". Clicking on that simple link leads us to a description of the complexities of this company. HOK considers itself "a global design, architecture, engineering and planning firm" (http://www.hok.com/about/). In the center of that page's horizontal menu, we find the link "Social Responsibility" and the following statement:

> "HOK IMPACT is our firmwide strategic approach to corporate social responsibility . . . Our triple bottom line approach—focusing on economic, ecological and social sustainability—aims for a promising future for the communities we serve around the world.
>
> We seek to promote architecture as a social work, using design to support and empower communities. By organizing our IMPACT into three distinct categories—professional services, charitable donations and volunteerism—we are raising the profile of the design profession and, we hope, making a difference. (http://www.hok.com/about/social-responsibility/)

The page's meta-name, the words we see at the very top of the browser window above any tabs or the URL, reads "HOK | A Global Design, Architecture, Engineering and Planning Firm". What we see placed next is the main menu with these symbols and words:

- a "+" sign in the same color as the HOK logo,
- "Design",
- the HOK logo,
- "Thought Leadership",
- "People", and
- "About". (www.hok.com)

The "+" sign at the top left opens to a rolling list of precepts displayed above the menu with bold-faced type for some numbers and words, primarily verbs, listing actions that help to reinforce values:

- **1,600** people in **24** cities living **4** values for **1** goal: **To use design to help our clients succeed.**
- We create exceptional environments that meet our clients' most complex design challenges.
- We inspire people through our work by expressing timeless cultural, organizational and personal values.
- We connect people and place with ideas that come from many minds and imaginations.
- We care about serving our clients, enriching lives, improving communities and protecting our natural environment through design.
- We are a global architecture, design, engineering and planning firm.

These values did not arise out of a vacuum. They were imprinted on the company early on in its infancy. Bill Valentine, recently retired former HOK chairman, explains the philosophy of Gyo Obata, one of HOK's three founding partners:

Gyo Obata embodies everything that's honorable about the architectural profession. Instead of designing for the fashions of the times or to make a personal statement, Gyo designs to improve lives. Imagine that. . . .

Our firm's design philosophy emerges directly from Gyo's vision that architects should listen to clients, work hard, and solve their problems with imaginative yet simple solutions. . . .

For years we have witnessed Gyo's philosophy come to life in every line he has drawn and in his every interaction with clients. His genuine desire to help the world by designing *socially conscious, sustainable buildings* [my emphasis] has transformed countless lives and made me eternally proud to be part of the HOK family. Gyo speaks softly but carries a big legacy. (Birkman, xi)

Everyday citizens passing by or through a building in their location may not always sense or understand that architects see their creations as partly metaphoric constructions that both embody and communicate ideas. Yet someone examining the HOK pages closely or reading through a reflective study like Marlene Birkman's about Gyo Obata cannot help but realize that most architects see their constructions as conveying particular philosophies to their observers. These may not necessarily be their own personal tenets, but I would imagine that working for a company with vastly differing values would prove uncomfortable at the very least. The philosophies may be ones that the architect is hoping to make evident to the consciousness of a group of people who may never before have had any occasion to hold such thoughts or who have never lived under circumstances that allowed such an idea to penetrate—for example, suggesting to Baku's people that their city is reinventing itself not only so that it participates in the global economy of the twenty-first century, but also becomes a global economic leader for many more centuries to come. Part of the purpose of the Baku Flame Towers, we recall, is to uplift the human condition, to give Baku's people hope for their future (see, again, http://www.cnn.com/video/#/video/world/2012/09/26/great-buldings-architecture-barry-hughes.cnn).

As Birkman's words above acknowledge, the now exigent condition of sustainability was always a concern for Gyo Obata long before it became today's trend. Obata himself explains:

As an architect practicing for more than 50 years, I understand how buildings can contribute to a pleasant or not so pleasant experience for people. I have learned about clear movement through buildings and how important daylight is to bring a space to life. The relationship to the outdoors and nature is so important and, at last, we are finally into sustainability. (Birkman, 3)

Exigency has elevated and drawn sustainability's situation to the forefront of HOK's list of most urgent concerns and dictated that the company address it, an action which they are best able to undertake through rhetorical fusion.

In order to persuade people to consider particular environmental values, HOK must then become a constructor and architect of ideas, not simply of physical spaces and buildings. Because our environment, furthermore, is now more obviously enmeshed in a globally precarious situation, this company subscribes to the philosophy that those able to see the exigency must address it. HOK's site works hard rhetorically to draw our attention to it and persuade us that the company's employees are, indeed, working hard to address it themselves. Situated in the middle of the main horizontal menu, just to the right of the company logo, a major category on the Web site's main menu is "Thought Leadership"; the position on the menu indicates its importance for viewers turning to the site:

> **We never stand still.** HOK works with clients and partners to conduct research, share this knowledge and imagine new ways to solve the challenges of our built environment. (http://www.hok.com/thought-leadership/)

The words "solve the challenges" suggest expending extra effort to analyze what that environment, the one we have already manipulated for centuries, can say to HOK's architects and employees, people with the idea of sustainability at the forefront of their designing consciousnesses. In a way, the site is directing our attention to two layers of environment, the natural environment before builders touch it, and the environment that takes shape as architects and engineers transform it. The visuals in this section also have two layers—in other words, we see a construction that architects and engineers have designed, but also one that now accounts for its environment in a conscious way because its own sustainability within the built environment has been part of that design. The sustainability of all projects is not always readily visible, so the site gives us images of certain projects, but must also use text and videos so that we completely understand what is "sustainable" about this traditional-looking structure. In point of fact, viewers of this section must do a double take, in other words actually view and then re-view, to recognize first what they're seeing and second what they must understand about how its rhetorical performance supports its claim about sustainability.

Now back to the topic of sustainability: under HOK's mission statement, we see an image above a series of four rectangles inscribed with subheadings; each rectangle names the work involved in one major area the company is focused on, each involving a different aspect of sustainability, each making full use of fused rhetoric to explain the concepts and illustrate exactly how HOK is handling them, and each is fused to an image. These four areas are: 1) Genius of Biome Report Now Available; 2) Enhancing Performance, Health & Wellness in the Workplace; 3) Helping airports prepare for natural disasters; 4) Algae powers process zero concept building. Moving a computer mouse slowly across the rectangles from left to right reveals a small pop-up image connected with that area of work. When we click on the rectangle, we move to a separate page where the image is central and the idea is explained in full. One previously featured project discussed using biomimicry + fit (Fully Integrated Thinking) to design healthy cities. The project has now been moved to a separate area on the site (http://www.hok.com/thought-leadership/algae-powers-process-zero-concept-building/).

Within the section covering the biome, for example, we find a series of questions embedded beneath thumbnail-size photos and a diagram of the biomimicry process. The entire section is an aggregate of photos, text, and diagrams, rhetorical fusion at its best. The questions are highlighted by bold face to emphasize the importance of the topics they introduce: natural ways to minimize erosion, adjusting to temperature changes within nature itself, cooperative relationships that evolve naturally—all challenges for people involved with creating, designing, and building structures, yet all challenges that nature has developed ways to cope with. The questions are not rhetorical, but they *are* rhetorically effective since they capture our attention immediately. The point of this section is to emphasize to all of us how much we can learn about sustainability by focusing on nature and analyzing then adapting ways through which it has already solved these intricate puzzles. It also emphasizes a report, "Genius of the Biome": "In collaboration with the biologists at Biomimicry 3.8, HOK designers explored innovative, place-based solutions to water, energy, materials, social and economic issues that were inspired by local flora and fauna of the temperate broadleaf forest in a new report called the *Genius of the Biome*." The description of the report is as follows:

> *Genius of the Biome* describes the strategies and designs adopted by living organisms found in a worldwide region of similar climate and vegetation. It describes the biological principles and patterns common to organisms and ecosystems within a biome. This biology is then translated into design principles that can be used to inspire innovations or identify more specific criteria for place-based design. (http://www.hok.com/thought-leadership/tapping-the-genius-of-the-biome/)

The entire section uses a mixture of images, charts, text, and diagrams to help explain, for example, climate solutions developed by leaves and bryophytes. The entire report has recently been published online (http://issuu.com/hoknetwork/docs/geniusofbiome?mode=window).

In another section having to do with sustainability titled "Algae powers process zero concept building", we find a description of a competition for young designers to see how they could work with a building that is now nearly half a century old to make it comply with President Obama's directive that by 2020 all federal agency buildings lower greenhouse gas emissions, to find "net zero energy solutions". HOK designers won this competition with a retrofit concept based on biomimicry:

> HOK / Vanderweil's "Process Zero: Retrofit Resolution," a retrofit design process, reduces the building's overall energy demand by 84 percent and generates the remaining 16 percent on-site. The design uses proven energy conservation and renewal strategies, including atria and light wells that bring daylight into workspaces, integrated louvers for natural ventilation, a new facade with 35,000 square feet of photovoltaic film, 30,000 square feet of rooftop solar collectors that circulate water through floors to help with climate control, and office equipment operated by a cloud computing system. (http://www.hok.com/thought-leadership/algae-powers-process-zero-concept-building/)

This project hints at another level of sustainability that we find explained more thoroughly in another section of the HOK Web site, and leads to a few more discussions explained in more detail below.

Sustainability as an exigent situation, however, includes more than the science of the biome, biomimicry, and retrofitting existing buildings to meet new environmental regulations. It also involves an ideological dedication to reaching out to places that have more difficult living conditions than we do in the US or the developed world, then to help build sustainable constructions and to pass on a legacy of sustainability. We find examples of sustainability as a legacy throughout the HOK site, but the best one involves a partnership between HOK and the US Green Building Council: rebuilding an orphanage in Haiti that was one of several destroyed by the January 2010 magnitude 7 earthquake west of Port-au-Prince. And, true to the technique of rhetorical fusion, we can only get a true sense of the physical and philosophical extent of the project by viewing the images, reading the text, and watching the videos connected with the Project Haiti Orphanage and Children's Center. The orphanage is a model for the world, one whose basic sustainable design concepts are replicable anywhere on the globe. It was an ideal project for HOK, considering the company's dedication to both sustainability and social responsibility, but most of all, enriching people's lives.

One of the most powerfully persuasive pieces illustrating the exigence of sustainability explains the project for a donation campaign in the form of a video posted on YouTube. The narrator Roger J. Limoges, Chief of Staff for the US Green Building Council, explains that Gina and Lucien Duncan, who brought the project to the Council, are

> transforming the lives of kids who have had absolutely nothing. For the first time in their lives, [these children] will be in a building that tells them they're valued, that they deserve to breathe good air, that they

deserve to be living in comfortable situations, and that they deserve to be cared about just like any other child any other place in the world. (http://www.youtube.com/watch? v=_rBYUKBIX-Q)

Additionally, Gina Duncan's words quoted on the HOK site point directly to sustainability as a legacy: "This green building is an amazing opportunity for Haiti. It's a legacy we're going to be leaving for the next generation" (http://www.hok.com/about/ sustainability/project-haiti-orphanage-and-childrens-center-/). If we did not understand the importance and exigence of sustainability for HOK, its site contains links to this project under two of its main menu topics: "Design" (http://www.hok.com/design/service/engineering/project-haiti/) and "About" (http://www.hok.com/about/social-responsibility/ project-haiti/).

While some of the general public might not consider architecture as being persuasive or conveying a message, more people than only architects certainly do. Roger Limoges' and Gina Duncan's words above tell us exactly what they believe the new orphanage in Port-au-Prince will say to its children. We can also listen to Bob Archibald, the former president of the HOK-designed Missouri History Museum, explaining that buildings are persuasive and speak directly to us, that they represent us and tell us stories about the values they embody as physical structures:

Everything is narrative. A story. We connect these stories together to make sense of our lives. And buildings are perhaps our most physical, pervasive narrative. Buildings and the communities they inhabit tell us what we hope for in the future. The addition to the Missouri History Museum was designed to physically represent our values. We wanted the new building to reach out to the community, and to be accessible and sustainable. We wanted the building to say, "People belong here. You belong here. This is your building." History is a narrative about people. (Birkman, 160)

Sustainability, then, is not only about buildings. It is about people and their spirit.

In his CNN interview discussing great buildings and, in particular, Baku's Flame Towers, Barry Hughes offers his belief that a great building can "make you feel more important—not the person who designed it, but everybody". Great architecture, he continues, "can uplift the human condition, make people feel better" (http://www.cnn. com/video/#/video/world/2012/09/26/great-buldings-architecture-barry-hughes.cnn).   So here at the end of this small section, I want to return to the idea of performance, in particular the type of orchestral performance I mentioned earlier in the chapter—one that includes a multitude of instruments and individual musicians all working together to convey one musical idea, the composer's, filtered through the conductor. A rhetorically strong Web site is its digital equivalent, fusing images, text, videos, charts, and diagrams, to convey an overall idea. In the case of the HOK Web site, that overall idea is sustainability. We see innumerable examples of people, places, and concepts all focused on that one idea. And, like an idea in an orchestral performance, that idea comes across not only through the concrete performance we witness on stage, read about in the performance program, and listen to with our ears and our minds. It comes across in the totality of the experience. Just so with this Web site: after analyzing the site rhetorically, we understand the idea that sustainability applies not only to architectural projects but also to the human spirit. Through its varied projects from the Flame Towers of Baku to the Project Haiti Orphanage and Children's Center, HOK helps us to understand that its mission is really to help sustain the human spirit. Through some of the most "concrete" objects in the world, then, some of the most abstract, yet necessary, emotions can be kindled—the spirit to understand and believe, if even for only a moment, that a better future is possible, that it is possible for any of us, no matter who we might be.

3) Apple: Delivery as Personality—Performing on the Cutting Edge

> At a time when the United States is seeking ways to sustain its innovative edge, and when societies around the world are trying to build creative digital-age economies, [Steve] Jobs stands as the ultimate icon of inventiveness, imagination, and sustained innovation. (Isaacson, xxi)

Apple Inc., the company, has in the recent past been almost synonymous with Steve Jobs, its former CEO. Apple's Web site, while not completely synonymous, has in many ways assumed the personality and character traits we associate with him—inventiveness, imagination, innovation, and a tendency to keep the world at an extremely long arm's length. Compared to many other companies, Apple has designed an opening splash page that picks up on these qualities, even down to keeping the world at arm's length. What I mean specifically is that the Web site's top level focuses our attention on recent innovative products, not any other activities or emotions that could be included, like supporting humanitarian causes or fostering specific corporate philosophies. These do occur late, but not here. Talking about the hard work behind an Apple product, the work that we never see, one employee could be explaining the reason why Apple's Web site is designed the way it is. We are meant to see the product rather than the years of hard work that went into its development. No one buys a product based on years of development. We buy it because of its performance and also the rhetorical performance delivered in its ad: "Certainly a hard work ethic is involved because there's so much work put into making anything, be it a product or a piece of marketing, or some software. What's presented to the consumer is this kind of effortless ease. You don't really know how much work goes on underneath the surface, but believe me. There's a lot" (http:// www.apple.com/jobs/us/corporate.html).

The type of performance we see on Apple's site is on its several embedded levels the opposite of what occurs on Chrysler's site. This polarity may result from the different corporate concerns of

- an economically viable company that has also provided a measure of stability to the nation's economy since becoming one of the country's most important corporations during the last few decades, versus
- a corporation striving to make a comeback after teetering on the brink of economic collapse.

Or it could be the simple difference between Steve Jobs and other people. I suspect it is the latter. Rather than focusing on uplifting an entire city like Chrysler, Apple uses its site to direct our attention to its success at staying on the cutting edge of technology and branding itself as a company concerned not simply with innovation, but a revolution that changes the way we all think. In a video discussed later in this chapter, an Apple employee explains: "The best part of working at Apple is actually the feeling that what you've brought to the table has contributed to something greater than yourself. In that way you're changing the world" (http://www.apple.com/jobs/us/corporate.html). The desire to contribute to a good greater than oneself and thereby change the world has always been part of Apple's philosophy. However, triggers for those emotions and persuading viewers about their value only emerge when we study the site more deeply, just as we would discover with a more private personality. In the technology world, sustained innovation is the primary exigent situation; the fused rhetoric of Apple's Web site works to convince its viewers that the company and everyone in it is not only located firmly on the edge of innovation but working hard to stay there because they want to be there.

Throughout Apple's corporate life, we have witnessed thought-provoking advertising campaigns that emphasized breaking molds while beckoning computer users out of their comfort zones. Apple's famous January 1984 Super Bowl commercial (http://www.youtube.com/watch?v= HhsW-zJo2sN4) builds on the theme of George Orwell's novel *1984* and takes direct aim at the reigning computer monopoly both figuratively and literally: figuratively through a sledge hammer thrown at a screen displaying a Hitlerian-type dictator addressing an audience of drones; literally by introducing a new, creative, personal computer alternative. The ad aggressively challenges the majority's computer choice and the company behind it all, that is, owners of PCs and the Microsoft Corporation: "1984 won't be like '1984'" (Isaacson, 162–165). Apple itself, furthermore, continues to valorize those who represent sustained innovation, not simply technological innovation, but the more elusive creative innovation fought for by those who can envision difference and change, those who strive to change the human condition. Apple devoted an entire ad series to this idea. The text of its "Think Different" campaign proclaims:

> Here's to the crazy ones. The misfits. The rebels. The troublemakers. The round pegs in the square holes. The ones who see things differently. They're not fond of rules. And they have no respect for the status quo. You can quote them, disagree with them, glorify or vilify them. About the only thing you can't do is ignore them. Because they change things. They push the human race forward. And while some may see them as the crazy ones, we see genius. Because the people who are crazy enough to think they can change the world are the ones who do. (Isaacson, 329)

Somewhere inside us all—especially the young, and probably many of us when we *were* young—is a bit of the rebel and the misfit. Those nearly forgotten parts of our psyches that dream we can change a heartless, rigid bureaucracy: Apple appeals to us and the notion, partly romanticized, but all too often true, that none of us can foresee, recognize, or implement this change while embedded comfortably in the middle of a group. The "misfits", "the round pegs in the square holes", the standing-at-the-edge-of-the-desert prophets, seem to be the only unencumbered ones free enough to remove their ideological blinders in order to find a new direction. Innovation is a struggle. Standing on the cutting edge is painful. If even a small part of our inner selves accepts that discomfort, then we will be primed for more than simply watching the performance. We will understand its message.

The second exigent situation the Web site addresses, then, is our tendency to remain satisfied with the status quo, what we already know, to resist change. We are often unprepared for the speed of change even while we support it philosophically. Apple uses its site to fight against complacency by celebrating the opposite quality and being a place where all of us, but especially the young, can find inspiration in change and being different. For this company, change is not blind; it has always been contemplated thoroughly with an eye to the distant, rather than the near, future. The Apple Web site is the main place where the company can prod us to change. In some ways, it gives its customers no choice since Apple constantly innovates by updating its products, thus forcing us to change whether we like it or not. I still remember being in a state of shock after I had to give up on floppy discs. I worry today about giving up on CD drives and moving files to a "cloud". All this while repeating my mantra, "Change. Yes, I like change. Change is good." Certainly Apple feeds the human desire to keep up with new trends, even while that desire constantly wars with the part of our selves that wants to stay in our comfort zones, not through a conservative aversion to change but more a lazy avoidance of learning new operating systems, new ways to access files and other documents, new movements like swiping a screen instead of clicking on a mouse.

The range of choices we see on the main horizontal menu of the Apple Web site's splash page (www.apple.com)—the Apple logo, then the words "store", "Mac", "iPod", "iPhone", "iPad", "iTunes", "support"—all give center stage to the iPhone. Links to the Apple online store and to support are located on the left and right sides of the menu, the spots with less immediate visual impact and thus less importance. Ordered in this way, the menu focuses on Apple's newer products and the newest version of those products. But product remains literally front and center. Apple's site differs greatly from Chrysler's and HOK's, both of which openly display their company philosophies for viewers to see, no digital digging involved. Not unlike Jobs himself, Apple's splash page stoically puts beliefs and commitments in places where we can find them later if we care to, just as Jobs himself would never reveal his personal philosophies to someone he just met. We cannot find them without a purposeful effort to scratch below this compelling surface advertising its technological edge or its eye-captivating images to discover what lies below. The main image on any iteration of Apple's splash page always points our attention to one or more newer products that appear whenever the screen is refreshed. Just below the main image we see a menu with images of other new products, some of which have been the iPad mini, the iPad with retina display, the iPhone 5, the Apple Worldwide Developers Conference, and once last year at the extreme right of the series appeared an item labeled "Supplier Responsibility" (http://www.apple.com/supplierresponsibility/). This is the closest Apple has ever come to revealing any of its philosophies on the top level of its Web site. While no longer linked to the opening page, the "Supplier Responsibility" page is still available. It opens to a section of the Apple site devoted to subjects covering "safe and ethical working conditions", with links to the following subjects: "Empowering Workers", "Labor & Human Rights", "Health and Safety", "Environment and Accountability". At the bottom of this page is a section labeled "Our Commitment to Transparency" containing reports on problems in factories supplying products for Apple.

No matter the amount of information each page contains, they all appear spare and uncluttered, giving the pages a Zen-like simplicity. Such a minimalist quality is another outgrowth of Steve Jobs' personality and character. Influenced by Zen Buddhism when he was young, Jobs carried its beliefs throughout his life even though he may not have claimed to be a practicing Buddhist. As Walter Isaacson tells it, Jobs rejected any kind of religious practices when he was 13. But, Isaacson adds, "He did, however, spend years studying and trying to practice the tenets of Zen Buddhism" (15). Isaacson mentions some of Jobs' Zen readings when Jobs was a college freshman. Isaacson states, however:

> Jobs's engagement with Eastern spirituality, and especially Zen Buddhism, was not just some passing fancy or youthful dabbling. He embraced it with his typical intensity, and it became deeply ingrained

in his personality. "Steve is very much Zen," said [Daniel] Kottke. "It was a deep influence. You see it in his whole approach of stark, minimalist aesthetics, intense focus." (35)

Even later, when Jobs dropped out of college, his interests at the time drew him to enroll in a calligraphy class. Isaacson quotes Jobs himself, who said, "I learned about serif and sans serif typefaces, about varying the amount of space between different letter combination, about what makes great typography great. It was beautiful, historical, artistically subtle in a way that science can't capture, and I found it fascinating" (40–41).

Not much about the Apple site focuses on history or the company's past, in part because that history is not as long and storied as, for instance, Chrysler's. But then, the point for Apple is not history. It's the future. Everything looks forward, not backward. One exception is the "timeline" of the iMac computer with successive images of the computer in profile ranging from 1998 to today that show visually how screen thickness decreased from the first model to the latest (http://www.apple.com/imac/design/). The timeline's heading reads "The evolution of iMac", the word "evolution" highlighting a move forward. Progress. Other references to the past mention improvements that make a product better today. Progress again. History for Apple, then, is only important insofar as it can help make a point about innovation taking place on the technological edge today and can be used to predict indirectly what might happen in the future. The ultimate progress. Web site viewers are always subtly reminded about Apple's success in regards to the exigent situation it faces daily, that it must stay at the cutting edge of technological invention, and that to do so its products must constantly be re-engineered and thinner, its display screens less reflective, its products more energy efficient, increasingly recyclable, and ultimately more environmentally friendly, all concerns that Apple knows its current consumers hold deeply. In fact, the slogan for the new iMac introduced at the end of 2012 reads: "The new iMac. Performance and design. Taken right to *the edge* [my emphasis]." Interesting word choice, this, especially given my repeated point about Apple and the cutting edge.

In addition to reflecting Steve Jobs' consuming desire to stay at the forefront of technological invention, the Apple site constantly reinforces Jobs' push to "think different" in its job descriptions for those seeking employment at Apple. Pages detailing "Job Opportunities at Apple" are not highlighted like the sections describing and selling its products: the small link sits at the very bottom of its splash page; viewers have to be looking for it (http://www.apple.com/jobs/us/). They have to want to dig below the site's surface. The main screen has a rotating series of photos showing people working at different Apple locations with a header and sub-header that read "Amaze yourself. Amaze the world. A job at Apple is unlike any other you've had. You'll be challenged. You'll be inspired. And you'll be proud. Because whatever your job is here, you'll be part of something big." Jobs' own obsessive attention to detail even emerges in part of the page's script: "Every detail matters."

The "corporate" link on the Apple employment pages fuses text, videos, and photos, all explaining and illustrating to potential jobs applicants what working at Apple would be like and how work goes on at Apple. If we watch the video, we get far more than an introduction to working at Apple. Now we get emotions and corporate philosophies. We listen to Apple employees themselves ranging from hardware engineers to a vice president of human resources and dean of Apple University to someone focusing on worldwide supply and demand telling us that:

- Apple is always about pushing the envelope, about doing the best thing possible.
- Apple will never give up because it's too hard or it's impossible.
- There's a belief in the power of small teams to do really great things.
- Thinking outside the box is funny. We don't even really think about the box. When we go out to do something we don't start by saying "What is everyone else doing? And therefore what are the best practices and what should we do?" I think we look to say "What's the best it can possibly be?"
- There's a lot of places you can find happiness. Work, when structured right, is one of the few places you can really find meaning. And I think what Apple gives the employees is the opportunity to be part of something really, really meaningful.

Above the video box is the following heading: "Imagine what you could do here." This heading is followed by the words: "At Apple, great ideas have a way of becoming great products, services, and customer experiences very quickly. Bring passion and dedication to your job and there's no telling what you could accomplish." And finally, next to the video on this corporate page we read:

> Be inspired every day. We're perfectionists, idealists. Inventors. Forever tinkering with products and processes, always on the lookout for better. A job at Apple is one that requires a lot of you, but it's also one that rewards bright, original thinking and hard work. None of us here at Apple would have it any other way. (http://www.apple.com/jobs/us/corporate.html)

These words could be talking about Steve Jobs himself, the ultimate perfectionist, idealist, and inventor, while they also loudly echo Apple's "Think Different" series of print ads and television commercials. Walter Isaacson explains:

> In addition to the television commercials, they created one of the most memorable print campaigns in history. Each ad featured a black-and-white portrait of an iconic historical figure with just the Apple logo and the words "Think Different" in the corner. Making it particularly engaging was that the faces were not captioned. Some of

them—Einstein, Gandhi, Lennon, Dylan, Picasso, Edison, Chaplin, King—were easy to identify. But others caused people to pause, puzzle, and maybe as a friend to put a name to the face: Martha Graham, Ansel Adams, Richard Feynman, Maria Callas, Frank Lloyd Wright, James Watson, Amelia Earhart.

Most were Jobs's personal heroes. They tended to be creative people who had taken risks, defied failure, and bet their career on doing things in a different way. (330)

The "Retail" link picks up on Steve Jobs' belief that technology and engineering themselves are not enough for true inspiration, that they need to be combined with the humanities: "I always thought of myself as a humanities person as a kid, but I liked electronics. . . . Then I read something that one of my heroes, Edwin Land of Polaroid, said about the importance of people who could stand at the intersection of humanities and sciences, and I decided that's what I wanted to do" (quoted in Isaacson, xix). Isaacson describes one of Jobs' final presentations at the March 2, 2011 launch of the iPad 2. This presentation ended with "one of the clearest expressions of [Jobs'] credo, that true creativity and simplicity come from integrating the whole widget—hardware and software, and for that matter content and covers and salesclerks—rather than allowing things to be open and fragmented" (526):

It's in Apple's DNA that technology alone is not enough. We believe that it's technology married with the humanities that yields us the result that makes our heart sing. Nowhere is that more true than in these post-PC devices. Folks are rushing into this tablet market, and they're looking at it as the next PC, in which the hardware and the software are done by different companies. Our experience, and every bone in our body, says that is not the right approach. These are post-PC devices that used to be even more intuitive and easier to use than a PC, and where the software and the hardware and the applications need to be intertwined in an even more seamless way than they are on a PC. We think we have the right architecture not just in silicon, but in our organization, to build these kinds of products. (527)

The main heading on the "Retail" employment page reads: "Where all talents apply". The header, like the one on the "Corporate" employment page, is followed by a movie about working retail at Apple. Next to text is this statement:

We're people who love technology and people who love people. We're also musicians, photographers, mountain climbers, students, and artists whose interests can't be defined by a job description. Whether you're analytical or creative, tech savvy or insightful, there's a place to share your talents while you learn, develop, and inspire. (http://www. apple.com/jobs/us/)

The entire section explaining employment at Apple truly reflects Jobs' personality and character, and most of all his belief in celebrating a humanities and electronics connection.

One final note here: performance and theater extend even to the packaging of Apple products. While packaging philosophy and drama are not part of the Web site, Isaacson's description of Jony Ive and Steve Jobs' focus on packaging offers us yet another bit of insight into the fact that dramatic performance is central to the tenets of Apple's ideology and permeates whatever the company produces, from products to its Web site to its packaging:

> Early on, Mike Markkula had taught Jobs to "impute"—to understand that people *do* judge a book by its cover—and therefore to make sure all the trappings and packaging of Apple signaled that there was a beautiful gem inside. Whether it's an iPod Mini or a MacBook Pro, Apple customers know the feeling of opening up the well-crafted box and finding the product nestled in an inviting fashion. "Steve and I spend a lot of time on the packaging," said Ive. "I love the process of unpacking something. You design a ritual of unpacking to make the product feel special. Packaging can be theater, it can create a story." (347)

Dramatic performance. Technological performance. Not wearing one's heart on one's corporate sleeve. Apple's Web site is thoroughly imprinted with Steve Jobs' character and personality, his audacity, his brilliance.

Whether they are fond of Steve Jobs or not, Apple Web site viewers, technology users, and this book's readers will have to admit, if they are being honest, that Apple pushed the tech industry to the place where it stands today and can claim responsibility for setting it on a trajectory that will be hard to stop, at least for the time being. Isaacson continues:

> Very few other companies or corporate leaders—perhaps none—could have gotten away with the brilliant audacity of associating their brand with Gandhi, Einstein, Picasso, and the Dalai Lama. Jobs was able to encourage people to define themselves as anticorporate, creative, innovative rebels simply by the computer they used. "Steve created the only lifestyle brand in the tech industry," Larry Ellison said. "There are cars people are proud to have—Porsche, Ferrari, Prius—because what I drive says something about me. People feel the same way about an Apple product." (332)

Apple's impact on the social as well as the tech world through its products and the rhetorical performance displayed on its Web site are undisputable, rhetorical communication at its best.

4) Howard Rambsy II: Blogging to Perform, Educate, Retain

If we work and teach on college campuses today, we would have to be asleep not to know the well-documented statistics about student success rates: 1) African American students on college campuses average lower retention rates than their white counterparts and 2) first-generation as well as minority college students often need the support of understanding mentors and professors to help them overcome obstacles to their academic success. Even just a cursory glance through journals such as the *Peabody Journal of Education*, the *Journal of Black Masculinity*, the *Harvard Educational Review*, the *Journal of Western Black Studies*, and the *Journal of African American Males in Education*, to name only a few, will confirm this situation.[4] Wynetta Y. Lee reports:

> All too often the wide-eyed optimism and enthusiasm that students bring to registration [at colleges and universities] dissipates and results in departure from the institution prior to degree completion. The 4-year degree requires considerably more time than that for completion for most students. . . . The degree completion rates are rather discouraging for students in general but are even more disheartening when considering African American students. (27)

In a quantitative study examining black students at both historically black colleges and universities and predominantly white colleges and universities, Walter R. Allen concludes:

> How bright the student is, his or her academic background or preparation, the intensity of his or her personal ambition and striving—all these factors will ultimately influence academic achievement. Beyond these personal traits, however, is a set of more general factors—characteristics that are more situational and interpersonal. Therefore, the student's academic performance will also be affected by the quality of life at the institution, the level of academic competition, university rules/procedures/resources, racial relations on the campus, *relationships with faculty and friends, and the extent of social support networks on campus* [my emphasis]. (40)

Directly involved in and attempting to address this situation are the African American/Black Studies programs in higher education across the country. While offering a variety of courses in disciplines such as history, literature, music, politics, sociology, and theater, these programs provide a social network and faculty role models to young people whose identities and attitudes about academia are still in flux. Black Studies programs thus become places where students can share ideas more openly and feel proud of their culture, the programs themselves perhaps influencing relationships and networks that can help such students succeed in college.

One program with a Web site clearly displaying an awareness of this exigent situation is located at Southern Illinois University, Edwardsville. The program's site is unusual simply because of the fact that it is a digital tool brought to bear on a critical situation; it becomes even more intriguing when we realize that the site is also combining technology and a fused rhetorical display to attract students, to keep them involved in both their studies and their community, and to employ the very technology that students will need to understand to help them navigate the current century successfully. Above and beyond the technology, however, the site encourages a mindset—not only for students but all viewers—that considers the future critically, then understands the challenges and varieties of knowledge that today's students need for success. The site states clearly that

> [t]he SIUE Black Studies Program comprises a field of knowledge that concentrates on African American progress and well-being. In the process of modernizing black studies to address twenty-first century challenges, the program seeks to produce useful, culturally distinct, and forward-thinking projects. The program also offers participants opportunities to develop or enhance their intellectual capabilities and problem-solving skills by collaborating on the implementation of research and interactive projects designed to benefit citizens in the region. (http://www.siue.edu/blackstudies/)

The program's Web site banner is not simply a design for its pages; it functions as a visual tool working with the site's text to establish a rhetorical ethos, logos, and pathos. Clearly evident in the Black Studies Program's Web banner are the Black Power movement's fist, a trumpet, a turntable, birds in flight, spiral designs, possibly fireworks, and a film reel, as well as a small diagram of a highway map—"The city-scape is there just to represent the idea of 'urban,' which persists in black cultural projects and production. The arrow is there representing moving in 'out' directions" (Rambsy, personal email, 11/1/12).

The program's Web site and its affiliated Blog, *Cultural Front: a notebook on literary art, digital humanities, and emerging ideas* (http: //www. culturalfront.org) directly address the exigent situation described by the scholars above, retaining African American students; the site and Blog give students places to develop relationships with their peers and faculty, support each other through social networks, and gain confidence in their ability to excel in an educational environment. The entire site also showcases work by students; one example appeared in a recent splash page photo of a student's extensive annotations of some poems she was studying; the photo serves as a concrete display showing exactly the tremendous amount of effort the student put into the project and also works as an example of what students need to do when studying a poem closely. Under a menu item labeled "Poetry", the site also displays several analytic entries by students

Figure 5.1   SIUE Black Studies Web page banner. Southern Illinois University, Edwardsville. Designed by Tristan Denyer and Marci Daniels for Howard Rambsy II's Black Studies Project. Courtesy: Howard Rambsy II.

examining individual poems. Praise for critical thinking plus modeling intellectual habits are thus reflected in the fused visual/textual example.

Among the SIUE Black Studies Program's projects are several that immerse participants in the types of communities and social networks that help them develop friendships, connections, and safety nets:

- **The African American Poetry Correspondence Project,** a letter-writing, poetry-sharing program that fosters communication between college students and high school students.
- **The East St. Louis Visual-Literary Project** (fall 2007), an extracurricular reading and interpretation program, which featured three different "visual-literary" exhibits and an exhibit catalogue. The exhibits appeared at the Lily-Freeman Elementary School, the Clyde C. Jordan Senior Citizens Center, and the East St. Louis Public Library.
- **Journey to SIUE,** sponsored by the Student Opportunities for Academic Results (SOAR) office and with coordination provided by the Black Studies Program, the project featured more than 400 SIUE travel narratives.
- **Blueprints for Progress Workshop,** a study group that involves various college students in discussions about the experiences and challenges confronting those who seek to pursue progressive lines of thinking during the contemporary era.
- **The Wright 100,** an interactive reading and composition activity that involves students at different schools in covering Richard Wright's autobiography *Black Boy (American Hunger)*. (http://www.siue.edu/blackstudies/research.html)

Even the simple act of posting this list online works, itself, as a tactic: a safeguard against student isolation because it gathers in one place a variety of choices for student involvement; no one has to go searching, exactly what a student feeling isolated would probably never do. The site advertises digital opportunities to the utmost. The combination of visuality with literacy plays an additional important role in the site, as we can see from the East St. Louis Visual-Literary Project described above. We can experience the full range of media the site draws on if we click on "media room" in the main menu, a section for storing videos, audio projects, and print projects involving photos such as the African American Health Initiative postcards displayed there.

The real gem of the SIUE Black Studies Web site for my purposes, however, is its affiliated Blog, *Cultural Front*, an exceptionally well-fused digital space. It extends far beyond mere textual postings on various subjects with an occasional photo inserted. The Blog describes itself as a place for intellectual exchanges about the "convergence of black studies, technology, and active citizenship". The space, intended to be educational as well as informative but far from pedantic, contains extended reflections and analyses of a variety of topics (such as black comic books and cartoon characters) and uses more than a simple sound or video clip but rather entire photographic displays and digital recordings to give us as complete an experience as we can have, after the fact of the original event. It exploits, in the most positive sense of that word, Web 2.0's capacity to educate through new media: its ability to embed audio and visual clips, its ability to link one part of a Web site to another area within that same site or to an external site, and ultimately its ability to hold massive amounts of information so that a portion of a particular site can become a digital file cabinet or storehouse containing records of important topics, discussions, events, exhibits, and histories.

A stellar example of digital fusion and the educational opportunities enabled through fusion occurs in an entry under the Blog's main horizontal menu item, "Poetry", then for October 22, 2012; the selection is titled "Amiri Baraka's scary wordless phrasings". Here we find a photograph of Amiri Baraka during a reading, a photo placed above an extended analysis of the way such utterances convey a certain ethos and emotion to poetry. We can look at this photo while we click on a link in a sentence just below the photo and listen to an mp3 file of Baraka reading the poem "In Walked Bud". Then immediately after, we can click on another link within that same sentence taking us to a YouTube file where we can listen to the Thelonious Monk Quartet performing a musical piece with the same name. The combination of visual material, expository text, and audio files for comparison creates an educational space impossible to duplicate through a single medium.

A cursory glance at the secondary, vertical menu list of the Blog's discussions reveals, among others, intriguing and relevant topics pertaining to this section's argument about rhetorical exigency:

- 28 Racial Barriers
- Black Men
- EBR Collection
- Education
- Visual Matters
    - Visual Matters VID (entry 2; Thursday April 15, 2010)
    - Blk Studies Visual Movements (entry 12; Friday October 10, 2008)

This section, furthermore, addresses an exigency within the already exigent situation of African American college students' precarious retention situations. The embedded exigency is the dearth of African American males enrolled in colleges and universities and the need to convince them to stay in college once they get there. Chance W. Lewis and Robert T. Palmer, in separate prefaces to two different issues of the *Journal of African American Males in Education*, both address the need to pursue research to study and improve the retention of African American males and to increase collaborative projects between K–12 and higher education for the same purpose: retention. Two related volumes edited by Henry T. Frierson, Willie Pearson, and James H. Wyche also approach the problem from other angles. While the number of black male role models on individual university campuses might vary from none to few, the *Cultural Front* Blog offers glimpses of important historical and contemporary black male figures; students can see their photos, listen to their speeches, read their work, or examine documents analyzing their contributions to black culture.

One of the topics listed above, "The EBR Collection", for example, documents the work and photographs of Eugene B. Redmond, a major figure in the Black Arts Movement of the 1960s and 70s. Students can view many images of black male role models, not only Eugene Redmond, but also the dozens of major writers and artists he has been photographing over the past six decades. We can hear and see Redmond reading his own work, sometimes even accompanied by a slideshow from his photographic collection illustrating the poem being read. One example, a poem titled "Mood Maya Kwansaba", shows us the text of the poem itself above a slideshow of images of Maya Angelou taken by Redmond starting in 1976. We also hear a jazz accompaniment in the background of the reading and slideshow. Finally, we also read an explanation of the poetic form used, a kwansaba (www.siueblackstudies.com/2010/ebr-discusses-maya-angelou.html).

Even more important than simply storing material, however, is the Blog's poly-vocal, dialogic quality. Students and other viewers of this Blog carry on conversations or start important threads that others respond to and develop. Students' ideas about their reading as posted under Blog topics are open to discussion and comment by others. A twenty-first century site for learning and thinking, the Blog, furthermore, serves as a digital vehicle to attract curious students and help them feel included in the blogging community if they choose to post their opinions and replies to posted statements then find that their ideas are being read by others.

The Blog is understated and innocuous in its opening pages; here is its entire description:

> This blog serves as a venue for extended conversations about African American literature and artistic culture. The site provides us with opportunities to exchange ideas about the convergence of black studies, technology, and active citizenship. This blog will also provide up-to-date information about the SIUE Black Studies Program: the minor, special projects, and knowledge-building opportunities. (http://www.culturalfront.org/)

One small example of this Blog's technological focus, purpose, and philosophy occurs under an entry titled "28 Ways of Thinking about Black Studies & Afrofuturism" posted on February 1, 2012:

Since becoming director of the program in 2007, I have worked to make technology central to the production of Black Studies @ SIUE. A framework known as afrofuturism, which highlights the intersections between race and technology, served as a crucial guiding force in my approaches to organizing certain kinds of projects and recruiting particular contributors.

For the month of February, we take a look at some of the ways that we have utilized a variety of new media, digital humanities, afrofuturist ideas, and concepts related to speculative narratives to expand knowledge about African American history, culture, and ideas. Perhaps black history month is as good a time as any to reflect on how technology and a framework for understanding African American engagements with the future have shaped our work over the past few years.

Entries:

- 1: Afrofuturism
- 2: The Malcolm X Mixtape
- 3: Music
- 4: Graphic Design
- 5: Listening Devices
- 6: The Black Studies Blog
- 7: The Interactive Reading Group
- 8: Mixed Media exhibits
- 9: Audio recordings
- 10: Past-future visions
- 11: Blogging about Katherine Dunham
- 12: Blogging about Black Women Poets (www.culturalfront. org/2012/02/28-ways-of-thinking-about-black-studies.html)

Sometimes a list is just a list. The one above, though? Maybe not. More of a jazz riff based on Wallace Stevens' poem "Thirteen Ways of Looking at a Blackbird", the 12 entries from the "28 Ways of Thinking" entry serving to whet our curiosity. Like any good riff, the list also weaves echoes of the past with contemporary sounds/creations/phrasings, musical and otherwise, to move out and beyond, always pointing towards the future. Finally, the list is highly rhetorical, its pathos, logos, and ethos persuading African American students that they have a valuable history surrounding and welcoming them if only they would simply choose to be part of such a group. If they accept the challenge, they will find that they can contribute to enriching the future of "black studies, technology, and active citizenship" (from the *Cultural Front* Blog description just above).

The person responsible for most of the Web site material and especially for the Blog postings is Howard Rambsy II, former Director of the SIUE Black Studies Program (see howardrambsy.com). A true child of the digital age—the kind who only reads his newspaper online, not on newsprint— and a young scholar, Rambsy understands only too well that capturing the attention of youth today and sparking their intellects involves using technology complete with all of its digital capacities available in the second decade of the twenty-first century. Not surprising to anyone who knows about his scholarship, Rambsy's work with this Blog is both an actual and virtual extension of his scholarly methodology and educational philosophy. Rambsy's work in African American literature focuses on examining factors that helped sustain and advance the Black Arts Movement of the 1960s and 70s—namely specific publishing venues and editorial practices. His study, *The Black Arts Enterprise and the Production of African-American Poetry*, has as its purpose

> to make vital, though regularly overlooked, publishing factors central to the operations of Black Arts Movement more apparent. In particular, this study seeks to *deepen our understanding of literary art by explaining significant ways that processes of transmission and socialization shaped the rise of* [my emphasis] black arts poetry. We will gain a broader knowledge concerning the production of poetry when *greater attention is paid to roles played by anthologies, literary magazines, and audio recordings* [my emphasis], for instance. (16)

Overlooked publishing factors important to the Black Arts Movement, processes of transmission in the past—those anthologies, literary magazines, and audio recordings—have become Web sites, online journals, blogs, YouTube, and mp3s. These are today's publishing venues that can likewise advance not only African American art, but all creative endeavors into vastly new terrain. We only need to remember to look at them, not overlook them, so we can study exactly how vital their roles will be for the arts movements of tomorrow. Howard Rambsy, however, is doing his best to remind us how important the new venues are.

Twenty-one years ago in 1992 Walter Allen urged educators to pay attention to the then- and still-exigent situation of African American students in higher education:

> Far-reaching, enduring change in higher education for African-American students will only come about when universities come to feel more keenly their responsibility for changing the system of unequal societal relationships based on race. Universities must also become more proactive and deliberate in the actions taken to address barriers to African American success within their institutions. Thus the challenge confronting U.S. colleges and universities now and into the twenty-first century is to achieve the promise of the high ideals of equality, representation, and solidarity in a culturally pluralistic society. If we fail to respond creatively and effectively to this challenge, not only will history judge us harshly, but this country will also continue to suffer the negative consequences, such as the loss of its competitive edge in

the world market, that have resulted from its failure to develop fully and utilize the talent of all its people, without regard to race, gender, or class. (42–43)

Part jeremiad and part plea, Allen's words still merit our serious attention. Howard Rambsy seems to have created his Southern Illinois University Edwardsville Black Studies affiliated Blog, *Cultural Front*, with these words in mind; however, since he only graduated with his undergraduate degree in 1999, he was not even a college student in 1992, much less a university professor. He was probably only one year into his high school career. It is, then, to his great credit that he and his Blog are today working tirelessly to do their parts in addressing social inequality through encouraging students who are this nation's future.

6   Border Work
Hybrid Texts and Analytic Fusion in Digital Space

The present epoch will perhaps be above all the epoch of space. We are in the epoch of simultaneity: we are in the epoch of juxtaposition, the epoch of the near and far, of the side-by-side, of the dispersed.

~ Michel Foucault

The underlying formal substratum of writing is not visual but spatial.

~ Roy Harris

As I have been arguing throughout this volume, our now multimodal world allows no surrender, no retreat into that bygone pastoral time of alphabetic-only text. We can't go back. We must both understand and teach rhetorical skills that translate to the digital, that help students to compose rhetorically in more than one medium, and that help them to analyze the multimodal texts they encounter. Chapter 6 extends my argument to claim that our analytic perceptions, abilities, and vocabularies must expand beyond two-dimensional surfaces to three-dimensional space. So if there's no going back from our multimodal world, there's also no going back from thinking about multimediated texts—those hybrid combinations of words and images—as textual space, especially as Foucault describes space above: simultaneous, juxtaposed, near and far, side by side, and dispersed. This chapter argues that digital sites, especially those preceded by or connected to an actual physical space like a museum, educational institution, or company are not only rhetorical artifacts, but that analytically fused rhetorical-spatial study can help us to better understand community, culture, and history.

In 1991, before the World Wide Web and multimodal texts became the commonplaces of 2012, Jay Bolter explored the traits of a then different space for writing—the electronic space—in his study *Writing Space: The Computer, Hypertext and the History of Writing.* Twenty-one years later, writing spaces have become digital, multimodal, and conceptually even more spatial. Bolter's words, however, still outline a way to explore one of our emerging rhetorical frontiers: digital space. Arguing that text is more a space than a linear progression of words, Bolter originally wrote: "How the writer and the reader understand writing is conditioned by the physical and visual character of the books they use. Each physical writing space fosters a particular understanding both of the act of writing and of the product, the written text" (11). Here is Bolter's text, as I revised and updated it for our world of digital space and for multimodal compositions even more unbounded by the two-dimensional theories applicable to a codex book and literature:

> How the [architect] and the [viewer] understand [digital space] is con-ditioned by the physical and visual character of the [Web space] they use. Each [digital multimodal] space fosters a particular understanding both of the act of [digital composing] and of the product, [the multi-modal space].

Jean Trumbo has differentiated between several types of space that designers and users must consider, saying, "A careful consideration of phys-ical, perceptual, conceptual, and behavioral space is a sound first step in the process of creating a navigable digital universe" (28). Below is my modified version of a chart that Trumbo sketches out in her essay (28):

- Physical Space: The size and shape of the space occupied by the mul-timedia project
- Perceptual Space: Our sense of the scale, distance, or proportion within the multimedia project
- Conceptual Space: The way in which the user understands or remem-bers the design space
- Behavioral Space: The way in which the user actually moves through the space

Furthermore, the ever-increasing visual and aural nature of the Web presses us to increase contact with other disciplines as well as with our own discipline's sub-specialties (see, for instance, the work of Cynthia Selfe—"The Movement of Air, the Breath of Meaning: Aurality and Multimodal Composing"—and a collection edited by Emily Golson and Toni Glover—*Negotiating a Meta-pedagogy: Learning from Other Disciplines*) whose theoretical bases can help us examine the Web more critically and more intelligently; semiotics, the fine arts, architecture, design, visual literacy, technical writing, and perhaps even geography are some of these disciplines. Trumbo's divisions suggest additional disciplines we may need to consult as we move toward a clearer understanding of what exactly might be involved today in digital rhetorical analysis. See Figure 6.1 below.

True, thinking about rhetoric and composition in connection with space entails inquiry into subjects outside the usual confines of our discipline. But such inquiry is not new to compositionists and rhetoricians. Early on,

PHYSICAL SPACE	PERCEPTUAL SPACE
GEOGRAPHY ARCHITECTURE ENGINEERING DESIGN GRAPHIC ART MEDIA STUDIES ART HISTORY	DESIGN STUDIES HYPERTEXT STUDIES TECHNICAL WRITING CARTOGRAPHY VISUAL CULTURE TYPOGRAPHY
CONCEPTUAL SPACE	BEHAVIORAL SPACE

COGNITION STUDIES
   EMBODIED COGNITION
   DISTRIBUTED COGNITION
   SITUATED COGNITION
DESIGN STUDIES
SEMIOTICS
PHILOSOPHY
LITERARY STUDIES
	MUSEUM STUDIES
	ANTHROPOLOGY
	CULTURAL STUDIES
	POPULAR CULTURE
	SOCIOLOGY
	HISTORY

Figure 6.1   Spatial types and related disciplines.

almost 30 years ago now, the field of composition studies adopted a cross-disciplinary predisposition: Janice Lauer published an important article in *Rhetoric Review* urging those of us in composition studies to accept the multidisciplinary nature of our discipline.

> Composition studies has maintained from the beginning what a number of disciplines are just starting to admit—that many of their most important problems can be properly investigated only with multiple research methods. Instead of assuming that it had to begin from *tabula rasa*, the field saw the value of building on relevant work in other fields and of using methods of investigation refined elsewhere. 25–26

Lauer dutifully pointed out both the pitfalls and advantages of multidisciplinarity. She cautioned us that we cannot simply borrow from another work in another field without understanding the "context, history, and status" of the work. She also added that those conducting such forays into another discipline also inherit the burden of mastery to a certain degree. But for Lauer, the advantages are worth the risk: our field thrives from a widening of intellectual scope while its members can become partners in intellectual exchanges among disciplines. Emily Golson and Toni Glover, more recently, agree: "When we mix traditional composition pedagogies with pedagogies and knowledge from other disciplines, the effect can be disorienting, but if we push past the demarcation that separates the familiar and unfamiliar, we can harness powerful new energy made possible by mixing disciplinary knowledge and composition pedagogy" (2). Such cross-disciplinarity is even more important for digital rhetoricians.

Some disciplines traditionally consulted for insight into multimodal composition are design, visual literacy, communication studies, typography, and media studies of film, television, video, and computer-generated texts (see, for example, Goldfarb; Handa, *Visual Rhetoric*; Hilligoss; and Wysocki). I propose here, however, that in order to better understand and help our students to analyze the overall construction of today's Web-based digital projects, we should consider these projects in spatial as well as solely verbal terms, particular with regard to overall site coherence—that is, the paths offered to viewers moving between digital Web pages on a site devoted to a single institution—then explore structural and spatial theories informing disciplines such as the ones listed above in Figure 6.1. Two that I want to focus on here are museum and exhibition studies and communication studies.[1] The ideas we find in such works can help us understand better how to analyze digital Web sites constructed with images as well as text and intended to be read more paratactically than hypotactically. In addition, imagining multimodal documents as three-dimensional spaces instead of two-dimensional surfaces—in other words, collections of rooms rather than flat pages bound within a book—may help our students compose and analyze Web sites in different ways: if they can connect Web navigation to the act of physically moving through geographic spaces, they may better understand and then construct online navigational paths within Web sites. Marita Sturken and Lisa Cartwright point out the ubiquity of images in virtual space, saying that they exist "not only on the Web but also as elements of video games, CD-Roms, and DVDs" (148). They then make the connection between museum space and virtual space. Navigation through visual images as part of a video game, they say,

> has also become a means through which art institutions such as museums are expanding their venues. Many contemporary museums now market CDs that are virtual galleries, through which viewers can move through images displayed in the museum on their computer. These digital image reproductions have the added dimension of virtual space

that encourages viewers to experience themselves as moving through actual museum space. (148)

Our students are accustomed to navigating through game space, so thinking of Web site navigation as moving through space should draw on already existing skills. Students may also begin to understand a few significant differences between the movement of ideas presented in bound texts going from one page to the next and the associative, multidimensional movement possible in three-dimensional, multimediated texts. These sometimes overlooked disciplinary sources can also help composition teachers and rhetoricians understand museum exhibits as forms of communication, the exhibit space itself as a rhetorical form of communication (for example, see B. Ferguson; McLuhan), and space's multidirectionality being rhetorically elucidated by considering it as a type of hypertext or three-dimensional structure. We need, in other words, to examine works that show us how to read space rhetorically. Such sources can help us determine what tools we can then use for digital spatial analysis that is fundamentally rhetorical.

This chapter proposes actions that educators should consider in order to establish rhetoric as equally important to digital studies as design and computer programming.

* * * * *

MUSEUMS AS SPATIAL FORMS OF RHETORICAL COMMUNICATION

> *If* [Marshall] *McLuhan can in fact be called a "founding father"* . . .
> *of postmodernism, it is precisely in having established* the spatial
> [my emphasis] *as the most significant dimension of postmodernist
> inquiry—including inquiry into communication.*
>
> ~ Richard Cavell

When Marshall McLuhan first began inquiring into the spatial aspects of communication in the 1960s, he was ahead of his time. In our day of Web 2.0 and multiply mediated texts, however, such inquiry is much easier to grasp.[2] Still, though, the ideas may seem odd to writing instructors who work primarily with traditional essay forms in their composition classes. Visualizing texts as spaces we move through, however, has recently become much more common. In January and February 2007, for example, during online commercials for their own network amid video replays of the current week's popular shows such as *NCIS*, *CSI*, and *Numb3rs*, CBS presented images of Web pages as walls of text, somewhat like moveable museum exhibit walls set at 90-degree angles to each other, three-dimensional boxes of text or individual panels that we could actually imagine navigating between and around, on foot.

A year later, during the 2008 election night coverage on major news networks such as CNN and NBC, broadcasters presented exit poll information, senate seat victories, and state electoral vote designations as multidimensional holograms, and even literally, as spaces people could walk through and around; NBC used the ice rink at its Rockefeller Plaza headquarters in New York City to place blue and red state cutouts onto a US map etched on the ice. Workers literally walked around the map putting the cutouts in place and communicating electoral votes tallies in three dimensions. Also recently, Google Maps has begun presenting directional maps called "street views" that look like renderings of three-dimensional spaces; in other words, instead of the two-dimensional views that we get with paper maps, Google attempts to give us dimensional views of the streets from an overhead angle with the buildings lining the streets drawn in perspective. By consulting these dimensional maps, we can anticipate the differing shapes and heights of those buildings as we drive or walk from point A to point B.

Even if viewers can begin imagining Web pages as similar to museum installation walls, however, the rhetorical nature of both might still elude these viewers. For these skeptics, Bruce W. Ferguson's "Exhibition Rhetorics: Material Speech and Utter Sense", appearing in a collection called *Thinking about Exhibitions*, specifically discusses rhetorical and cultural theories related to museum exhibits. Ferguson explains exactly how we might approach a spatial, three-dimensional exhibition rhetorically. He begins by considering an exhibition a "communications performance", exactly the type of performance we could equate with an Internet Web site:

> Who speaks TO and FOR WHOM and UNDER WHAT CONDITIONS as well as WHERE and WHEN the particular utterance occurs are significant questions that can be asked of any communications performance. By asking who speaks it is possible to establish the gender, ethnicity, race, age and cultural background and the history of texts of the speaker. By asking TO WHOM and FOR WHOM we can establish the administrative nature of the relationship: whether it is commercial or casual, individually professional or institutionally mediated, intimate or formal, a teacher to a student, a slave to a master, and so on. In other words how is this particular voice filtered and mediated by its connections to other people, other institutions, other kinships and networks of influence? (183–184)

Ferguson additionally connects these museum exhibitions to groups he calls the consciousness industries—that is, most media today. But if the physical locations/spaces of the museums are part of such industries, then, I would add, so are their online representations/spaces—their Web sites—because they contain not just practical information, but also cultural information in the form of images and text that help us interpret the exhibitions themselves.

SPACE CAN COMMUNICATE

If we examine two relatively recent museum sites, we can begin to understand how Ferguson's questions help yield a richer understanding of these spaces. The Birmingham Civil Rights Institute in Birmingham, Alabama, and the Japanese American National Museum in Los Angeles, California, were constructed late in the second half of the twentieth century, post-World War II and the civil unrest of the 1960s (both opened their doors in 1992). In both cases, the groups that conceived of and founded these institutions are the US citizens who experienced some of the more horrific atrocities perpetrated in the country. As they worked to achieve their human and civil rights, their right to vote, their right to be treated with dignity, African Americans endured verbal abuse, physical beatings, fire-hose spraying, dog attacks, bombings, lynch mobs, and murder. At the beginning of the US' involvement in World War II, President Roosevelt's Executive Order 9066 named Japanese Americans, all of whom were US citizens, as enemies of the country, thereby authorizing their forced removal from their homes; stripped of their property and possessions, they were herded into buses and trains, then incarcerated in concentration camps scattered across the more desolate areas of the US. Both physical museums speak on behalf of, and in the voices of, those citizens who experienced the atrocities, as well as the descendants of those citizens. Both museums speak more broadly to all people in the nation, most who did not experience them, and some who were born after these occurrences.

Each of these museums also presents rhetorical arguments to those who move through their online sites as well as their physical spaces, arguments conveyed especially through the museums' online mission statements. While both Web sites include pictures of each museum's physical exhibits and rooms containing important documents and historical objects such as one of the Freedom Riders' buses, each digital site focuses a viewer's attention rhetorically by including these mission statements. The Birmingham Civil Rights Institute's mission is: "To promote civil and human rights worldwide through education". Elsewhere in the online documents, we find this addendum:

> As summarized in its Mission Statement, the Institute sets out to "focus on what happened in the past, to portray it realistically and interestingly, and to understand it in relationship to the present and future developments of human relations in Birmingham, the United

States and perhaps the world." (http://www.bcri.org/ information/his-tory_of_bcri/history6.html)

The Japanese American National Museum's online mission statement reads:

> The mission of the Japanese American National Museum is to promote understanding and appreciation of America's ethnic and cultural diversity by sharing the Japanese American experience.
> We share the story of Japanese Americans because we honor our nation's diversity. We believe in the importance of remembering our history to better guard against the prejudice that threatens liberty and equality in a democratic society. We strive as a world-class museum to provide a voice for Japanese Americans and a forum that enables all people to explore their own heritage and culture.
> We promote continual exploration of the meaning and value of ethnicity in our country through programs that preserve individual dignity, strengthen our communities, and increase respect among all people. We believe that our work will transform lives, create a more just America and, ultimately, a better world. (http://www.janm.org/about)

The rhetorical configurations of both institutions' Web sites support and expand on those mission statements which, in terms used to instruct students in writing classes, serve as the main arguments or thesis statements of each site.

Despite its multidimensionality and hypertextually inclined structure, then, space does communicate rhetorically. In the cases of these two museum Web sites, their online spaces, aided by their mission statements, focus our attention on the argument each one presents as we view digital, online images of exhibits that also exist in the actual, physical museum locations.[3]

CONNECTIONS TO RHETORIC AND COMPOSITION

I contend here that writing teachers can apply ideas from museum scholarship to help us frame our writing instruction in two specific areas: 1) more in-depth rhetorical analysis, and 2) the analysis and construction of Web documents.

According to a recently posted study including data about writing students' success or difficulty with 16 different writing objectives, students in a variety of writing classes have the least amount of success at close, deep analysis of the sources they choose to cite for their research. Students do less analyzing of references—as sources, and in context (Haas, Losh, and Strenski, 2–3). For example, they do not investigate possible bias or perform the close textual analysis that might cause them to investigate their sources' contexts or to question the reliability of the people they paraphrase or quote. Viewing Web sites *of* museum exhibitions and then analyzing these sites *as* actual, physical museum exhibitions might be one possible avenue to help them better understand how to conduct such analysis in all their college studies since our students are 1) more open to and eager about multimedia analysis than most other types of closer reading (even though very few students have conducted any digital media analysis), and 2) have more experience analyzing dimensionality as it shows up in online gaming.

USEFUL FRAMING

Bruce Ferguson clearly establishes that a physical exhibit in the space of a museum is rhetorical, and that museums themselves are rhetorical spaces. If we take the questions Ferguson asks above about museums as communications performances, modify them slightly for students examining online educational spaces, and apply them to a Web site, we get a slightly different angle than the one Anne Wysocki works with to help her students become more visually literate through concentrating on design issues as students write and create multimodal documents. Wysocki focuses on the tools students use and the materiality of students' texts. That is, the production of texts by means of certain tools affects those texts themselves and what we are able to do with them. As Wysocki argues, "[W]riting teachers help others consider how the choices we make in producing a text necessarily situate us (or can try to avoid situating us) in the midst of ongoing, concrete, and continually up-for-grabs decisions about the shapes of our lives" (7). Wysocki presents us with exercises for understanding the materiality and design elements of texts. She gives us exercises that help us to understand how even a choice of writing tool will affect our textual outcomes (see in particular 27–31). Wysocki does have suggestions for analyzing readings containing theories about technology (see 34–37). Her ideas about "mapping" the major ideas of readings, combined with the processes I describe below, would make an interesting exercise for students; they could begin by "reading" an online document as a physical space, and they could end up trying to construct an actual, concrete "map" of that space.

The chief departure, however, from the questions we are already asking about Web sites is that having students examine online documents by using rhetorical tools and questions prompts them to consider organization as a form of architecture that engineers their moves through space so that 1) this movement ends in conveying a persuasive message and 2) this same movement places them contextually in a position to understand a part of their culture. Ferguson's questions above, modified and put into list form, then, would follow along these lines:

1. Who speaks to whom?
2. Who speaks for whom?
3. Under what conditions is this speaker speaking?

4. Where is the speaking occurring?
5. When is the speaking occurring?
6. Can we determine the gender, ethnicity, race, age, and cultural background of the speaker?
7. Can we determine the history of texts of the speaker?
8. By asking who is speaking and determining for whom the speaking is occurring, can we establish the administrative nature of the relationship?
9. Is it commercial or casual?
10. Is it individually professional or institutionally mediated?
11. Is it intimate or formal (i.e. a student to a student, a teacher to a student, an employee to a manager or CEO)?
12. How is this particular voice filtered and mediated by its connections to other people, other institutions, other kinships and networks of influence?

Because I have written elsewhere about conducting an in-class rhetorical analysis using Ferguson's questions on a museum and university Web site,[4] I will not repeat that study here; what I will show instead is the importance of a fused rhetorical analysis of the geographical and digital spaces of a monument with a particularly conflicted history.

MEMORIALS AS SPATIAL FORMS OF RHETORICAL COMMUNICATION

While not an enclosed space like a museum, the memorial as a free-standing object within a given geographical space can communicate rhetorically just as much as a museum does. A memorial's Web site, additionally, serves the same important function as a museum's. Earlier in this chapter I argued that online representations of physical spaces like museums contain important cultural information in addition to more practical data like location, hours of operation, and admission costs. For memorials with contested histories, a fused rhetorical analysis accounting for both the physical space plus the text and images within its related online spaces is especially important. The online sites discussed below are crucial in conveying cultural information that may not be at all clear to someone visiting the geographical space.

Analyzing three-dimensional objects as cultural statements is not a new practice. Marita Sturken's profound study of the Vietnam Veteran's Memorial is one good example. Sturken explains that in forms of remembrance such as this memorial, "we can see acts of public commemoration as moments in which the shifting discourse of history, personal memory, and cultural memory converge. Public commemoration is a form of history-making, yet can also be a contested form of remembrance" ("The Wall," 163). Sturken shows how those clashing forms of remembrance influenced the monument's creation and reception. She uses the metaphor of a screen to show how various definitions of that word explain what happens when viewers look at the memorial.[5]

Studying the Web sites associated with the memorial reveals just how contested the space of the monument remains to this day. A search through library catalogs, online bookseller inventories, and search engines like Google and Bing for histories of the Vietnam Veterans Memorial yields few results. Codex books exist, but most are primarily aimed at children. There are also photographic histories. But very few histories for adults exist.[6] In this case, then, the story and the history reside in the monument itself and in the online Web sites. Analyzing the online material therefore becomes even more important. In our age of the "dispersed", to use Foucault's language in this chapter's epigraph, we need to "juxtapose" the spaces of several sites in addition to the space of the search site itself—an extremely important action for geographical places with online spaces and little historical documentation otherwise available—because the list of Web sites unearthed by search engines acts like a table of contents: it previews the variety of online documents and differing points of view available for analysis. Such a move is always important, too, for people who cannot actually visit the geographical place in person. In addition, online searchers must review with care the list of Web sites that turn up in a search because to date there is no one authoritative representative site like there is for a museum or a company or a retail store. In fact the individual sites for this memorial may give viewers a skewed sense of what the physical space actually looks like. Web sites like the one sponsored by the National Park Service and others by various Vietnam Veterans groups seem to be competing for the distinction of being the authoritative site. A rhetorical look at these sites shows that the conflict we see portrayed comes down to differing senses of ethos, rhetorical context, and epideictic rhetoric.

ETHOS, CONTEXT, EPIDEICTIC RHETORIC

From its beginning, expectations, assumptions, race, gender, a generation gap, and architectural traditions complicated the question of ethos within the space of the Vietnam Veterans Memorial. In opening a competition for their memorial's design to be judged by a panel of art experts, the Vietnam Veterans group in charge of the memorial fund did not consider the possibility that more than one kind of person—namely a war veteran—could speak credibly through a memorial (or that there could even be any question about ethos), that the rhetorical context of such a conflicted war and historical period would not show itself in the memorial, and that notions of the epideictic rhetoric projected by a memorial could differ so much. Jack Selzer's definition of epideictic rhetoric is that it is "ceremonial discourse used to create and reinforce community values (at a given *present* moment)" (284). The commissioning group simply expected this memorial to express and reinforce traditional war-time values—ones that they forgot became increasingly contested as this war progressed.

As Sturken explains:

> At the time her anonymously submitted design was chosen by a group of eight art experts, Maya Ying Lin was a twenty-one-year-old undergraduate at Yale University. She had produced the design for a funerary architecture course. She was not only young and uncredentialed but also Chinese-American and female. Initially, the veterans of the VVMF were pleased by this turn of events; they assumed that the selection of Lin's design would only show how open and impartial their design contest had been. However, the selection of someone with "marginal" cultural status as the primary interpreter of a controversial war inevitably complicated matters. Eventually, Maya Lin was defined, in particular by the media, not as American but as "other." This otherness became an issue not only in the way she was perceived by the media and some of the veterans, it became a critical issue of whether or not that otherness had informed the design itself. ("The Wall," 168)

To get any sense of this conflict and to be able to reply to the rhetorical questions Ferguson asks, we need to go online. We need, furthermore, to analyze both the texts and images we see there, but we need, especially, to analyze the list of sites turned up by whatever search tool we use (and it is best to use more than one) as guides to the history and cultural clashes embedded in the monument's geographic site. The top five sites that the search engine Bing listed on July 8, 2011 were:

1. Amtrak Goes to Memorial
2. Vietnam Veterans Memorial, Washington
3. The Vietnam Veterans Memorial Wall Place
4. Vietnam Veterans Memorial—Wikipedia
5. Vietnam Veterans Memorial National Monument

While the first site, upon very close inspection, is actually an ad, I include it here because nothing separates the ad visually from the other listings, neither font style, size, nor design. This lack of distinguishing features that should visually mark the listing as an advertisement for Amtrak is a deliberate rhetorical omission that indicates the extent to which commercial interests prevail on this site. The top five sites on Google for the same date were:

1. The Vietnam Veterans Memorial Wall Place
2. Wall Information—the Vietnam Veterans Memorial Wall Page
3. Vietnam Veterans Memorial—Wikipedia

4. News for Vietnam Veterans Memorial
5. Images for Vietnam Veterans Memorial

As to be expected, the ethos projected from the different sites listed by both search engines belongs to the sponsoring organization, at first primarily the Vietnam Veterans groups and the National Park Service. The Wikipedia site aims for the ethos of a relatively objective encyclopedia entry. The most interesting entry because of its pertinence to this study of digital fusion is the row of the memorial's images on Google's search list. Clicking on each thumbnail image, one would expect a larger image to open up. And one does. But behind that image is a shadowed text. If we close the image, the shadow clears and we can then see the Web site where the photo originated, complete with that site's description and history of the memorial: for example, three of the different images dissolve to show 1) the Wikipedia entry, 2) an "Art & Culture" blog, and 3) an "Essential Architecture" page complete with a bibliography of further reading along with many additional photos and Web sites for other images. In a very real sense, then, the most important parts of the monument, what it tells us about ourselves and our history, are not visible unless we adopt an expanded notion of space and of this monument's space especially—that previously mentioned hypertextual-type space linking both geographic and digital spaces—plus an expanded notion of analysis that encompasses both image and text.

If we ask "Who speaks to whom?" and "Who speaks for whom?" we get a different answer depending upon the part of the geographic memorial we direct our question to: the wall itself, Frederick Hart's addition of the three soldiers, the women's memorial, or the flag. In the case of the original wall, Maya Lin and the soldiers named are speaking to families, visitors, and the country, and Maya Lin is speaking for those soldiers. If we look at the group of three solders added later, the Vietnam Veterans group is speaking to the country and speaking for all the veterans of the war, and in the case of the women, that part of the monument is speaking to female veterans and the country and is speaking for the women who also lost their lives or who served and returned to their country.

The geographic monument's lack of rhetorical focus also emerges when we ask "Under what conditions is this speaker speaking?" because each piece speaks under different conditions. The wall is speaking under the condition of a university architecture class and then under the condition of the prize-winning piece selected to represent and memorialize the many lives lost in the war. The three soldiers are speaking under the condition of a contested memorial and an attempt to redirect/refocus attention on traditional art and a traditional heroic interpretation of war. The third part of the memorial, the women, speaks under the condition of the forgotten women who also fought, served, and died in the war.

Bruce Ferguson's final question about the "particular voice filtered and mediated by its connection to other people, other institutions, other kinships and networks of influence" can be answered only in part by visiting the geographical space. Seeing the different pieces of the memorial today might give a student of rhetoric some inkling that for the geographic memorial, a connection to other people, other institutions, and other networks of influence have led to competing foci as well as different degrees of and kinds of pathos. Ferguson's question will be answered fully by visiting the online spaces that can explain why the memorial has its particular form today.

All of the Vietnam Veterans Memorial spaces, digital and physical, are needed to get a true sense of the monument. Just as the online spaces give more cultural history (logos), the geographical site gives an overwhelming sense of loss and of the great sacrifice of the thousands who gave their lives (pathos). Seeing images online is not the same as walking slowly past the names—one name at first then more and more and more as a visitor moves from either side then reaches the center point where the two walls converge and literally overwhelm the visitor with the height of the walls and by the numbers of names of the dead. The Web spaces cannot give that same sense of loss.

How much history from now on will need to account for both geographical and online spaces? How important or necessary will be our ability to convey that history to a generation that turns to the Web first for nearly every type of information before it turns to paper documents?

CONNECTIONS IN THE END

Museum and exhibition studies provide compositionists with sources that can help us better envision Web sites, multimodal documents, and ultimately all writing as designed spaces, terrain that conveys information in rhetorical ways we may never before have considered while also yielding important cultural and historical information. While composition scholars have not usually drawn from these spatially oriented disciplines, such fields can now provide us with new points of view for analyzing the rhetorical aspects of written compositions.[7]

Studying online Web spaces designed as companion digital sites for physical museum and memorial spaces like the Civil Rights Institute in Birmingham, the Japanese American Museum in Los Angeles, or the Vietnam Veterans Memorial in Washington, DC, additionally, illustrates how much rhetorical-spatial textual study can help us to better understand community, culture, and history. Victoria Gallagher has argued that studying the rhetorical aspects (including a rhetor's goals and rhetorical success) of material artifacts extends our vocabulary for understanding from the purely linguistic to include the visual:

> In the case of memorials, the consequences of materiality include issues of partisanship, particularly institutionalization of memory and, thereby, value. As a result, the highly contested nature of race relations

and civil rights in the United States means that related memorials enact a dialectical tension between reconciliation and amnesia, conflicts resolved and conflicts simply reconfigured. Analysis of the [Birmingham Civil Rights] Institute's visual vocabularies and material presence provides a way to illuminate this tension and determine its implications. (304)

Such analytic goals are undoubtedly lofty, but they begin by providing students with tools for further rhetorical analysis. What these questions and exercises can push students to see and understand are:

- Complicated questions of speaker and audience
- How much a speaker is embedded in complexities even though, at first glance, a speaker might seem to be operating alone
- The degree to which a speaker can be embracing or rejecting the conditions within which he/she is contextualized
- How much a context shapes a person
- What obligations a speaker assumes or neglects in regard to readers and future readers, viewers and future viewers

As writing teachers, we aim to show our students how important their own writing is and how it can make some impact on the world. This seems a good way to begin in order to reach such an end.

Bruce Ferguson emphasizes for us the analytic value of studying museum exhibition scholarship:

The consciousness industries are contemporary forms of traditional rhetoric, complex expressions of persuasion through complex transmissions of voice and image. Like rhetoric itself, they might be best described as strategic systems of representation; strategies whose aim is the wholesale conversion of its audiences to sets of prescribed values to alter social relations.

And this is precisely what an exhibition is—a strategic system of representations. The system of an exhibition organizes its representations to best utilize everything, from its architecture which is always political, to its wall colorings which are always psychologically meaningful, to its labels which are always didactic (even, or especially, in their silences), to its artistic exclusions which are always powerfully ideological and structural in their limited admissions, to its lighting which is always dramatic (and therefore an important aspect of narrativity and the staging of desire), to its security systems which are always a form of social collateral (the choice between guards and video surveillance, for example), to its curatorial premises which are always professionally dogmatic, to its brochures and catalogues and videos which are always literacy-specific and pedagogically directional, to its aesthetics which are always historically specific to that site of presentation rather than to individual artwork's moments of production. In other words, there is a plan to all exhibitions, a will, or teleological hierarchy of significances, which is its dynamic undercurrent. . . . The will to influence is at the core of any exhibition. (178–179)

BORDERS—MARGINALITY VERSUS LIMINALITY

Simultaneity, juxtaposition, near-and-far, side-by-side, dispersed: both geographic and digital spaces are all of these. More and more we need to place our selves and our digital research on the borders between both physical and digital spaces and on the borders between rhetoric and those disciplines that can only enrich our rhetorical study. These days with battles against illegal immigrants occurring in so many states, both the word "border" and the notion of any border crossing carry negative connotations and conjure up frightening images. We need to remember, however, that a border can be seen in many ways. It can be limiting—that is, a line to contain what is within and to mark all that is outside as marginal or "other", and not worth our consideration. But a border can also be considered differently. Instead of limi*ting*, it can be seen as limi*nal*, a space that is a threshold more than a guarded crossing with armed troops ordered to keep out anyone who looks remotely like an "other".

In an entire chapter devoted to examining the complex state of liminality from an anthropological perspective, Victor Turner defines such a state as one that "represents the midpoint of transition in a status-sequence between two positions" (237). Turner's definition arises from his work in cultural anthropology and examinations of classes within cultures. More recently in 2009, an entire special issue of *International Political Anthropology* (2, no. 1) has been devoted to the subject of liminality. In their introduction to this issue, editors Agnes Horvath, Bjørn Thomassen, and Harald Wydra state that liminality is "a major concept in cultural and social anthropology [important to] the understanding of wider processes of social and political change" (3). One of the issue's essays, Bjørn Thomassen's "The Uses and Meanings of Liminality", traces the concept's intellectual history.

For those of us rhetoricians working with the digital, striving to stay on the borders— between text and image, between print and digitality, between geographic and Internet spaces—is a crucial balancing act for the wider process of change and insight that must mark our work.

THE PROBLEM OF EPHEMERALITY FOR RESEARCH AND STUDY

In the end, online spaces can provide important historical material for those of us who are not experts and who never intend to become scholars in a field. But also in the end, the biggest problem is certainly the ephemerality of those online spaces because Web sites can come and go. Luckily the problem of history and the ephemerality of Web space is being studied by Michael L. Nelson and his team of researchers at Old Dominion University. To show how difficult Nelson's task is, Jie Jenny Zou at the *Chronicle of Higher Education* quoted Alexis Rossi, a Web-collections manager of one of the archives used by Nelson on the subject of his team's efforts: "It's such a moving target—the web is expanding all the time. . . . People are coming to the realization that if nobody saves the Internet, their work will just be gone." Zou's piece continues:

> For Mr. Nelson, the study is another step toward creating a browsing experience that links the past to the present: where users can replay events as they unfolded, such as media coverage of hurricane Katrina in 2005 or 2007's Virginia Tech shootings.
>
> "You relive the experience in a way that a summary page can't even begin to capture," Mr. Nelson said, imagining a day when such historical searches become common. (http://chronicle.com/blogs/wiredcampus/old-dominion-u-researchers-ask-how-much-of-the-web-is-archived/32068)

Only when keeping in mind rhetoric's range, components, and goals can we begin understanding how the multimediated texts of today speak to us on many levels while revealing complexities about ourselves and our surrounding cultures that will remain hidden unless we equip ourselves to understand the pieces of the delicate online rhetorical fusion that is now here to stay.

Notes

NOTES TO THE INTRODUCTION

1. This Chair's address to the conference membership was later published in *College Composition and Communication* 50 no. 3 (1999), where my quotation originates on page 414. It is the foundation for an entire monograph published later in 1999 by Southern Illinois University Press.
2. See, for example, Richard Lanham ("Digital Literacy," 1995), Lee Brasseur ("Visual Literacy in the Computer Age," 1997), David Reinking *et al* (*Handbook of Literacy and Technology*, 1998), Bill Cope and Mary Kalantzis (*Multiliteracies*, 2000), Gunther Kress (*Literacy in the New Media Age*, 2003), Ilana Snyder (*Silicon Literacies*, 2002), Barbara Warnick (*Critical Literacy in a Digital Age*, 2002), Gail Hawisher and Cindy Selfe (*Literate Lives in the Information Age*, 2004), Stuart Selber (*Multiliteracies for a Digital Age*, 2004).
3. For an explanation of the "profound cultural shift" that Napster represents and an argument about Napster's significance for composition teachers, see DeVoss and Porter's essay "Why Napster Matters to Writing."

NOTES TO CHAPTER 1

1. For an extended study of this generation, the differences between its members and all previous generations including baby-boomers, see Don Tapscott's *Grown Up Digital: How the Net Generation is Changing Your World* (New York: McGraw-Hill, 2009), especially "Part One: Meet the Net Gen," 1–119, where Tapscott elaborates on this Net Gen's characteristics.
2. See Aristotle, *On Rhetoric: A Theory of Civic Discourse*, trans. and intro. George A. Kennedy (New York: Oxford UP, 1991).
3. Doug Brent, "Rhetorics of the Web: Implications for Teachers of Literacy," *Kairos: A Journal for Teachers of Writing in Webbed Environments* 2, no. 1 (Spring 1997). http://www.technorhetoric.net/2.1/binder.html?features/ brent/ wayin.html (see "A Way In" subsection).
4. See for example, Rudolph Arnheim, "A Plea for Visual Thinking," in *The Language of Images*, ed. W.J.T. Mitchell (Chicago: The University of Chicago Press, 1980), 171–179; Barbara Maria Stafford, *Good Looking: Essays on the Virtue of Images* (Cambridge, MA: The MIT Press, 1996); John Ruskiewicz, "Word and Image: The Next Revolution"; Kathleen E. Welch, *Electric Rhetoric: Classical Rhetoric, Oralism, and a New Literacy* (Cambridge, MA: The MIT Press, 1999).

5. See work by Diane S. Hope (*Visual Communication: Perception, Rhetoric, and Technology*); Lester Olson ("Benjamin Franklin's Pictorial Representations of the British Colonies in America: A Study in Rhetorical Iconology" and *Benjamin Franklin's Vision of American Community*); and Sonja Foss ("Rhetoric and the Visual Image: A Resource Unit"). Olson and Foss in particular have been studying visual rhetoric since the 1980s.

6. For an early, perceptive discussion of connections between poetry, the visual, and hypertext, see William Dickey, "Poem Descending a Staircase: Hypertext and the Simultaneity of Experience," in *Hypermedia and Literary Studies*, ed. Paul Delany and George P. Landow (Cambridge, MA: The MIT Press, 1991), 143–152.

7. See William C. Mann and Sandra A. Thompson, "Rhetorical Structure Theory," *Text* 8, no. 3 (1988): 243–281.

8. See also Nicholas C. Burbules, "Rhetorics of the Web: Hyperreading and Critical Literacy," in *Page to Screen: Taking Literacy into the Electronic Era*, ed. Ilana Snyder (London: Routledge, 1998), 102–122; also Christy Desmet, "Reading the Web as Fetish," *Computers and Composition* 18, no. 1 (March 2001), 55–72.

9. See Jane Yellowlees Douglas, "Will the Most Reflexive Relativist Please Stand Up: Hypertext, Argument and Relativism," in *Page to Screen: Taking Literacy into the Electronic Era*, ed. Ilana Snyder (London: Routledge, 1998), 144–162; and Doug Brent, "Rhetorics of the Web."

10. See Lanham's *Handlist*, pages 167–168 for 28 topics of argument, many of which lend themselves to the visual.

11. See *Iconology: Image, Text, Ideology* (Chicago: The University of Chicago Press, 1987), *The Language of Images* (Chicago: The University of Chicago Press, 1980), and *Picture Theory: Essays on Verbal and Visual Representation* (Chicago: The University of Chicago Press, 1994).

NOTES TO CHAPTER 2

1. This quotation comes courtesy of Sister Miriam Joseph, page 32, who used a translation edited by W.R. Ross and published by Oxford (1928).

2. Between them, these two scholars cite Quntilian, Donatus, Bede, Heinrich Lausberg, Harry Caplan, Puttenham, Peacham, Morris W. Croll, Jonas Barish, and George Williams, among others to show the extent of the debate over the meanings of tropes and figures. See Sister Miriam Joseph, 31–34, and Richard Lanham (*Handlist*, 155–156).

3. Mathematics, computer science, and engineering, disciplines that involve mathematical "language", use the term "syntax" quite liberally. See for example http://math.stackexchange.com/; entering the word "syntax" in the search tool yields, among other results, a question: "Where to learn the syntax of mathematics?" with replies and examples of mathematical syntax. Also see http://en.citizendium.org/wiki/Syntax_%28computer_science%29 for an explanation of syntax in programming languages. *Software Language Engineering: Creating Domain-Specific Languages Using Metamodels* by Anneke G. Kleppe (Upper Saddle River, NJ: Addison-Wesley Professional/Pearson Education, 2008) contains an entire chapter titled "Concrete Syntax".

4. For much more expansive explanations and extended discussions of these fields, see D'Andrade on culture and cognition, Deignan (*Metaphor and Corpus Linguistics* and "Conceptual Metaphor Theory") on conceptual metaphor theory, Eubanks on metaphor specifically and figurative thought generally,

Fahnestock on rhetoric and cognitive science, Hutchins on situated cognition, Lakoff and Johnson on metaphor, Lakoff and Turner on metaphor, and Mark Turner on English and cognitive science. By referring to this variety of fields, I hope to avoid confusing my use of the term "cognition" with the approach to cognition traditionally taken some decades ago by compositionists and composition researchers. Influenced by cognitive psychology and artificial intelligence research, this earlier approach is visible in the process-oriented studies of the late 1970s and 1980s. See Deborah McCutchen, Paul Teske, and Catherine Bankston's "Writing and Cognition: Implications of the Cognitive Architecture for Learning to Write and Writing to Learn."

5. See Ihab Hassan's *The Postmodern Turn: Essays in Postmodern Theory and Culture*, 91–92, for a schematic chart outlining the differences between modernism and postmodernism.

NOTES TO CHAPTER 3

1. Lanham's explanation of this distinction can be found throughout his work, from *The Electronic Word* to *Analyzing Prose* to *The Economics of Attention*. See in particular Lanham's "Preface to the Second Edition" of *Analyzing Prose*, page xii, and Chapter 9 in *Analyzing Prose*, "Opaque Styles and Transparent Styles," especially pages 207 through 209.
2. Paul Harvey's radio program "The Rest of the Story" aired on ABC Radio Networks until 2008.
3. For current information on community college funding, see *Delta Cost Project on Postsecondary Education Costs, Productivity, and Accountability* (http://www.deltacostproject.org); Donna M. Desrochers and Jane V. Wellman, *Trends in College Spending 1999–2009: Where Does the Money Come From? Where Does It Go? What Does It Buy?* (A Report of the Delta Cost Project, Washington, DC: Delta Cost Project, 2011); Richard Kahlenberg, "How to Boost Spending on Community Colleges," *The Chronicle of Higher Education* (28 January 2012) (http://chronicle.com/blogs/innovations/how-to-boost-spending-on-community-colleges/30394); California Legislative Analyst's Office, "Higher Education," *2011 Cal Facts: California's Economy and Budget in Perspective* (http://www.lao.ca.gov/reports/2011/calfacts/calfacts_010511.aspx#zzee_link_ 39_1294170707); Tamar Lewin, "Spending Inequity in Colleges Has Risen," *The New York Times* (14 September 2011) (http://www.nytimes.com/2011/09/14/education.14delta.html); Grace Chen, "State Spending Impacting Graduation Rates at Community Colleges across the Country," *Community College Review* (14 July 2011) (http://www.communitycollegereview.com/articles/367); and Brian Burnsed, "Community Colleges Get Squeezed" *Bloomberg Businessweek* (15 January 2009) (http://www.businessweek.com/bschools/content/jan2009/ bs20090115_797474.htm).
4. See Clair Potter's TEDx talk "Classrooms of the Future" for more thoughts about the recession's influence on diversity, or the actual lack thereof, in education. Thanks to Will Hochman for this reference (http://tedxtalks.ted.com/video/TEDxConnecticutCollege-Claire-P).
5. See Paul Fain, "Community College Chancellor Opposes Differential Tuition," *Inside Higher Ed* (5 April 2013) (www.insidehighered.com/news/2013/04/05/california-community-college-chancellor-opposes-differential-tuition); Michael Higham, "Community College Enrollment Decline Continues in California," *Independent Voter Network* (29 March 2013) (http://ivn.us/progress-report/2013/03/29/community-college-enrollment-decline-

continues-in-california/); Nannette Miranda, "Community College Fee Rising to $46 Per Unit," *KABC-TV/DT California News* (18 December 2011) (http://abclocal.go.com/kabc/story? section=news/ state&id=8471836); and Carla Rivera, "California's Community Colleges Staggering during Hard Times," *LATimes.com* (22 September 2012) (http://latimes.com/news/local/la-me-college-overview-20120923,0,3310236.story).

6. For more background on community colleges, their missions, and their funding, see Arthur M. Cohen and Florence B. Brawer, *The American Community College*, 5th ed. (San Francisco, CA: Jossey-Bass, 2008); George B. Vaughan, *The Community College Story*, 3rd ed. (Washington, DC: Community College Press, 2006); George A. Baker, III, ed., Judy Dudziak and Peggy Tyler, technical eds., *A Handbook on the Community College in America: Its History, Mission, and Management* (Westport, CT: Greenwood Press, 1994); Barbara K. Townsend and Kevin J. Dougherty, eds., "Community College Missions in the 21st Century," *New Directions for Community Colleges*, issue no. 136 (winter 2006), 5-99; and Josh M. Beach, *Gateway to Opportunity: A History of the Community College in the United States* (Sterling, VA: Stylus Publishing, LLC, 2011.

NOTES TO CHAPTER 4

1. Detroit's history and its collapse during the past few decades as one of the country's great urban centers have been chronicled in studies such as: *The Origins of the Urban Crisis: Race and Inequality in Postwar Detroit* (Princeton Studies in American Politics) by Thomas J. Sugrue, rev. ed. (Princeton, NJ: Princeton University Press, 2005); *Detroit Divided* by Reynolds Farley (New York: Russell Sage Foundation Publication, 2002); *Whose Detroit? Politics, Labor, and Race in a Modern American City* by Heather Ann Thompson (Ithaca, NY: Cornell University Press, 2001).

2. A short segue here about this motto and the rhetorical figure "anaphora": we can understand how anaphora works in spoken or written texts—that is, repetition of a word or phrase at the beginnings of successive phrases or clauses—to emphasize an idea or object so that we cannot forget it as a focal point. Furthermore, just as anaphora can hold together a sermon rhetorically and increase an emotional impact, the fused motto "Imported from Detroit" with its accompanying winged Chrysler logo laces together the entire Chrysler Web site.

3. More about the complications of ethos and more detailed explanations and examples can be found in Sister Miriam Joseph's work, in particular Chapter 9 of *Shakespeare's Use of the Arts of Language* titled "Pathos and Ethos". Section 2 on Ethos begins on page 393.

4. For more on the banking model of education, see Chapter 2 of Paulo Freire's *Pedagogy of the Oppressed*.

NOTES TO CHAPTER 5

1. For an overview of delivery as conceived and studied historically, see Ray Nadeau's "Delivery in Ancient Times: Homer to Quintilian," *Quarterly Journal of Speech* 50, no. 1 (February 1964): 53–60, as well as Martin Jacobi's "The Canon of Delivery in Rhetorical Theory: Selections, Commentary, and Advice," in *Delivering College Composition: The Fifth Canon*, edited

by Kathleen Blake Yancey (Portsmouth, NH: Boyton/Cook Publishers, Inc., 2006), 17–29.

2. My musings on delivery and performance were triggered by a casual aside that Richard Lanham made during his March 2012 Conference on College Composition and Communication presentation "'That Stuff Hasn't Changed Much in 2500 Years, Has It?': Rhetorical Terms in an Attention Economy." He mentioned Tom Beghin's work on Haydn, performance, and rhetoric. That comment connecting rhetoric and music was too intriguing to pass up, mainly because I had never thought of musical performances being rhetorical. But it certainly makes sense. While *Haydn and the Performance of Rhetoric* (edited by Tom Beghin and Sander M. Goldberg, Chicago: The University of Chicago Press, 2007) contains several intriguing chapters, the ones I found the most compelling for my own thinking about digital presentations are the ones by the editors themselves: Beghin and Goldberg's "Introduction" (1–13), Goldberg's "Performing Theory: Variations on a Theme by Quintilian" (39–60), and Beghin's "'Delivery, Delivery, Delivery!' Crowning the Rhetorical Process of Haydn's Keyboard Sonatas" (131–171).

3. For a detailed report on the resonance of the Smith/Carlos raised fist salute, see in particular Oliver Brown's 12 July 2012 report from the 2012 London Olympics "London 2012 Olympics: Tommie Smith and John Carlos' famous Black Power salute still resonates 44 years on," published in the *Telegraph* (http://www.telegraph.co.uk/sport/ olympics/9393260/London-2012-Olympics-Tommie-Smith-and-John-Carlos-famous-Black-Power-salute-still-resonates-44-years-on.html); and a film by Matt Norman, *For the Record, Salute: The Story behind the Image* (Film Finance Corporation Australia Limited, 2008; Warner Bros., 2012) with a brief introduction and details about availability on the film's Web site (http://salutethemovie.com/).

4. For only a small sampling, see Walter R. Allen, "The Color of Success: African-American College Student Outcomes at Predominantly White and Historically Black Public Colleges and Universities," *Harvard Educational Review* 62 no. 1 (Spring 1992): 26–44; Henry T. Frierson, Willie Pearson, and James H. Wyche, eds., *Black American Males in Higher Education: Diminishing Proportions*, Diversity in Higher Education 6–7 (Bradford, UK: Emerald Group Publishing Ltd, 2009); Wynetta Y. Lee, "Striving toward Effective Retention: The Effect of Race on Mentoring African American Students," *Peabody Journal of Education* 74 no. 2 (2000): 27–43; Chance W. Lewis, "The Decision: Maximizing Our Position within the Academy to Improve Educational Outcomes of African American Males," *Journal of African American Males in Education* 2 no. 1 (Feb/Mar 2011): 1–4; Robert T. Palmer, "A Strong Focus on Collaborations between K–12 and Higher Education to Increase Enrollment and Success of Black Men in Postsecondary Education," *Journal of African American Males in Education* 3 no. 1 (Summer 2012): i–ii; and Dominique L. Thomas, Chauncey D. Smith, Bryant T. Marks, and Brandon Crosby, "Institutional Identity and Self-Esteem among African American Males in College," *Journal of African American Males in Education* 3 no. 1 (Summer 2012): 1–11.

NOTES TO CHAPTER 6

1. Geoff Sirc has broached the subject of "writing as museum exhibit" in his chapter, "Box-Logic," in *Writing New Media*. Sirc focuses on ways to help students envision text as less linear and essayistic. For him, students should

be introduced to text as Duchampian box or collage, that is, fragmentary, synecdochic collections of text and images that convey students' particular intellectual passions and that resemble museum exhibits.

If we (finally) journey away from the linear norm of essayist prose, which the texts of the everyday world implore us to do, where do we go, especially in a composition classroom? What sorts of formal and material concerns guide a newly-mediated pedagogical practice? . . . In terms of transcending essayist prose, then, and all its conventions/ restrictions/impediments, the [Duchampian] box offers a grammar which could prove useful . . . it allows both textual pleasure, as students archive their personal collections of text and imagery, and formal practice in learning the compositional skills that seem increasingly important in contemporary culture . . . . So, as readers, we might best take the anticipatory stance towards texts: ready to enter an exhibit; students as curators, mounting another show of the ever-evolving permanent collection at their musées imaginaries. Text, then as a collection of retrojective idiosyncratic dream-moments, now electronically gathered, framed, and exhibited. (114–116)

While Sirc proposes the idea of student as curator and writing as art exhibit, our foci in this volume are different: I am therefore concentrating more on our students as readers of such texts, as visitors to others' exhibits, and as analytic viewers of texts taking the form of Web sites.

2. Marjorie Ferguson explains in "Marshall McLuhan Revisited: 1960s Zeitgeist Victim or Pioneer Postmodernist?" that "McLuhan's mythos apprehended media as art forms to be studied as symbolic structures with their own language and grammar and subsequently expanded into trans-historical social metaphors" (75). Later in this essay Ferguson adds:

In expanding media 'languages' into social metaphors about Western civilization, McLuhan combined *exploration* with interpretation. From his earliest critiques of American advertising and popular culture in the 1940s, his 'reading' of the symbolic universes of comics, cars, ironing boards and clothes, predates by a considerable margin the discovery of ontological truth and epistemological certainty in advertisements, television, blue jeans and the built environment by writers from Barthes (1957) onwards. In this sense McLuhan was a founding father, pointing the way for later practitioners of the texts, rhetorics or discourses of popular cultural artifacts and media technologies. (83)

3. Other museums and memorials that might lend themselves to such analysis and study are the National Civil Rights Museum in Memphis, Tennessee; the Journey Museum in Rapid City, South Dakota; the US Holocaust Memorial Museum in Washington, DC; and the Martin Luther King Jr. National Memorial in Washington, DC.

4. For a more detailed explanation of exactly how to structure such an exercise, see my chapter in Golson and Glover, especially pages 28–36.

5. Sturken's more recent work is an entire volume on different aspects of the Vietnam War: *Tangled Memories: The Vietnam War, the AIDS Epidemic, and the Politics of Remembering* (Berkeley: The University of California Press, 1997).

6. Two that do are Patrick Hagopian's study *The Vietnam War in American Memory: Veterans, Memorials, and the Politics of Healing* (Amherst: The University of Massachusetts Press, 2009); and director Freida Lee Mock's film *Maya Lin—A Strong Clear Vision* (New York: New Video Group, 1995).

7. I would like to point out that scholars in other disciplines besides museum/ exhibition studies must think in terms of space as they construct knowledge. Physicists, for instance, must construct visual, spatial representations of their ideas, and they must communicate within these "spaces". Applied linguists Elinor Ochs, Sally Jacoby, and Patrick Gonzales have studied physicists' means of communication as they are working in graphic space: "Interpretive Journeys: How Physicists Talk and Travel through Graphic Space," *Configurations* 2, no. 1 (1984): 151–171.

Bibliography

Academy of American Poets. http://www.poets.org.

Allen, Walter R. "The Color of Success: African-American College Student Outcomes at Predominantly White and Historically Black Public Colleges and Universities." *Harvard Educational Review* 62, no. 1 (Spring 1992): 26–44.

American River College. www.arc.losrios.edu.

Apple. www.apple.com.

———. *1984 Macintosh Commercial*. http://www.youtube.com/watch?v=HhsWzJo2sN4.

———. "Jobs at Apple." http://www.apple.com/jobs/us/.

———. "Jobs at Apple: Corporate." http://www.apple.com/jobs/us/corporate.html.

———. "The Story behind Apple's Environmental Footprint." http://www.apple.com/environment/.

———. "Supplier Responsibility at Apple." http://www.apple.com/supplierresponsibility/.

Aristotle. *On Rhetoric: A Theory of Civic Discourse*. Translated by George A. Kennedy. New York: Oxford University Press, 1991.

Arnheim, Rudolph. "A Plea for Visual Thinking." In *The Language of Images*, edited by W.J.T. Mitchell, 171–179. Chicago: The University of Chicago Press, 1980.

Bach, Johann Sebastian. *Suites for Violoncello Solo*, BWV 1007–1012, 6–7. Performed by Anner Bylsma. New York: Sony Music Entertainment, Inc., 1992. Compact Discs: S2K 48047.

Baker, George A. III, ed., Judy Dudziak and Peggy Tyler, technical eds. *A Handbook on the Community College in America: Its History, Mission, and Management*. Westport, CT: Greenwood Press, 1994.

Barthes, Roland. *Image | Music | Text*. Translated by Stephen Heath. New York: Hill and Wang, 1977.

Beach, Josh M. *Gateway to Opportunity: A History of the Community College in the United States*. Sterling, VA: Stylus Publishing, LLC, 2011.

Beghin, Tom. "'Delivery, Delivery, Delivery!' Crowning the Rhetorical Process of Haydn's Keyboard Sonatas." In *Haydn and the Performance of Rhetoric*, edited by Tom Beghin and Sander M. Goldberg, 131–171. Chicago: The University of Chicago Press, 2007.

Beghin, Tom and Sander M. Goldberg. "Introduction." In *Haydn and the Performance of Rhetoric*, edited by Tom Beghin and Sander M. Goldberg, 1–13. Chicago: The University of Chicago Press, 2007.

Berlin, James A. *Rhetorics, Poetics, and Cultures: Refiguring College English Studies*. Urbana, IL: National Council of Teachers of English, 1996.

Biomimicry Group, Inc. and HOK Group, Inc. *Genius of Biome.* Available at Issuu. com. http://issuu.com/hoknetwork/docs/geniusofbiome?mode=window.

Birkman, Marlene Ann. *Gyo Obata: Architect | Clients | Reflections.* Mulgrave, Australia: Images Publishing Group Pty Ltd, 2010.

Birmingham Civil Rights Institute. http://www.bcri.org/.

Blair, Anthony J. "The Possibility and Actuality of Visual Arguments." *Argumentation and Advocacy* 33 (1996): 23–39.

Bodmer, Paul. "Is It Pedagogical or Administrative? Administering Distance Delivery to High Schools." In *Delivering College Composition: The Fifth Canon,* edited by Kathleen Blake Yancey, 115–126. Portsmouth, NH: Boynton/Cook Publishers, Inc., 2006.

Bolter, Jay David. "Hypertext and the Question of Visual Literacy." In *Handbook of Literacy and Technology: Transformations in a Post-typographic World,* edited by David Reinking, Michael C. McKenna, Linda D. Labbo, and Ronald D. Kieffer, 3–13. Mahwah, NJ: Lawrence Erlbaum Associates, 1998.

———. "Hypertext and the Rhetorical Canons." In *Rhetorical Memory and Delivery: Classical Concepts for Contemporary Composition and Communication,* edited by John Frederick Reynolds, 97–111. Mahwah, NJ: Lawrence Erlbaum Associates, Inc., 1993. Digital printing, New York: Routledge, 2009.

———. *Writing Space: The Computer, Hypertext and the History of Writing.* Hillsdale, NJ: Lawrence Erlbaum Associates, Inc., 1991.

Bolter, Jay David and Richard Grusin. *Remediation: Understanding New Media.* Cambridge, MA: The MIT Press, 1999.

Bose Corporation. www.bose.com.

Bowker, Geoffrey C. and Susan Leigh Star. *Sorting Things Out: Classification and Its Consequences.* Cambridge, MA: The MIT Press, 2000.

Brasseur, Lee. "Visual Literacy in the Computer Age: A Complex Perceptual Landscape." In *Computers and Technical Communication: Pedagogical and Programmatic Perspectives,* edited by Stuart A. Selber, 75–96. Greenwich, CT: Ablex Publishing Corp., 1997.

Brent, Doug. "Rhetorics of the Web: Implications for Teachers of Literacy." *Kairos* 2, no. 1 (Spring 1997). http://kairos.technorhetoric.net/2.1/binder. html?features/brent/wayin.html.

Bristol Community College. www.bristolcc.edu.

Brooke, Collin Gifford. *Lingua Fracta: Toward a Rhetoric of New Media.* Cresskill, NJ: Hampton Press, 2009.

Brown, Oliver. "London 2012 Olympics: Tommie Smith and John Carlos' Famous Black Power Salute Still Resonates 44 Years On." *The Telegraph* (12 July 2012). http://www.telegraph.co.uk/sport/olympics/9393260/London-2012-Olympics-Tommie-Smith-and-John-Carlos-famous-Black-Power-salute-still-resonates-44-years-on.html).

Brown University. www.brown.edu.

Browne, Sir Thomas. *Urne-Burial.* London: Penguin Books Ltd, 2005.

Buchanan, Richard. "Declaration by Design: Rhetoric, Argument, and Demonstration in Design Practice." In *Design Discourse: History, Theory, Criticism,* edited by Victor Margolin, 91–109. Chicago: The University of Chicago Press, 1989.

Burbules, Nicholas C. "Rhetorics of the Web: Hyperreading and Critical Literacy." In *Page to Screen: Taking Literacy into the Electronic Era,* edited by Ilana Snyder, 102–122. London: Routledge. 1998.

Burnsed, Brian. "Community Colleges Get Squeezed." *Bloomberg Businessweek,* (15 January 2009). http://www.businessweek.com/bschools/content/jan2009/bs20090115_797474.htm.

California Legislative Analyst's Office. "Higher Education." *2011 Cal Facts: California's Economy and Budge in Perspective.* http://www.lao.ca.gov/reports/2011/calfacts/calfacts_010511.aspx#zzee_link_39_1294170707.

Carpenter, Edmund and Marshall McLuhan, eds. *Explorations in Communication.* Boston: The Beacon Press, 1960; 1966.

Cavell, Richard. "McLuhan and Spatial Communication." *Western Journal of Communication* 63, no. 3 (Summer 1999): 348–363.

Chen, Grace. "State Spending Impacting Graduation Rates at Community Colleges across the Country." *Community College Review* (14 July 2011). http://www.communitycollegereview.com/articles/367.

Chrysler Group LLC. *The Chrysler 300: A Legendary Pedigree.* http://www.chrysler history.com/IconicVehicles/Content.aspx?topic-The-Chrysler-300.

———. www.chrysler.com.

———. *Imported from Detroit: Videos.* www.importedfromdetroit.com/videos/.

Cohen, Arthur M. and Florence B. Brawer. *The American Community College.* 5th ed. San Francisco, CA: Jossey-Bass, 2008.

Columbia University. www.columbia.edu.

Cope, Bill and Mary Kalantzis. *Multiliteracies: Literacy Learning and the Design of Social Futures.* London: Routledge, 2000.

Cornell University. www.cornell.edu.

Cowboy Poets Society International. http://www.cowboyrudy.com/cbyptsoc.htm.

Crick, Nathan, Loretta Pecchioni, and Joni Butcher. *Deconstructing Communication: An Introduction to Rhetorical, Performance, and Communication Theory.* Boston: Pearson Custom Publishing, 2007.

D'Andrade, Roy Goodwin. "The Cultural Part of Cognition." *Cognitive Science* 5 (1981): 179–195.

Dartmouth College. www.dartmouth.edu.

Deignan, Alice. "Conceptual Metaphor Theory." *Metaphor Analysis Project.* The Centre for Research in Education and Educational Technology. UK: The Open University, 2005. http://creet.open.ac.uk/projects/metaphor-analysis.

———. *Metaphor and Corpus Linguistics.* Amsterdam: John Benjamins, 2005.

Delta Cost Project on Postsecondary Education Costs, Productivity, and Accountability. http://www.deltacostproject.org.

Desmet, Christy. "Reading the Web as Fetish." *Computers and Composition* 18, no. 1 (March 2001): 55–72.

Desrochers, Donna M. and Jane V. Wellman. *Trends in College Spending 1999–2009: Where Does the Money Come From? Where Does It Go? What Does It Buy?* A Report of the Delta Cost Project. Washington, DC: Delta Cost Project, 2011.

DeVoss, Danielle Nicole and James E. Porter. "Why Napster Matters to Writing: Filesharing as a New Ethic of Digital Delivery." *Computers and Composition* 23, no. 2 (May 2006): 178–210.

Dickey, William. "Poem Descending a Staircase: Hypertext and the Simultaneity of Experience." In *Hypermedia and Literary Studies,* edited by Paul Delany and George P. Landow, 143–152. Cambridge, MA: The MIT Press, 1991.

Douglas, Jane Yellowlees. "Will the Most Reflexive Relativist Please Stand Up: Hypertext, Argument and Relativism." In *Page to Screen: Taking Literacy into the Electronic Era,* edited by Ilana Snyder, 144–162. London: Routledge, 1998.

Douglas, Mary. *How Institutions Think.* Syracuse, NY: Syracuse University Press, 1986.

Dragga, Sam. "The Ethics of Delivery." In *Rhetorical Memory and Delivery: Classical Concepts for Contemporary Composition and Communication,* edited by

John Frederick Reynolds, 79–95. Mahwah, NJ: Lawrence Erlbaum Associates, Inc., 1993. Digital reprinting, New York: Routledge, 2009.

Elkins, James. "Problems of Classification." In *The Domain of Images*, 82–91. Ithaca, NY: Cornell University Press, 1999.

Eubanks, Philip. *Metaphor and Writing: Figurative Thought in the Discourse of Written Communication*. Cambridge, England: Cambridge University Press, 2011.

Fahnestock, Jeanne. "Rhetoric in the Age of Cognitive Science." In *The Viability of Rhetoric*, edited by Richard Graff, 159–180. New York: State University of New York Press, 2005.

Fain, Paul. "Community College Chancellor Opposes Differential Tuition." *Inside Higher Ed*, (5 April 2013). www.insidehighered.com/news/2013/04/05/california-community-college-chancellor-opposes-differential-tuition.

Farley, Reynolds. *Detroit Divided*. New York, NY: Russell Sage Foundation Publication, 2002.

Ferguson, Bruce W. "Exhibition Rhetorics: Material Speech and Utter Sense." In *Thinking about Exhibitions*, edited by Reesa Greenberg, Bruce W. Ferguson, and Sandy Nairne, 175–190. London: Routledge, 1996.

Ferguson, Marjorie. "Marshall McLuhan: 1960s Zeitgeist Victim or Pioneer Postmodernist?" *Media, Culture and Society* 13, no. 1 (1991): 71–90.

Forster, E.M. *Howards End*. New York: Random House, 1921. Reprint, New York: Vintage Books, 1921.

Foss, Sonja K. "Rhetoric and the Visual Image: A Resource Unit." *Communication Education* 31, no. 1 (1982): 55–67.

———. "A Rhetorical Schema for the Evaluation of Visual Imagery." *Communication Studies* 45 (Fall–Winter 1994): 213–224.

———. "Visual Imagery as Communication." *Text and Performance Quarterly* 12 (1992): 85–96.

Foucault, Michel. "Of Other Spaces." Translated by Jay Miskowiec. *Diacritics* 16, no. 1 (1986): 22–27.

Freire, Paulo. *Pedagogy of the Oppressed*. Translated by Myra Bergman Ramos. New York: Continuum, 1993.

Frierson, Henry T., Willie Pearson, and James H. Wyche, eds. *Black American Males in Higher Education: Diminishing Proportions*. Diversity in Higher Education, Volume 6. Bradford, UK: Emerald Group Publishing Ltd, 2009.

———. *Black American Males in Higher Education: Research Programs in Academe*. Diversity in Higher Education, Volume 7. Bradford, UK: Emerald Group Publishing Ltd, 2009.

Gaines, Robert N. "An Introduction to Rhetorical Delivery." http://www.arsrhetorica.net/gaines/delivery.html.

Gallagher, Victoria J. "Memory and Reconciliation in the Birmingham Civil Rights Institute." *Rhetoric & Public Affairs* 2, no. 2 (1999): 303–320.

Gallop, Jane. "The Historicization of Literary Studies and the Fate of Close Reading." *Profession* (2007): 181–186.

Geertz, Clifford. *The Interpretation of Cultures*. New York: Basic Books, Inc., 1973.

Gencarella, Stephen Olbrys and Phaedra C. Pezzullo, eds. *Readings on Rhetoric and Performance*. State College, PA: Strata Publishing, Inc., 2010.

Goldberg, Sander M. "Performing Theory: Variations on a Theme by Quintilian." In *Haydn and the Performance of Rhetoric*, edited by Tom Beghin and Sander M. Goldberg, 39–60. Chicago: The University of Chicago Press, 2007.

Goldfarb, Brian. *Visual Pedagogy: Media Cultures in and between the Classroom*. Durham, NC: Duke University Press, 2002.

Golson, Emily and Toni Glover, eds. *Negotiating a Meta-pedagogy: Learning from Other Disciplines*. Newcastle upon Tyne, UK: Cambridge Scholars Publishing, 2009.

Goody, Jack. "What's in a List?" In *Literacy: A Critical Sourcebook*, edited by Ellen Cushman, Eugene R. Kintgen, Barry M. Kroll, and Mike Rose, 32–51. Boston: Bedford/St. Martin's, 2001.

Haas, Lynda, Elizabeth Losh, and Ellen Strenski. "Learning Outcomes of the UCI Lower-Division GE Writing Requirement: The Capstone Research Paper in WR 39C and Humanities 1C." 25 September 2006. Composition Program: The University of California, Irvine. http://eee.uci.edu/programs/comp/.

Hagopian, Patrick. *The Vietnam War in American Memory: Veterans, Memorials, and the Politics of Healing*. Amherst: The University of Massachusetts Press, 2009.

Handa, Carolyn. "Digital Space: Crossing Untraditional Frontiers." In *Negotiating a Meta-pedagogy: Learning from Other Disciplines*, edited by Emily Golson and Toni Glover, 21–38. Newcastle upon Tyne, UK: Cambridge Scholars Publishing, 2009.

———, ed. Special Issues on Visual Rhetoric. *Computers and Composition* 18, nos. 1 & 2 (2001).

———, ed. *Visual Rhetoric in a Digital World: A Critical Sourcebook*. Boston: Bedford/St. Martin's, 2004.

Harold Washington College. www.ccc.edu/colleges/Washington/.

Harris, Roy. *Signs of Writing*. London: Routledge, 1995.

Harvard University. www.harvard.edu.

Hassan, Ihab. *The Postmodern Turn: Essays in Postmodern Theory and Culture*. Columbus, OH: The Ohio State University Press, 1987.

Hawhee, Debra. "The Visible Spoken: Rhetoric, Athletics, and the Circulation of Honor." In *Bodily Arts: Rhetoric and Athletics in Ancient Greece*, 162–187. Austin, TX: The University of Texas Press, 2004.

Hawisher, Gail E. "Blinding Insights: Classification Schemes and Software for Literacy Instruction." In *Literacy and Computers: The Complications of Teaching and Learning with Technology*, edited by Cynthia L. Selfe and Susan Hilligoss, 37–55. New York: The Modern Language Association of America, 1994.

Hawisher, Gail and Cynthia L. Selfe. *Literate Lives in the Information* Age: *Narratives of Literacy from the United States*. Mahwah, NJ: Lawrence Erlbaum Associates, Inc., 2004.

Heaney, Seamus. "From the Frontier of Writing." In *The Haw Lantern*, 6. New York: Farrar Straus Giroux, 1987.

Higham, Michael. "Community College Enrollment Decline Continues in California." *Independent Voter Network* (29 March 2013). http://ivn.us/progress-report/2013/03/29/community-college-enrollment-decline-continues-in-california/.

Hilligoss, Susan. *Visual Communication: A Writer's Guide*. New York: Longman, 1999.

Hilligoss, Susan and Sean Williams. "Composition Meets Visual Communication." In *Digital Writing Research: Technologies, Methodologies, and Ethical Issues*, edited by Heidi A. McKee and Danielle Nicole DeVoss, 229–247. Cresskill, NJ: Hampton Press, Inc., 2007.

Hinde, Robert A. *Non-verbal Communication*. Cambridge, England: Cambridge University Press, 1972.

Hocks, Mary E. and Michelle R, Kendrick, eds. *Eloquent Images: Word and Image in the Age of New Media*. Cambridge, MA: The MIT Press, 2005.

Hodge, Robert and Gunther Kress. "Classification and Control." In *Language as Ideology*, 62–84. 2nd ed. London: Routledge, 1993.

HOK: Helmuth, Obata, Kassabaum. "Design Practice." http://www.hok.com.

Hope, Diane S. *Visual Communication: Perception, Rhetoric, and Technology*. Cresskill, NJ: Hampton Press, Inc., 2006.

Horn, Robert. *Visual Language: Global Communication for the 21st Century.* Bainbridge Island, WA: MacroVU, Inc., 1998.

Horvath, Agnes, Bjørn Thomassen, and Harald Wydra. "Introduction: Liminality and Cultures of Change." *International Political Anthropology* 2, no. 1 (2009): 3–4.

Hutchins, Edwin. *Cognition in the Wild.* Cambridge, MA: The MIT Press, 1996.

Internet Poetry Archive. http://www.ibiblio.org.

Isaacson, Walter. *Steve Jobs.* New York: Simon & Schuster, 2011.

Jacobi, Martin. "The Canon of Delivery in Rhetorical Theory: Selections, Commentary, and Advice." In *Delivering College Composition: The Fifth Canon,* edited by Kathleen Blake Yancey, 17–29. Portsmouth, NH: Boynton/Cook Publishers, Inc., 2006.

Janof, Tim. "Conversation with Anner Bylsma." *Tutti Celli* 4, no. 6 (November/December 1998): 1–12. http://www.cello.org/Newsletter/Articles/bylsma.htm.

Japanese American National Museum. http://www.janm.org/.

Joseph, Sister Miriam. *Shakespeare's Use of the Arts of Language.* Philadelphia: Paul Dry Books, 2005.

Journey Museum. http://www.journeymuseum.org.

Joyce, Michael. "Siren Shapes: Exploratory and Constructive Hypertexts." *Academic Computing* 3, no. 4 (1988): 10–14, 37–42. Also available in *Of Two Minds: Hypertext Pedagogy and Poetics,* 39–69. Ann Arbor, MI: The University of Michigan Press, 1995.

Kahlenberg, Richard. "How to Boost Spending on Community Colleges." *The Chronicle of Higher Education* (28 January 2012). http://chronicle.com/blogs/innovations/how-to-boost-spending-on-community-colleges/30394.

Kaufer, David S. and Brian S. Butler. *Designing Interactive Worlds with Words.* Mahwah, NJ: Lawrence Erlbaum Associates, 2000.

———. *Rhetoric and the Arts of Design.* Mahwah, NJ: Lawrence Erlbaum Associates, 1996.

Keedy, Jeffery. "The Rules of Typography according to ~~Crackpots~~ Experts." In *Looking Closer 2: Critical Writings on Graphic Design,* edited by Michael Beirut, William Drentell, Steven Heller, and D.K. Holland, 49–52. New York: Allworth Press, 1997.

Keller, Josh. "Colleges Rehab Their Web Sites for Major Payoffs." *The Chronicle of Higher Education* 57, no. 33 (22 April 2011): A10–A11.

Kimme Hea, Amy C. "Destabilizing the Categories of New Media Research." *JAC: A Journal of Rhetoric, Culture, & Politics* 28, no. 3–4 (2008): 738–749.

———, ed. *Going Wireless: A Critical Exploration of Wireless and Mobile Technologies for Composition Teachers and Researchers.* Cresskill, NJ: Hampton Press, 2009.

———. "Riding the Wave." In *Digital Writing Research: Technologies, Methodologies, and Ethical Issues,* edited by Heidi A. McKee and Danielle Nicole DeVoss, 269–286. Cresskill, NJ: Hampton Press, Inc., 2007.

Kinross, Robin. "The Rhetoric of Neutrality." In *Design Discourse: History | Theory | Criticism,* edited by Victor Margolin, 131–143. Chicago: The University of Chicago Press, 1989.

Klein, Julia. "Review of *Detroit: A Biography* by Scott Martelle." Special to the *Los Angeles Times* (26 April 2012). http://latimes.com/entertainment/news/la-et-book-scott-martelle-20120426,0,781969.story.

Kleppe, Anneke G. *Software Language Engineering: Creating Domain-Specific Languages Using Metamodels.* Upper Saddle River, NJ: Addison-Wesley Professional/Pearson Education, 2008.

Kolowich, Steve. "No Laughing Matter." *Inside Higher Ed* (4 August 2011). http://www.insidehighered.com/news/2010/08/04/websites.

Kress, Gunther. *Literacy in the New Media Age*. London: Routledge, 2003.

Lakoff, George. "The Importance of Classification." In *Women, Fire, and Dangerous Things: What Categories Reveal about the Mind*, 5–11. Chicago: The University of Chicago Press, 1987.

Lakoff, George and Mark Johnson. *Metaphors We Live By*. Chicago: The University of Chicago Press, 1981.

Lakoff, George and Mark Turner. *More Than Cool Reason: A Field Guide to Poetic Metaphor*. Chicago: The University of Chicago Press, 1989.

Landow, George. *Hypertext—The Convergence of Contemporary Critical Theory and Technology*. Baltimore, MD: John Hopkins University Press, 1992.

Lanham, Richard A. *Analyzing Prose*. 2nd ed. London: Continuum, 2003.

———. "Digital Literacy." *Scientific American* 273, no. 3 (September 1995): 198, 200.

———. *The Economics of Attention: Style and Substance in the Age of Information*. Chicago: The University of Chicago Press, 2006.

———. *The Electronic Word: Democracy, Technology, and the Arts*. Chicago: The University of Chicago Press, 1993.

———. *A Handlist of Rhetorical Terms*. 2nd ed. Berkeley: The University of California Press, 1991.

———. "'That Stuff Hasn't Changed Much in 2500 Years, Has It?': Rhetorical Terms in an Attention Economy." Featured speaker at the 2012 Conference on College Composition and Communication, 63rd Annual Convention. St. Louis, MO. 21–24 March 2012.

Lauer, Janice. "Composition Studies: Dappled Discipline." *Rhetoric Review* 3 (1984): 20–28.

Lawson, Alexander. *Anatomy of a Typeface*. Boston: David R. Godine Publisher, Inc., 1990.

Leach, Edmund. "The Influence of Cultural Context on Non-verbal Communication in Man." In *Non-verbal Communication*, edited by Robert A. Hinde, 315–347. Cambridge, England: Cambridge University Press, 1972.

Lee, Wynetta Y. "Striving toward Effective Retention: The Effect of Race on Mentoring African American Students." *Peabody Journal of Education* 74, no. 2 (2000): 27–43.

Lemke, J.L. "Metamedia Literacy: Transforming Meanings and Media." In *Handbook of Literacy and Technology: Transformations in a Post-typographic World*, edited by David Reinking, Michael C. McKenna, Linda D. Labbo, and Ronald D. Kieffer, 283–301. Mahwah, NJ: Lawrence Erlbaum Associates, 1998.

———. "Multiplying Meaning: Visual and Verbal Semiotics in Scientific Text." In *Reading Science: Critical and Functional Perspectives on Discourses of Science* edited by J.R. Martin and Robert Veel, 87–113. London: Routledge, 1998.

Lewin, Tamar. "Spending Inequity in Colleges Has Risen." *The New York Times* (14 September 2011). www.nytimes.com/2011/09/14/education.14delta.html.

Lewis, Chance W. "The Decision: Maximizing Our Position within the Academy to Improve Educational Outcomes of African American Males." *Journal of African American Males in Education* 2, no. 1 (Feb/Mar 2011): 1–4.

Light, Pamela. "Interior Design: Tailor Made." *HOK Knowledge Center*. http://www.HOK.com.

Lorain County Community College. www.lorainccc.edu.

Manjoo, Farhad. "Overdone: Why Are Restaurant Websites So Horrifically Bad?" *Slate* (9 August 2011). http://www.slate.com/articles/technology/technology/2011/08/ overdone.html.

Mann, William C. and Sandra A. Thompson. "Rhetorical Structure Theory." *Text* 8, no. 3 (1988): 243–281.

Martelle, Scott. *Detroit: A Biography*. Chicago: Chicago Review Press, Inc., 2012.

Martin Luther King Jr. National Memorial. http://www.mlkmemorial.org/.

Mazurs, Edward G. *Graphic Representations of the Periodic System during One Hundred Years*. Tuscaloosa, AL: The University of Alabama Press, 1957.

McCorkle, Ben. *Rhetorical Delivery as Technological Discourse: A Cross-Historical Study*. Carbondale, IL: Southern Illinois University Press, 2012.

McCutchen, Deborah, Paul Teske, and Catherine Bankston. "Writing and Cognition: Implications of the Cognitive Architecture for Learning to Write and Writing to Learn." In *Handbook of Research on Writing: History, Society, School, Individual, Text*, edited by Charles Bazerman, 451–470. New York: Routledge, 2010.

McLean, Ruari. *The Thames and Hudson Manual of Typography*. London: Thames and Hudson, 1980.

McLuhan, Marshall. "Classroom without Walls." In *Explorations in Communication*, edited by Edmund Carpenter and Marshall McLuhan, 1–3. Boston: The Beacon Press, 1960; 1967.

Meramec College. www.stlcc.edu/mc/.

Miranda, Nannette. "Community College Fee Rising to $46 Per Unit." *KABC-TV/ DT California News* (18 December 2011). http://abclocal.go.com/kabc/story?section=news/state&id=8471836.

Mishra, Punyashloke. "The Role of Abstraction in Scientific Illustration: Implications for Pedagogy." *Journal of Visual Literacy* 19, no. 2 (1999): 139–158.

Mitchell, Lee Clark. *Westerns: Making the Man in Fiction and Film*. Chicago: The University of Chicago Press, 1996.

Mitchell, W.J.T. *Iconology: Image, Text, Ideology*. Chicago: The University of Chicago Press, 1987.

———. *The Language of Images*. Chicago: The University of Chicago Press, 1980.

———. *Picture Theory: Essays on Verbal and Visual Representation*. Chicago: The University of Chicago Press, 1994.

Mitra, Ananda and Elisia Cohen. "Analyzing the Web: Directions and Challenges." In *Doing Internet Research: Critical Issues and Methods for Examining the Net*, edited by Steven G. Jones, 179–202. Thousand Oaks, CA: Sage Publications, Inc., 1999.

Mock, Freida Lee, director. *Maya Lin—A Strong Clear Vision*. DVD. New York: New Video Group, 1995. Film.

Moulthrop, Stuart. "The Politics of Hypertext." In *Evolving Perspectives on Computers and Composition Studies*, edited by Gail E. Hawisher and Cynthia L. Selfe, 253–271. Urbana, IL: National Council of Teachers of English, 1991.

———. "Reading from the Map: Metonymy and Metaphor in the Fiction of Forking Paths." In *Hypermedia and Literary Studies*, edited by Paul Delany and George P. Landow, 119–132. Cambridge, MA: The MIT Press, 1991.

Munroe, Randall. "University Website." *xkcd*. http://imgs.xkcd.com/comics/university_website.png.

Nadeau, Ray. "Delivery in Ancient Times: Homer to Quintilian." *Quarterly Journal of Speech* 50, no. 1 (February 1964): 53–60.

National Civil Rights Museum. http://www.civilrightsmuseum.org.

Neff, Joyce Magnotto. "Getting Our Money's Worth: Delivering Composition at a Comprehensive State University." In *Delivering College Composition: The Fifth Canon*, edited by Kathleen Blake Yancey, 48–59. Portsmouth, NH: Boynton/Cook Publishers, Inc., 2006.

Neiman Marcus. http://www.neimanmarcus.com/.

New London Group. "A Pedagogy of Multiliteracies: Designing Social Futures." *Harvard Educational Review* 66, no. 1 (1996): 60–92.

Norman, Matt. *Salute: The Story behind the Image.* Film Finance Corporation Australia Limited, 2008; Warner Bros., 2012. Available on iTunes, Amazon Instant Video, and Netflix.

Northcut, Kathryn. "Images as Facilitators of Public Participation in Science." *Journal of Visual Literacy* 26, no. 1 (Spring 2006): 1–14.

Occupy Wall Street. http://occupywallst.org.

Ochs, Elinor, Sally Jacoby, and Patrick Gonzales. "Interpretive Journeys: How Physicists Talk and Travel through Graphic Space." *Configurations* 2, no. 1 (1884): 151–171.

Olson, Lester C. "Benjamin Franklin's Pictorial Representations of the British Colonies and America: A Study in Rhetorical Iconology." *Quarterly Journal of Speech* 73 (1987): 18–42.

———. *Benjamin Franklin's Vision of American Community.* Columbia, SC: University of South Carolina Press, 2004.

Palmer, Robert T. "A Strong Focus on Collaborations between K–12 and Higher Education to Increase Enrollment and Success of Black Men in Postsecondary Education." *Journal of African American Males in Education* 3, no. 1 (Summer 2012): i–ii.

Porter, James E. "Recovering Delivery for Digital Rhetoric." *Computers and Composition* 26, no. 4 (December 2009): 207–224.

Potter, Claire. "Classrooms of the Future." TEDx Talks. http://tedxtalks.ted.com/video/TEDxConnecticutCollege-Claire-P.

Preminger, Alex, Frank Warnke, and O.B. Hardison, assoc. eds. *Princeton Encyclopedia of Poetry and Poetics.* Princeton, NY: Princeton University Press, 1965.

Princeton University. www.princeton.edu.

Prior, Paul, Janine Solberg, Patrick Berry, Hannah Bellwoar, Bill Chewning, Karen J. Lunsford, Liz Rohan, Kevin Roozen, Mary P. Sheridan-Rabideau, Jody Shipka, Derek Van Ittersum, and Joyce Walker. "Re-situating and Re-mediating the Canons: A Cultural-Historical Remapping of Rhetorical Activity." *Kairos* 11, no. 3 (2007). http://kairos.technorhetoric.net/11.3/binder.html?topoi/prior-et-al/index.html.

Rambsy, Howard II. *The Black Arts Enterprise and the Production of African American Poetry.* Ann Arbor: The University of Michigan Press, 2011.

———. *Cultural Front Blog.* http://www.culturalfront.org/.

———. howardrambsy.com.

———. Personal email. 1 November 2013.

Redd, Teresa. "Keepin' It Real: Delivering College Composition at an HBCU." In *Delivering College Composition: The Fifth Canon,* edited by Kathleen Blake Yancey, 72–88. Portsmouth, NH: Boynton/Cook Publishers, Inc., 2006.

Reinking, David, Michael C. McKenna, Linda D. Labbo, and Ronald D. Kieffer, eds. *Handbook of Literacy and Technology: Transformations in a Post-typographic World.* Mahwah, NJ: Lawrence Erlbaum Associates, 1998.

Reynolds, John Frederick. "Delivery." In *Encyclopedia of Rhetoric and Composition: Communication from Ancient Times to the Information Age,* edited by Theresa Enos, 174–175. New York: Garland Publishers, Inc., 1996.

———. "Memory Issues in Composition Studies." In *Rhetorical Memory and Delivery: Classical Concepts for Contemporary Composition and Communication,* edited by John Frederick Reynolds, 1–15. Mahwah, NJ: Lawrence Erlbaum Associates, Inc., 1993. Digital reprinting, New York: Routledge, 2009.

Rice, Jeff. "Folksono(me)." *JAC: A Journal of Rhetoric, Culture, & Politics* 28, no. 1–2 (2008): 181–208.

Ridolfo, Jim and Danielle Nicole DeVoss. "Composing for Recomposition: Rhetorical Velocity and Delivery." *Kairos: A Journal for Teachers of Writing in Webbed Environments* 13, no. 2 (2009). http://kairos.technorhetoric.net/13.2/topoi/ridolfo_devoss/index.html.

Rivera, Carla. "California's Community Colleges Staggering during Hard Times." *LATimes.com* (22 September 2012). http://latimes.com/news/local/la-me-college-overview-20120923,0,3310236.story.

Rosch, Eleanor. "Principles of Categorization." In *Cognition and Categorization,* edited by Eleanor Rosch and Barbara B. Lloyd, 27–40. Hillsdale, NJ: Sage Publications, Inc., 1978.

Rosch, Eleanor and Barbara L. Lloyd. *Cognition and Categorization.* Mahwah, NJ: Lawrence Erlbaum Associates, 1978.

Ruskewicz, John. "Word and Image: The Next Revolution." *Computers and Composition* 5, no. 3 (1988): 9–15.

Rutz, Carol. "Delivering Composition at a Liberal Arts College: Making the Implicit Explicit." In *Delivering College Composition: The Fifth Canon,* edited by Kathleen Blake Yancey, 60–71. Portsmouth, NH: Boynton/Cook Publishers, Inc., 2006.

Said, Edward W. *Culture and Imperialism.* New York: Vintage Books, 1994.

Saks Fifth Avenue. http://www.saksfifthavenue.com.

Scott, Linda M. "Images in Advertising: The Need for a Theory of Visual Rhetoric." *Journal of Consumer Research* 21 (September 1994): 252–273.

Selber, Stuart. *Multiliteracies for a Digital Age.* Carbondale, IL: Southern Illinois University Press, 2004.

Selfe, Cynthia L. "The Movement of Air, the Breath of Meaning: Aurality and Multimodal Composing." *College Composition and Communication* 60, no. 4 (2009): 616–663.

———. "Technology and Literacy: A Story about the Perils of Not Paying Attention." *College Composition and Communication* 50, no. 3 (1999): 411–436. 1998 Conference on College Composition and Communication Chair's Address.

———. *Technology and Literacy in the Twenty-First Century: The Importance of Paying Attention.* Carbondale, IL: Southern Illinois University Press, 1999.

Selzer, Jack. "Rhetorical Analysis: Understanding How Texts Persuade Readers." In *What Writing Does and How It Does It,* edited by Charles Bazerman and Paul Prior, 279–307. Mahwah, NJ: Lawrence Erlbaum, 2004.

Shauf, Michele. "The Problem of Electronic Argument: A Humanist's Perspective." *Computers and Composition* 18, no. 1 (2001): 33–37.

Shelton State College. www.sheltonstate.edu.

Shirk, Henrietta Nickels. "Hypertext and Composition Studies." In *Evolving Perspectives on Computers and Composition Studies,* edited by Gail E. Hawisher and Cynthia L. Selfe, 177–202. Urbana, IL: NCTE, 1991.

Sierra College. www.sierracollege.edu.

Sirc, Geoffrey. "Box-Logic." In *Writing New Media: Theory and Applications for Expanding the Teaching of Composition,* edited by Anne Frances Wysocki, Johndan Johnson-Eilola, Cynthia L. Selfe, and Geoffrey Sirc, 111–146. Logan, UT: Utah State University Press, 2004.

Slowick, Kenneth. "The *Servais* Stradivarius Cello." Booklet accompanying *J.S. Bach Suites for Violoncello Solo,* BWV 1007–1012, 6–7. Performed by Anner Bylsma. New York: Sony Music Entertainment, Inc., 1992. Compact Discs: S2K 48047.

Snyder, Carol. "Classifications: Foucault for Advanced Writing." *College Composition and Communication* 35, no. 2 (1984): 209–216.

Snyder, Ilana, ed. *Silicon Literacies: Communication, Innovation and Education in the Electronic Age.* London: Routledge, 2002.

Solomon, Martin. "The Power of Punctuation." In *The Idea of Design: A Design Issues Reader,* edited by Victor Margolin and Richard Buchanan, 113–117. Cambridge, MA: The MIT Press, 1995.

Sosnoski, James. "Configuring as a Mode of Rhetorical Analysis." In *Doing Internet Research: Critical Issues and Methods for Examining the Net,* edited by Steven G. Jones, 127–143. Thousand Oaks, CA: Sage Publications, Inc., 1999.

Soto, Gary. *Gary Soto Web site.* http://www.garysoto.com.

———. *Gary Soto Web site* (pre-2007). http://web.archive.org/web/199811111 84507/http://garysoto.com/.

Southern Illinois University Edwardsville. "Research and Programs." *SIUE Black Studies Program.* http://www.siue.edu/blackstudies/research.html.

———. *SIUE Black Studies Program.* http://www.siue.edu/blackstudies/.

Stafford, Barbara Maria. *Good Looking: Essays on the Virtue of Images.* Cambridge, MA: The MIT Press, 1996.

———. *Visual Analogy: Consciousness as the Art of Connecting.* Cambridge, MA: The MIT Press, 1999.

Stafford, Kim R. "Foreword." In *Between Earth and Sky: Poets of the Cowboy West,* edited by Anne Heath Widmark, 11–12. New York: W.W. Norton, 1995.

Star, Susan Leigh. "Grounded Classification: Grounded Theory and Faceted Classification." *Library Trends* 47, no. 2 (1998): 218–232.

Storey, John. *Cultural Theory and Popular Culture: An Introduction.* 4th ed. Athens, GA: The University of Georgia Press, 2006.

Stroupe, Craig. "The Lost Island of English Studies: Globalization, Market Logic, and the Rhetorical Work of Department Web Sites." *College English* 67, no. 6 (2005): 610–635.

Sturken, Marita. *Tangled Memories: The Vietnam War, the AIDS Epidemic, and the Politics of Remembering.* Berkeley: The University of California Press, 1997.

———. "The Wall, the Screen and the Image: The Vietnam Veterans Memorial." In *The Visual Culture Reader,* edited by Nicholas Mirzoeff, 163–178. London: Routledge, 1998.

Sturken, Marita and Lisa Cartwright. *Practices of Looking: An Introduction to Visual Culture.* Oxford, England: Oxford University Press, 2001.

Sturken, Marita and Douglas Thomas. "Introduction: Technological Visions and the Rhetoric of the New." In *Technological Visions: The Hopes and Fears that Shape New Technologies,* edited by Marita Sturken, Douglas Thomas, and Sandra J. Ball-Rokeach, 1–18. Philadelphia: Temple University Press, 2004.

Sugrue, Thomas J. *The Origins of the Urban Crisis: Race and Inequality in Postwar Detroit.* Princeton Studies in American Politics. Princeton, NJ: Princeton University Press, 2005.

Sutton, John. "Remembering." In *The Cambridge Handbook of Situated Cognition,* edited by Philip Robbins and Murat Aydede, 217–235. Cambridge, England: Cambridge University Press, 2009.

Tapscott, Don. *Grown Up Digital: How the Net Generation is Changing Your World.* New York: McGraw-Hill, 2009.

Taylor, Todd. "Design, Delivery, and Narcolepsy." In *Delivering College Composition: The Fifth Canon,* edited by Kathleen Blake Yancey, 127–140. Portsmouth, NH: Boynton/Cook Publishers, Inc., 2006.

Thomas, Dominique L., Chauncey D. Smith, Bryant T. Marks, and Brandon Crosby. "Institutional Identity and Self-Esteem among African American Males in College." *Journal of African American Males in Education* 3, no. 1 (Summer 2012): 1–11.

Thomassen, Bjørn. "The Uses and Meanings of Liminality." *International Political Anthropology* 2, no. 1 (2009): 5–27.

Thompson, Heather Ann. *Whose Detroit? Politics, Labor, and Race in a Modern American City.* Ithaca, NY: Cornell University Press, 2001.

Tidewater Community College. www.tcc.edu.

Townsend, Barbara K. and Kevin J. Dougherty, eds. "Community College Missions in the 21st Century." *New Directions for Community Colleges* 136 (Winter 2006): 5–99.

Trimbur, John. "Delivering the Message: Typography and the Materiality of Writing." In *Rhetoric and Composition as Intellectual Work*, edited by Gary A. Olson, 188–202. Carbondale: Southern Illinois University Press, 2002.

Trumbo, Jean. "The Spatial Environment in Multimedia Design: Physical, Conceptual, Perceptual, and Behavioral Aspects of Design Space." *Design Issues* 13, no. 3 (1997): 19–28.

Turner, Mark. *Reading Minds: The Study of English in the Age of Cognitive Science.* Princeton: Princeton University Press, 1991.

Turner, Victor. *Dramas, Fields, and Metaphors: Symbolic Action in Human Society.* Ithaca, NY: Cornell University Press, 1974.

UCLA. www.ucla.edu.

United States Holocaust Memorial Museum. http://www.ushmm.org/.

The University of Pennsylvania. www.penn.edu.

Valentine, Bill. "The Power of Less." *HOK Knowledge Center.* http://www.HOK.com.

Vaughan, George B. *The Community College Story.* 3rd ed. Washington, DC: Community College Press, 2006.

Venturi, Robert, Denise Scott Brown, and Steven Izenour. *Learning from Las Vegas: The Forgotten Symbolism of Architectural Form.* Revised ed. Cambridge, MA: The MIT Press, 1994.

Walmart. http://www.walmart.com/.

Warnick, Barbara. *Critical Literacy in a Digital Age: Technology, Rhetoric, and the Public Interest.* Mahwah, NJ: Lawrence Erlbaum Associates, Inc., 2002.

———. *Rhetoric Online: Persuasion and Politics on the World Wide Web.* New York: Peter Lang, 2007.

Weiser, Irwin. "Faculties, Students, Sites, Technologies: Multiple Deliveries of Composition at a Research University. In *Delivering College Composition: The Fifth Canon*, edited by Kathleen Blake Yancey, 30–47. Portsmouth, NH: Boynton/Cook Publishers, Inc., 2006.

Weiser, Michael J., Chad D. Foradori, and Robert J. Handa. "Estrogen Receptor Beta in the Brain: From Form to Function." *Brain Research Reviews* 57, no. 2 (14 March 2008): 309–320. Also available online through http://www.elsevier.com/ locate/brainresrev.

Welch, Kathleen E. *Electric Rhetoric: Classical Rhetoric, Oralism, and a New Literacy.* Cambridge, MA: The MIT Press, 1999.

———. "Reconfiguring Writing and Delivery in Secondary Orality." In *Rhetorical Memory and Delivery: Classical Concepts for Contemporary Composition and Communication*, edited by John Frederick Reynolds, 17–30. Mahwah, NJ: Lawrence Erlbaum Associates, Inc., 1993. Digital reprinting, New York: Routledge, 2009.

Wertheim, Margaret. *The Pearly Gates of Cyberspace: A History of Space from Dante to the Internet.* New York: W.W. Norton, 1999.

Widmark, Anne Heath, ed. *Between Earth and Sky: Poets of the Cowboy West.* New York: W.W. Norton, 1995.

Williams, Sean. "Thinking out of the Pro-verbal Box." *Computers and Composition* 18, no. 1 (2001): 21–32.

Wysocki, Anne Frances, Johndan Johnson-Eilola, Cynthia L. Selfe, and Geoffrey Sirc. *Writing New Media: Theory and Applications for Expanding the Teaching of Composition.* Logan: Utah State University Press, 2004.

Yakima Valley Community College. www.yvcc.edu.

Yale University. www.yale.edu.

Yancey, Kathleen Blake. "Delivering College Composition: A Vocabulary for Discussion." In *Delivering College Composition: The Fifth Canon,* edited by Kathleen Blake Yancey, 1–16. Portsmouth, NH: Boynton/Cook Publishers, Inc., 2006.

———.*Writing in the 21ˢᵗ Century: A Report from the National Council of Teachers of English.* Urbana, IL: National Council of Teachers of English, February 2009. Available at http://www.ncte.org.

Wired Campus. *The Chronicle of Higher Education* (6 July 2011). http://chronicle.com/blogs/wiredcampus/old-dominion-u-researchers-ask-how-much-of-the-web-is-archived/32068.

Zou, Jie Jenny. "Old Dominion U. Researchers Ask How Much of the Web is Archived."

Index

Note: 'N' after a page number indicates a note; 'f' indicates a figure.

For Product Safety Concerns and Information please contact our
EU representative GPSR@taylorandfrancis.com Taylor & Francis
Verlag GmbH, Kaufingerstraße 24, 80331 München, Germany